Penguin Books

ARGUMENTS FOR DEMOCRACY

Tony Benn, former Chairman of the Labour Party and of the Fabian Society, and present Chairman of the Labour Home Policy Committee, has held six ministerial posts in five Labour governments: Postmaster-General in 1964; Minister of Technology in 1966; Minister of Power in 1969; Secretary of State for Industry and Minister of Posts and Telecommunications in 1974; and Energy Secretary from 1975 to 1979. In 1977 he was President of the Council of Energy Ministers of the E.E.C. Since 1950 he has been elected twelve times as Member of Parliament for Bristol South-East. He was candidate for the leadership of the Labour Party in 1976; and for the deputy leadership in 1971 and 1981. His previous books include *The Regeneration of Britain*, *Speeches* and *Arguments for Socialism* (Penguin 1980).

Tony Benn

Arguments for Democracy

Edited by Chris Mullin

Penguin Books

Penguin Books Ltd, Harmondsworth, Middlesex, England
Penguin Books, 625 Madison Avenue, New York, New York 10022, U.S.A.
Penguin Books Australia Ltd, Ringwood, Victoria, Australia
Penguin Books Canada Ltd, 2801 John Street, Markham, Ontario, Canada L3R 1B4
Penguin Books (N.Z.) Ltd, 182–190 Wairau Road, Auckland 10, New Zealand

First published by
Jonathan Cape Ltd 1981
Published in Penguin Books 1982

Printed and bound in Great Britain by
Cox & Wyman Ltd, Reading

Once again with love and gratitude to
Caroline and the whole family

Contents

Editor's Note

No one in British public life is more roundly vilified by the establishment than Tony Benn. Mention of his name is liable to send a wave of hysteria not merely through the boardrooms of the City of London or the drawing room of the Athenaeum, but even through the smoke-filled rooms where the establishment of the Labour movement prefers to do business. There have been times during the last few months when the entire resources of Her Majesty's Opposition seem to have been devoted, not to opposing the Tories, but to stopping Tony Benn becoming deputy leader of the Labour Party.

Yet outside the golden triangle bounded by Fleet Street, the Palace of Westminster and Hampstead a quite different appreciation of Mr Benn prevails. His public meetings draw larger and more enthusiastic crowds than those of any other contemporary politician. His last book, *Arguments for Socialism*, became a bestseller. Year after year he tops the poll in the elections for the constituency section of the Labour Party executive.

How do we explain the contradictory emotions that Mr Benn arouses? Very simple: Mr Benn asks questions that a lot of important and influential people would rather were not raised. Questions which large numbers of people who do not enjoy power or influence are very keen to see raised. What is more, he has not been bought or silenced by office or the prospect of office.

In *Arguments for Democracy* Mr Benn takes us on a conducted tour of the establishment. He examines the power of Downing Street, the civil service, the press barons, the security services. He demonstrates how these institutions have become the servants of consensus and argues for radical change. This book is based on speeches, lectures and articles written or delivered in the two years up to April 1981. My job has been to produce a coherent narrative by eliminating repetition, updating statistics, adding footnotes and plugging the occasional gap. I would like to thank Janet Sandall and Linky Somes for typing the manuscript with speed and efficiency, and Deborah Shepherd of Jonathan Cape for her rigorous copy-editing which greatly improved the final manuscript.

May 1981 Chris Mullin

Preface

This book has been written for those of us who want to see the people of this country take control of our own destinies and use the power of democracy to resolve the many pressing problems we face in our daily lives, including unemployment, injustice and the threat of war. It identifies some of the obstacles which now prevent us from taking effective action and is intended as a practical guide rather than an academic study.

My arguments are based upon experience acquired as a long-serving member of Parliament and Cabinet minister. This provided a close-up view of the way power is really exercised by those who at present determine the course of events.

In searching for the reasons why our society is now experiencing a crisis we should not look for individual scapegoats upon whom all the blame for our troubles can be heaped. To seek out a group of supposedly guilty men and women and demand their replacement by others would not get to the root of the problem. The real answer requires the wide redistribution of political and economic power. The obstacles that now stand in the path of such a redistribution occur in the institutions of state power as well as in those which uphold private power. They exist inside the Labour and trade union movement as well as in the forces of capital. They are to be found abroad as well as at home. And they are also in our own minds in so far as we lack the self-confidence to attempt what has to be done because of apathy or fear or because we do not understand what is happening and why.

Democracy is much more than a mechanism by which an electorate can appoint and remove those who govern them –

essential as that is. Institutional devices that merely siphon off public discontent by providing a 'constitutional' remedy are not what democracy is all about. Popular demands for political, economic and social rights have been a constant theme throughout our history. Since these demands were for equality in the control of political power it follows that when that power is acquired the next demand will be to use it to achieve greater equality of treatment in every aspect of life. This is the bridge which links democracy with socialism and merges the arguments for one with the arguments for the other. It is not possible to conceive of a socialist society with any future that denies political democracy, nor is it conceivable that real political democracy could fail to lead to greater social equality and socialism.

Herein lies both the weakness and the vulnerability of all dictatorships, of the right or of the left. Those who seek to justify authoritarianism of all kinds are forced to base their argument upon a false justification for an inherent inequality of political power. They deny the right of people to correct policy errors at the top or remove those who make them. All totalitarian societies fear the emergence of democratic challenges and so do many societies in the West.

What terrifies the establishment today is not, as they contend, that democratic socialism may endanger personal freedom, but that they realise that at last they are facing a democratic challenge to the legitimacy of their own undemocratic privileges. In short, the real enemy now perceived by the British establishment is democracy itself. To fight off the challenge they have had to pretend that capitalism and democracy are inextricably bound up together and that both are now facing an attack by anti-democratic socialists. It is a measure of the power and influence of establishment propaganda, regularly put out by the media, that many good people have been persuaded to accept that false analysis which is the direct opposite of the truth.

Even within the Labour movement the debate about democracy, which has at last produced some real changes, has been characterised by the use of some false arguments by those who oppose change. As the issues have been revealed it has become crystal clear that the reform movement that has been so widely denounced as anti-democratic is in truth the champion of democracy.

It is a pity, however, that the nature of the argument about socialism should have been so narrowly conceived in terms of industrial, economic and administrative policies. If democracy is based on a moral claim to equality, the issues opened up are as wide as life itself. Inequality in Britain is not by any means confined to the class relations deriving from the ownership of capital, though that remains a central obstacle which must be overcome if any real progress is to be made. But there is a whole philosophy of inequality embedded in the moral values which underpin capitalism and the social relations which it requires for success. Women, who represent more than half our total population, experience inequality in ways that go beyond their specially disadvantaged position as workers. The ethnic communities are in a similar position, experiencing inequalities which arise from racial discrimination. Other minorities such as gays are also victims of discrimination.

If democracy and socialism are both rooted in the moral claim for equality, these issues must be faced too. All the moral questions which arise within human experience must be capable of illumination and clarification in the light of socialist teaching.

This book makes no claim to be comprehensive. It is based upon speeches, articles and lectures written and delivered in the two years that followed the election of 1979. The ideas in it are based upon experience of ministerial office in the 1960s and 1970s. I hope that readers may draw new energy from reading an account of how, despite all the achievements of which the Labour movement can be proud, real power has eluded us and how important it is that we should take up the struggle for democracy again with renewed faith and commitment. The right to speak freely, to organise freely and to work for justice are basic rights. Even when the ballot box is added to those rights we must never forget that socialist and democratic values are necessary to help us use our newly won power wisely.

The world can never be changed by leaders, however wise. Until the people as a whole can be brought to see that we alone have the capacity to shape our own destiny, nothing real can be achieved. When that realisation spreads among the people and we resolve to build a different future, no power on earth can stop us.

May 21 1981 — Tony Benn

THE POWER OF THE ESTABLISHMENT

I

Britain as a Colony

For those of us who are trying to understand the tragedy which has overtaken this country and its people, there are three different levels to which we must address our minds. They are the practical, the moral and the constitutional levels, all closely interconnected but each requiring separate analysis if the nature of the crisis is to become intelligible, and if it is to be overcome.

The practical aspects are plain enough to see: an accelerating spiral of decline into chronic mass unemployment; the dismantling of essential public services; a widening gap between rich and poor, with growing social tensions; the erosion of the rights of women, trade unions, and the black communities; mounting attacks upon civil liberties; and the increasing risk of nuclear war.

The moral aspects are equally apparent for anyone who takes the trouble to reflect upon them: the worship of profit as the truest test of human achievement; the elevation of financial gain above human needs; the belittling of service to others as being an indication of weakness; the sanctification of status and power; the encouragement of cynicism; and the positive stimulation of public hostility against those who seek to point out these obvious facts to the public at large.

We cannot allow this state of affairs to continue. Our response must be to pursue reforms which lead to new and different policies based upon the reassertion of decent moral values. Such reforms will not be achieved by allowing the political argument to rotate around the narrow question of which party has the best management team to administer the present economic system, rooted as it is in a degenerate materialism, and packaged and presented for public consumption as 'moderation in the defence of capitalist freedom'. If these reforms are to be carried through, then we must look to the means by which this can be done. What power do we have to make the necessary changes? By what mechanism can they be implemented? What structures are available for those who seek peaceful reform by general consent? It is in seeking the answers to those questions that the third – or constitutional – level of the crisis becomes clear.

The decline of British democracy

Despite all that is said about British democracy and our traditional freedoms, the people of Britain have much less control over their destiny than they are led to believe; far less than they are entitled to expect and to demand; and a great deal less than they had a generation ago. In short, the powers which control our lives and our future have become progressively more concentrated, more centralised, more internationalised, more secretive and less accountable. The democracy of which we boast is becoming a decorous façade behind which those who have power exercise it for their own advantage and to the detriment of the public welfare. This growing political and economic impotence has been sensed rather than understood over a number of years and has expressed itself in many symptoms of discontent. The extent to which we have all been effectively disfranchised has been concealed from us, so that the blame for our frustrations has been directed into harmless and divisive channels.

The establishment has played its cards with exceptional skill in diffusing and defusing our anger, so as to preserve its own position. We are told that our economic difficulties are caused by our low productivity and lack of competitiveness; that our trade unions are destructive; that socialism is subversive; that our whole nation is afflicted by some malaise; and that our people are irresponsible and decadent. These are the themes that come through much of the media coverage of events. They add up to a barrage of propaganda designed to legitimise the present balance of power and to lead people to believe that an even greater centralisation of authority is desirable, to impose a tougher law and order regime, would discipline us to accept our fate, by stimulating fear of the future, suspicion of our neighbours, and distrust of all those who offer a different analysis.

These systematic attempts to persuade us to accept the establishment's explanation of what is happening have not been completely successful, and some of the frustrations that people experience are being directed at the *real* obstacles to advance. The rapidly growing anti-nuclear movement is based upon a legitimate fear that the military, which purports to defend us from foreign attacks upon our liberties, is a potential domestic threat to our freedom; and could get so far out of hand as to destroy the human race, perhaps by accident. The deep-seated and ineradicable hostility in Britain to the Common Market stems from a realisation that we are now governed by those we do not elect, and cannot remove. Public anxiety about state power, which has a role in meeting our economic, industrial and social needs, is based upon the knowledge that much of that power is managed by people who are not adequately accountable for what they do. Even the disenchantment with democracy itself derives from the failure of democratic institutions to get to the root of thc problems of society. Instead the people who run our institutions take refuge in the ins-and-outs game of electoral politics, concealing their failure by aggressive personal rhetoric.

Industrial workers who are thrown on the scrap heap when their employers – sometimes multinationals – decide to close their factory know quite well that something is wrong with a system that protects the making of speculative gains and denies recognition to those who create wealth. Nurses, teachers and social workers who face redundancy imposed by governments at the dictates of the bankers, and are then condemned to witness the misery it causes to their clients and themselves, protest at what has happened but may be driven back to hopelessness when they contemplate the strength of the forces they are opposing. As these experiences mount up, more and more people are beginning to see through the distortions of the press and have identified the subtle and persistent bias of the

BBC and commercial television. But, in the absence of an alternative commentary on events, they may lack the confidence to struggle against what is happening. Thus it is that while the situation steadily worsens and the morality we are asked to accept becomes less and less convincing, we are simultaneously realising that our democratic instruments for change have become weaker and weaker.

The struggle for reform must be engaged at the practical, moral and constitutional levels. There is no alternative to the intensification of the national and local campaigns to protect jobs and services; to the defence of women's rights and trade union rights and the rights of black people. We must expose and resist the attacks upon civil liberties and the drift to war. We must reassert and preach the morality upon which socialism is founded, and challenge the rotten and decaying values which underpin the present system. But we must also take up the democratic issues afresh and alert people to the reasons why they seem to have so little power to change their future; and show them how that democratic power can be won to allow them to take control for themselves. The winning of democratic control must be perceived as a major task, to be conceived and executed on a majestic scale as the necessary precondition for all advance.

Britain faces a national liberation struggle

What we have to do is comparable to a national liberation struggle, of which we have seen many examples in the era of de-colonisation which followed 1945. These colonial struggles were motivated by the desire for universal adult suffrage, self-government and political independence – all of which we regard as our natural rights. They involved prolonged, bitter and often bloody battles against many of the same forces which now govern us at home, discreetly, behind the lace curtains hung by the Mother of Parliaments so that those outside cannot see what is happening inside.

Is Britain then a colony like any other? On the face of it this may seem an outlandish question to pose. In 1945 London was the centre of the largest empire the world had ever known.

Those colonies have left us, but how can it be said that we have become a colony ourselves? And if so, to which empire do we belong and who governs us? Those are the questions to which we should now be turning our minds.

Britain – the last colony in the British Empire

The British Empire came into existence before the British system of government had developed into a political democracy as we know it today. The conquest of our overseas colonies and their settlement under the control of the British Crown put them under the same system of law that existed at home; and British subjects were governed by the same methods as were practised overseas. Every school-child knows of the old American colonists' resistance to 'taxation without representation', but few make the connection with the position of the British people who in 1776 were also taxed without representation, since the House of Commons was then composed of MPs elected by only 2 per cent of the population, all men. Moreover, the role of the military in defeating colonial rebellions also found a parallel at home. After the French Revolution, barracks were built in many industrial towns in Britain to maintain law and order at a time when unrest among industrial workers threatened to get out of control. Indeed, as Field Marshal Lord Carver made clear, in a remarkable television interview after his retirement, until just before the Second World War the army saw its main function as being to maintain law and order at home, and regarded the fighting of foreign wars as its secondary role.[1]

As colony after colony won its freedom, culminating in the establishment of an independent Zimbabwe in 1980, the British people found themselves virtually alone as subjects of the Crown. Of course the struggle of the Chartists and the suffragettes had, by 1928, extended the franchise to every man and woman at twenty-one, and by 1970 the age had been lowered to eighteen. Of course the growth of trade unionism, the creation of the Labour Party, its adoption of socialism, and the election of majority Labour governments made possible significant advances for working people in sustaining full employment and building the welfare state. But these advances made far less impact upon the formal and legal structures of constitutional power in Britain than we have ever cared to admit.

A hereditary House of Lords, topped up by the pliable recipients of prime ministerial patronage, still has great power to delay or obstruct the policies adopted by an elected House of Commons; it also has an unfettered veto, in law, to protect itself from abolition. The Crown still retains an equally unfettered legal authority to dismiss an elected government, dissolve an elected House of Commons, and precipitate a general election at any time it chooses. To do so, it need only call upon its prerogative powers as used by the Governor-General of Australia in 1975 when the Labour Government of Gough Whitlam was dismissed.

These prerogative powers are also used to sidestep the House of Commons whenever it suits Her Majesty's ministers. No treaty entered into by a British government, not even the treaty joining us to the Common Market, is submitted to the elected Commons for formal ratification. Similarly, all those laws under which we are governed which derive from international treaties are enacted by the prerogative, without having to pass through Parliament. All Cabinet ministers derive their executive authority, in its legal sense, not from election as leaders of the majority party in the Commons, but as members of Her Majesty's Government formed by a prime minister at the Crown's invitation. Each, individually, is sworn into Her Majesty's Privy Council and bound to secrecy by a personal oath administered by the Clerk of the Council. Both the courts and the armed forces swear their allegiance to the Crown and not to the elected government. Even Members of Parliament swear the same oath and the Royal Assent is necessary for the enactment of Bills that have been passed 'by and with the advice and consent of the Lords Spiritual and Temporal and the Commons of the United Kingdom in Parliament assembled'.

This formal constitutional structure is now widely presented as being of little more than academic interest, because most people believe that real power has long been transferred in practice to a wholly democratic parliamentary system. However, in its annual handbook entitled *Britain* which contains factual information of many kinds, the Central Office of Information until 1977 still described Britain as a 'monarchical state' and not as a parliamentary democracy.

If a government elected by a clear majority on a mandate of reform were to introduce legislation to complete the process of democratic advance to the point where it became comparable to de-colonisation, it might encounter opposition in a number of forms. The Lords' veto, the prerogatives of the Crown to dismiss and dissolve, and the loyalties of the courts and the services to adjudicate upon legitimacy and to enforce those judgments might all be used to defend the status quo against the parliamentary majority elected to transform it. This may seem far-fetched, but at least those forces opposed to democratic reforms could argue that they were operating in accordance with the letter of the constitution, even though in no sense within its spirit.

Unlike countries where the overthrow of elected governments by a non-elected military elite has to take place in open defiance of the constitutional safeguards enjoyed by the people, and is thus seen to be illegal, the British Constitution reserves all its ultimate safeguards for the non-elected elite. The democratic rights of the people can, in a crisis, be adjudicated to be illegal, thus legitimising the military in extinguishing them. Within that essential legal difference between the British Constitution and the constitutions of other parliamentary democracies lies part of the proof of the continuing colonial status of the British people. In examining that potential conflict and its potential outcome, we have done no more than point to the limitations upon democracy that we have allowed to remain in a century and a half of political reform.

Britain under the influence of economic imperialism

Our colonial status under the ultimate authority of the surviving remnants of British feudalism is only a part of the present structure of extra-parliamentary power which now supervises and controls the governments we elect. Private economic, financial and industrial power in Britain has never been accountable to the electorate for the decisions it has made. Even acts of nationalisation have only touched some 20 per cent of our national output of goods and services; and many nationalised sectors, including the Bank of England and the great public corporations, have continued to operate much as the private corporations which they replaced had done in the past.

Meanwhile the growth of private monopoly has gone on apace, and so has the international growth of industrial and financial power. These global corporations – in oil, engineering and minerals – have long since outgrown nation states in the sheer size of their wealth and income and the world-wide scale of their operations. They perceive their prime responsibility to lie with their shareholders, and they have the power to maximise their return on capital by deploying their resources without regard to frontiers. This applies with equal force to those multinationals whose home base is Britain, since they feel no allegiance to the nation from within whose territory they grew. Profits made in one country can be exported to another where perhaps wage rates or taxes are low, and by transfer pricing or the skilful manipulation of currencies they can conduct their financial transactions with great advantage to themselves but with damaging consequences for employment, production, or the balance of payments of countries in which they operate.

My personal experience of this kind of conduct, from the mid-1960s as Minister of Technology to the late 1970s as Secretary of State for Energy, convinced me of the colonial status which the multinationals have succeeded in imposing upon Britain.

The same is true of international financial power, now symbolised by the International Monetary Fund. Two Cabinets in which I served went to the IMF for bridging loans, one after the 1967 devaluation and the second in 1976. The IMF sent a team to examine Britain's economic policy and laid down the most rigid prescription for corrective measures to be adopted before either instalment of aid was made available. For tactical reasons, and to avoid a charge of dictation, the IMF operates by seeking a 'letter of intent' from a suppliant government before agreeing to the loan. A British Chancellor of the Exchequer is therefore obliged to pretend to volunteer economic policy changes, having in fact agreed them secretly in advance, knowing that only these pre-negotiated terms will release the necessary cash.

The humiliation that IMF imperialism imposes upon colonial Britain is deepened, rather than lessened, by the knowledge that our government has been compelled to pretend that it wished to follow policies that have in fact been imposed by the pressure of world bankers. To make matters worse, the restoration of 'confidence' is described as if it had some objective reality, whereas in truth 'confidence' is nothing more than a political prize awarded by world bankers when they are satisfied that governments are pursuing policies acceptable to the international financial community.

Britain's subordinate role within the American global defence system

Parallel with the colonisation of post-war Britain by the multinationals and the bankers, came the much more specifically political supervision of another area of our policy – defence – by the United States. Relations between the USA and Britain are exceptionally close, exceedingly complicated, and are shrouded in secrecy.

As the leading power in the English-speaking world, Americans recognise their indebtedness to British history, language, culture and traditions. As rebels against George III, they retain a certain inherited hostility to the British Empire. President Roosevelt, for example, offered little encouragement to Winston Churchill in his desire to re-establish the British Empire after the Second World War.[2] As Britain's commercial rival, America was quite ready to exploit British weakness in Iran, the Middle East and elsewhere, for its own advantage.[3] But these factors are of little account compared to the 'special relationship' between the UK and the US, whereby the situation before 1776 has been reversed, so that Britain is now to a large extent a colony in an American empire.

Some of this colonial relationship is expressed through the multinationals and the IMF, which are overwhelmingly dominated by the USA as the most powerful country in the capitalist world. But it is in the area of defence policy that

American dominance has become most pronounced. In analysing this process, I am basing my argument upon my personal experience as a minister who has had many dealings with the United States administration.

It began during the war, when Washington and London were the twin pillars of the Western Alliance. Britain desperately needed American support – financial and industrial as well as military – and we got it but on strict terms laid down by the USA. Lend/Lease sustained us, but at a cost of selling our overseas assets.[4] The post-war American loan was granted on condition that the UK adopted a policy of convertibility which collapsed as soon as it was tried.[5] Our military mission in Washington became a major arm of Whitehall government, and the integration of our research into atomic weapons was purchased at a very heavy price that came to be paid after the war.

UK/US atomic cooperation, through which our own scientific skills were merged with those of America together with her technological capacity to build the Hiroshima and Nagasaki bombs, was halted at the end of the war. It only restarted on the basis of complete American supervision of Britain's security arrangements. Through these supervisory arrangements, which are still in force, the Americans are entitled to lay down the framework of our intelligence systems and to have access to what they produce; in return they provide some information from their own world-wide intelligence network. In the field of atomic research we are both dependent upon their skills and obliged to seek their consent for our own developments. On one occasion I was required to appear before the United States Atomic Energy Commission to explain, and in effect to seek their consent for, changes in the structure of the British Atomic Energy Authority for which I was responsible. On another occasion it was necessary to clear a technical development with the US authorities.

This close relationship certainly assisted the build-up of Britain's own nuclear weapons. It also alienated the French and triggered off de Gaulle's first veto of Britain's application to join the EEC.[6] But its most important effect was to give the USA a commanding position in the deployment of its own nuclear weapons in Britain. Though I have been the minister responsible for the Atomic Research Centre at Aldermaston, and have served in four Cabinets and on occasions as a member of the key Overseas Policy and Defence Committee, as well as other, smaller committees dealing with nuclear policy, I was never told, and still do not know, the basis upon which US nuclear weapons sited in the UK can be fired. The general assumption is that guidelines have been drawn up that constitute a working agreement governing their use and provide for consultation between president and prime minister, if that is practical. No Cabinet in which I have served has ever been told the true position and I can only suppose that the key US/UK arrangements are in effect only known to the president and the prime minister.

The essence of national sovereignty and independence lies in the capacity for a nation and its parliament to decide to go to war or to make peace. I believe that the sovereign right has long been ceded in law through a secret agreement with the USA; and in practice, by the very fact that no limitation on the use of US nuclear weapons based in Britain would be enforceable. Yet every student learning about the British Constitution is told how Parliament won from a reluctant Crown the right of control over the 'purse and the sword'. That is to say it demanded, and obtained, the right to an annual vote of all moneys required by the government; and the right to renew annually or not to renew the military discipline laws which gave our forces their legitimacy. Today, both these democratic safeguards have gone. The expenditure on nuclear weapons and the programmes for which they are designed are concealed from Cabinets as well as Parliament; and we have on our soil the armed forces of a foreign power, armed with weapons of mass destruction that can be fired without Parliament's approval.

Those are, in effect, colonial arrangements under which, in a crucial area of government, we are a part of an American world-wide military system. They will soon be supplemented by a US-inspired Rapid Deployment Force within which British troops will be engaged in operations never explicitly authorised by our elected representatives.[7]

One final comment needs to be made here. The 1980 Labour

Party Conference resolved that all US nuclear bases in the UK shall be closed and that Britain shall adopt a non-nuclear defence strategy.[8] If that policy were to be incorporated in the manifesto upon which the next Labour government is elected, and formal representations were made to Washington to withdraw those weapons and close those bases, it is not at all clear that the US administration would agree to do so. They would almost certainly respond by pointing to agreements reached with earlier British governments under which these bases were made available and express their view that these agreements must be upheld and could not be unilaterally abrogated by a British government.

Only at that stage would the British House of Commons and the British people be made aware of the surrender of sovereignty and democratic control by Parliament over peace and war which has already taken place secretly, reducing us to colonial status in our relations with the US and its armed forces.

Britain's formal surrender to the Common Market

The most formal surrender of British sovereignty and parliamentary democracy that has ever occurred in our history took place in January 1972, when Mr Heath signed the Treaty of Accession which bound Britain to the Treaty of Rome and subordinated our key law-making and tax-gathering powers to the Common Market. The Commons had earlier voted in favour of entry in principle. A sufficient number of Labour MPs defied a three-line whip to give Mr Heath his majority.[9] Without those votes by Labour MPs – some of whom have now left the party to lead the Social Democrats – Britain would still be a parliamentary democracy.

Both Houses passed a Bill providing the legislative authority needed to enforce Community laws. The House of Lords, which often claims that its constitutional function is to provide a breathing space to allow the electors to express their view, allowed this major constitutional change to go through without demanding an election, so that the electorate were denied their rights, only gaining a retrospective judgment on withdrawal in a referendum three years later.

It is impossible to exaggerate the nature of the change wrought in our system of parliamentary democracy by entry into the Common Market. European laws – whether made in secret under prerogative powers in the Council of Ministers, or by the non-elected Commission, or by the Court – take precedence over all laws passed by our Parliament, where the two conflict. European laws are also enforceable by the British courts even to the point of declaring the actions of an elected British government illegal in British law. They cannot be repealed by British Acts of Parliament and the only remedy lies in complete withdrawal by domestic legislation and the abrogation of the Treaty of Accession to free us from the Treaty of Rome.

Britain is now, in law and in practice, a colony of this embryonic West European federal state. The economic and industrial price we are paying for our abdication of sovereignty is now becoming apparent.

This, then, is an outline of the evidence for asserting that Britain has been reduced by successive governments to colonial status.

How the British establishment persuaded the British people to abandon parliamentary democracy

How was this achieved? Why did we not see in time what was happening to us? Why were the safeguards of parliamentary democracy and national independence yielded so easily by a nation that supposedly prided itself on their maintenance? The answer lies in the skilful exercise of power by the establishment in cooperation with the media over the whole of this period. The British establishment concluded years ago that the ballot box, combined with a strong and united Labour movement, was going to prove capable of introducing Britain to socialism by democratic means through Parliament. Those who belittle the role of parliamentary democracy in the transition to socialism by pointing to the slow progress made so far, do not understand that the establishment has never been in favour of parliamentary democracy and has always seen the potential for socialism by consent as a serious threat. The establishment also knows that the only real obstacle to the transformation they fear has been the reluctance of the parliamentary leadership of the Labour Party to carry through the changes which the Labour movement wants to see; and not in any inherent incapacity to make those changes.

They have therefore responded to the challenge in three ways, each of which have depended upon the use of the media. First, the establishment and the media have sustained a continuing and largely successful campaign to keep the leadership of the Labour movement separate from their active supporters, projecting the leadership as responsible and moderate and the rank and file as irresponsible and anti-democratic.

Second, the establishment and the media have cooperated to cover up the systematic transfer of powers from the British Parliament to the Common Market, the Pentagon, the IMF and the multinationals. They have presented those who have opposed those moves as being hostile to parliamentary democracy while the truth was the very opposite. It was the establishment itself which betrayed our heritage of democracy, because they feared for their power and privileges if it was allowed to continue. They opted for survival as the colonial administrators of a subject Britain rather than accept displacement by the democratic process within Britain.

Third, the establishment and the media have conducted a long and reasonably successful campaign to win public assent for their strategy by undermining the self-confidence of the British people and their faith in the vitality and efficacy of our democratic institutions. Socialists and trade unionists are familiar with the media bias directed against socialism and trade unionism. But few people seem to realise that the underlying drift of media bias has been to present democratic institutions themselves in an unfavourable light. The media have presented the British people as being so irresponsible as to be unfit to exercise ultimate control, and Britain as so weak in the world as to make self-government virtually meaningless.

In this way our people became confused and diverted from an understanding of what was really happening, while our democratic rights were taken from us and we were reduced to colonial status.

The campaign for self-government must be led by the Labour movement

This needs to be stated if we are to understand the magnitude of the task which faces us. It is not only that our public morality is being debased and degraded by shallow materialism, or that our practical problems need to be tackled with renewed faith and vigour. If we are to attempt serious reforms, we shall find that we need to restore democracy by taking back our rights of self-government. We shall need to rebuild our self-confidence as a nation, to build it upon a clearer and better concept of human values, and to take charge of our own economic and political destiny. To attempt all that is, in effect, to embark upon a national liberation struggle.

The strength of the powers that will be ranged against us have to be identified before we start. But the analysis of our opponents' power must not be used to suggest that victory is impossible. There is no power on earth that can stop a determined people when they resolve to change the conditions under which they live. If all the other colonies in the British Empire were able to win their freedom from the tyranny of the British establishment, how much more easier will it be for us to liberate ourselves? All the pressures from Washington, Brussels or Zurich could not prevent us from shaping our own future once they realised that we were in earnest.

The greatest obstacle lies not in external forces that might frustrate us, but in ourselves for our tardiness in attempting to free ourselves and our unfounded self-doubt about the outcome if we tried. Once we set upon our course, we can certainly win. The only question is how long must we wait before we start. This is the true challenge confronting the Labour movement and the socialists within it, and all believers in democracy. The role of the British Labour movement must be to offer leadership in that liberation struggle to end our colonial status, and to allow the people to enter into their rightful inheritance.

2

The Case for a Constitutional Premiership

The argument in outline

After eleven years' service as a member of four Labour governments, I have reached the conclusion that the range of powers at present exercised by a British prime minister, both in that capacity and as party leader, is now so great as to encroach upon the legitimate rights of the electorate, undermine the essential role of Parliament and usurp some of the functions of collective Cabinet decision-making. In addition, a Labour prime minister can neutralise much of the influence deriving from the party's internal democracy – which is necessary to serve the interests of its membership. In short, the present centralisation of power in the hands of one person has gone too far and amounts to a system of personal rule in the very heart of our parliamentary democracy. The prime minister and party leader must be made more accountable to those over whom he or she exercises power, so that we can develop a constitutional premiership in Britain. To transform an absolute premiership into a constitutional premiership would involve making some fundamental changes in its functions comparable to those made, over the years, when the Crown was transformed from an absolute monarchy into a constitutional monarchy. The arguments for change are based upon experience of the way the present system works in practice. Many of the decisions of government, which are now thought to be the result of collective decision-making, actually reflect a personal view of what should be done, by a prime minister who has the power to get his or her own way.

The need to restate the case for democracy

One advantage of looking at the top of the tree for the causes of some of Britain's political problems, rather than at the electorate as a whole, is that it makes a welcome and healthy change. The more commonly expressed theory, that Britain is afflicted with a national malaise so serious that no amount of wise leadership has been able to bring the nation to its senses, is not very convincing. Even if it were true, I could not accept the only remedy on offer: to limit the democratic process and hand even more power to the people at the top.

Democracy means that the electorate can remove their government. It does not mean that political leaders can take over power from the electors because they are disappointed with the electors' performance in exercising responsibility for their own affairs. Power and responsibility must necessarily go together and it is my argument that, if the people are supposed to lack responsibility, it may be because they have too little power. Perhaps the remedy lies in decentralising power by moving it down from the top, instead of shifting more of it to the top. That is the basic case for democracy and it needs to be restated in this generation, beginning with a very critical look at the premiership, where so much power now resides.

The origins of prime ministerial power

Britain's political history has been marked by a long series of struggles to wrest powers away from the centre and redistribute them to a wider group of interests. After the truly absolutist monarchy of William the Conqueror, who ruled by the sword with which he came to power, there was a succession of bitter battles from which the monarchy emerged with its powers trimmed, first by the feudal barons at Runnymede, then by the House of Lords and, later still, by the revolution of the gentry at the time of Cromwell. The growing power of the House of Commons after the abdication of James II in 1688, and the development of Cabinet government in the century that followed, led to the situation under which the Crown's own ministers were required to command a majority in the elected chamber.

After the Reform Act of 1832 the processes of extending the franchise were carried to the point which we have reached today, when ministers are accountable to a House of Commons chosen in an election at which all adults may vote.[1] Under this textbook version of the development of our constitutional monarchy, within a parliamentary democracy, the powers of the prime minister can be seen as a great achievement because they have been wrested away from the Throne, and are now only exercised at the will of the electorate. But that analysis leaves out of account the impact that the powers of the prime minister may have on the rights of those in Parliament, and in the political parties which offer candidates for Parliament, and on the electorate as a whole. The establishment of an 'elected monarch' who has succeeded in drawing to himself or herself such an array of personal powers and patronage may reproduce, in a significant sense, the very system of personal rule which earlier struggles were intended to end. Indeed, it is quite legitimate to ask whether we have not, accidentally, made a good job of reproducing feudalism, complete with a new generation of barons, who owe their positions to a new 'monarch' dispensing power and status of a much more significant kind, as well as the old honours.

This is not to suggest that all the solid achievements of British democracy have been eroded by these tendencies. The ultimate power of the House of Commons to topple a prime minister remains unaffected, as does the even greater power of the voters to get rid of both governments and the MPs who support them. The very fact that these powers are there operates to restrict and restrain the exercise of power by premiers and their ministers. But, within that broad framework of public and parliamentary control, there has certainly been a greater centralisation of personal power in the hands of one man or woman than outward appearances would suggest.

The Labour Party and parliamentary democracy

To complete the background history of the development of parliamentary democracy in Britain it is necessary to look at the growth of the party system. For this purpose, I will confine my comments to the Labour Party, because it grew outside Parliament and the links that bind it to the parliamentary process are different from those of other parties. The Labour movement in the nineteenth century saw itself as representing working people before they had the vote, and campaigned with the Chartists to extend the franchise. It was only after the vote had reached working men that the trade unions saw the need for working men to be put up as candidates to represent their class. Later the Labour Party was born out of the Labour Representation Committee.[2] The Constitution of the party, as agreed in 1918, has as its first purpose:

> To organise and maintain in Parliament and in the country a political Labour Party.

The basis of the deep commitment of the Labour Party to the parliamentary system lies in the belief that, by the adoption of candidates who are pledged to policies agreed at annual conference, the party rank and file can, subject to the will of the electors in a general election, win a majority to carry through those policies in a peaceful and democratic way. Thus the link between the party in the country and Labour MPs lies at the very root of the party's concept of how parliamentary democracy should work. A whole range of issues bearing upon that relationship are up for discussion within the party at this moment. But for present purposes it is the link between the party and the party leader that is most relevant.

The Labour Party in Parliament was the first party to have any sort of election for its leader. Indeed, the very idea of MPs of any party electing their leader was seen as revolutionary not so very long ago, when it was widely believed that the Crown had retained the prerogative right to ask anyone it chose to form a government. Now that all three main parties elect their leaders the Crown accepts that its choice of prime minister will be made for it by the majority party in Parliament. Only in very exceptional circumstances, such as a hung Parliament, would the Crown have any discretion in the choice of premier.

The reason that this is such a sensitive political issue for the Labour Party is that the whole existence of, and justification for, the party depends upon its ability to trust the Labour prime minister of the day to provide the last link in the process by which its policies get implemented, after they have been hammered out at conference, and have won approval at a general election.

This is not the place to discuss the method of election of the leader, which is a separate issue, and has nothing whatever to do with the powers that any leader might have, however he or she is elected. I now intend to set out these powers and examine them in some detail.

The powers of the party leader in opposition

The powers that a Labour leader has while the party is in opposition are of course far less significant than when the party is in government. But they raise the same questions of democratic accountability.

1 Power to allocate shadow portfolios

Though the Parliamentary Committee (Shadow Cabinet) is elected by the whole parliamentary Labour Party, when the party is in opposition, the leader, at present, chooses which elected MP is to shadow which department – and he or she can reshuffle his or her team at any time without consulting either the Parliamentary Committee or the MPs. This power is based upon the practice of appointing, or reshuffling, ministers when a Labour government is in office. The main difference is that no MP elected to the Parliamentary Committee can actually be removed by the leader. The relationship of Parliamentary Committee members to the leader is, therefore, quite different from the relationship of ministers to the prime minister. Even so, the allocation of these shadow portfolios is very important in that it amounts to real patronage – carrying, as it does, at least a hint of what office a person might expect to hold if a government was formed. Moreover any person chosen to speak for the party from the front bench will find that his pronouncements carry great weight and can actually blank out the policy decided by the party nationally.

In the case of MPs who are unsuccessful in winning a place on the Parliamentary Committee, the leader of the party has an unrestricted right to appoint them to shadow for a department either as principal or secondary spokesmen. These appointments now number forty-five, excluding the whips. Such non-elected spokesmen are in a different position from their elected fellow front benchers in a number of respects. They do not attend the Parliamentary Committee as a matter of course, though they can be asked to attend, if needed. Their places are entirely at the disposal of the leader, and to this extent they are more like non-Cabinet ministers in their total dependency upon his wishes. Admittedly they have a certain freedom from 'Shadow Cabinet responsibility' on any subject other than the one which they speak about from the front bench. The full members of the Parliamentary Committee are expected to follow the line agreed at the committee. Members of the Parliamentary Committee are not allowed to speak at meetings of the parliamentary Labour Party except on their own front bench responsibilities, and then only in line with the decisions of the committee.

2 *Power to nominate for peerages*

It had long been the custom for the prime minister of the day to offer to the leader of the opposition the right to nominate people for peerages to 'strengthen the opposition in the House of Lords'. This was done during the war and became institutionalised when life peerages were started in 1958. Following that innovation it became a habit to put an asterisk against the names of persons whose nominations came from opposition party leaders. Whatever the justification for this new development, it opened up an important new source of much-prized patronage in the hands of the leader of the Labour Party, whether in or out of office. A peerage carries with it a seat in Parliament for life, a daily attendance allowance and – in the case of former MPs – the right to use the facilities of the House of Commons, save only the right to enter the chamber. Many Labour peers work very hard indeed for the party in the House of Lords, watching the passage of every bill, and putting up opposition to those clauses which the party has opposed in the Commons. Nothing I have said is intended to be in any way a criticism of their work.

3 *The power of patronage*

The problem of patronage, however, is really a problem that begins long before the honour has been awarded. It stems from the relationship that is set up between the party leader – as donor – and those who may wish – as applicants – to receive the award. This relationship lies at the heart of the matter and extends the influence of patronage far beyond the number of people who, in the event, actually receive an honour. For every Labour peer who is created there may be many more who hope that they will be. At any one time, there may be dozens of Labour MPs – or others – who want what only the leader can give them. Human nature being what it is, it is inevitable that the knowledge that their heart's desire can only be realised by their remaining in favour with the leader will affect some people's conduct on issues upon which the leader has definite views.

This is how patronage can shift someone's interests away from representing constituents or the party, to the quite different concern of pleasing the leader. It follows that in such cases the leader gains from the hopefuls a voting strength and influence in the parliamentary Labour Party which could possibly be used to frustrate the policies of the party outside. If this analysis is valid it does not imply any criticism of leaders who exercise this power, or of the recipients of the patronage. But what it does show is that the system of patronage – whether in the appointment of ministers or peers – is an important element in the apparatus of power which surrounds the prime minister and party leader.

4 *Power of the leader over the contents of the manifesto*

The party constitution provides that the manifesto shall be drawn up by the Labour Party National Executive Committee and the Parliamentary Committee sitting together. But the power of the party leader is greater than the formal constitutional position suggests. For he or she is a permanent member of the NEC and does not have to wait to use his or her power until the actual manifesto meeting takes place. In the past the leader has argued that there is a formal veto which he or she can exercise over the manifesto, or any part of it which he or she is not prepared to agree should be put to the electorate.

5 *Power of the timing of the manifesto*

Moreover, since the leader's consent is held to be necessary for the approval of the manifesto, his or her agreement is also needed before any joint meeting between the NEC and the parliamentary leaders to draft the manifesto can be arranged. In this way the leader can effectively block early work on the manifesto and defer the discussion and agreement until the general election is imminent. This timing point is crucial to the content of the manifesto and its role in the campaign. If the manifesto is drawn up early, free from the pressure of an impending campaign, the NEC is in a much more favourable position to press for conference policies to be included; and if the draft manifesto can actually be published as a campaign document before the election is announced, the party has much more time to get its proposals across to the electorate. This happened in 1974 when a campaign document was issued and the voters knew, well in advance of the election, what policies Labour candidates would be advocating. If, however, the manifesto is left to the last minute, as happened in 1979, as the leader can insist that it is, then there can be no certainty as to what commitments will be included in it before the campaign has begun.

6 *The power to threaten resignation*

Moreover, since the natural desire for unity within the party is at its peak at the beginning of a campaign, the leader's veto is absolute. He or she only has to hint that, if a certain pledge were included, he or she would feel obliged to resign the leadership and ask the party to pick a new leader to carry it into the campaign, for all pressure for that pledge to subside at once. In this way the leader's veto over manifesto commitments passes unchallenged and his or her wishes are complied with as a simple expression of confidence on the eve of battle. To this extent the veto power of the leader greatly exceeds the veto power of the House of Lords over Labour legislation. For while a clear Labour majority in the Commons can override the delaying power of the Lords, even an overwhelming majority on the manifesto committee of the Labour Party cannot override or by-pass in any way the leader's veto.[3]

By an extension of this absolute power, the leader can, in effect, actually set aside any draft prepared by the NEC and substitute a draft of his or her own and insist that the meeting address itself to his or her draft manifesto instead of to the NEC draft.

The powers of the prime minister in office

All the powers enjoyed by a party leader in opposition are, of course, retained when he or she becomes prime minister, and indeed are reinforced by virtue of his or her office. In addition he or she acquires a formidable battery of new powers which are so numerous as to make it difficult to compress the list down to manageable proportions. Of all these powers the authority to appoint and dismiss ministers, without any constitutional requirement to get these changes approved by Parliament or the party, is the most decisive. For by the use, or threat of use, of this authority all the other powers described below fall into the hands of the prime minister alone; to exercise as he or she thinks best.

1 Power to appoint, reshuffle or dismiss ministers

This power derives from the formal constitutional position that the Crown entrusts the task of forming an administration to an individual who is then solely responsible for nominating his or her Cabinet and all other ministers. The number of ministerial appointments made between 1945 and 1976 was 1,494, made up of 309 Cabinet and 1,185 non-Cabinet ministers, and by seven prime ministers.[4]

2 *Power to create peers*

This power too derives from the general right to advise the Crown on the use of its prerogative. From 1945 to 1976, 568 hereditary and life peers were created on the advice of seven prime ministers. Each peer is a member of Parliament. For comparison, it takes 40 million electors to elect 635 members of the House of Commons. Though a Political Honours Scrutiny Committee examines these nominations, the process cannot be said to involve any genuine accountability.

3 *Powers over honours generally*

The prime minister has of course considerable powers over a much wider range of honours included in the New Year and Queen's Birthday Lists. In all, 64 lists were issued from 1945 to 1976, excluding Special Lists such as are produced after a dissolution. These seven prime ministers created 118 baronetcies and 264 knighthoods during that period.

4 *Power to appoint the chairmen of nationalised industries*

The prime minister expects to be consulted, personally, on appointments of all chairmen of nationalised industries; and in effect enjoys the right to insist upon the appointment of the person he wishes to go forward. The same seven prime ministers were responsible for 85 such appointments from 1945 to 1976. These chairmanships confer real power in that the nationalised industries account for about 20 per cent of the nation's output, employ some 1.75 million people and have an aggregate turnover of over £15 billion a year.

In addition, during the same period 35 chairmen of royal commissions were appointed.

5 *Further powers of appointment*

So far we have identified 2,564 major appointments or patronage awards made by seven men over a thirty-one-year period. The scale of the patronage is breathtaking and no medieval monarch could compare with it, either in numbers or in importance. Nor could an American president approach this level of personal patronage. But there is more to come, since prime ministers also appoint permanent secretaries; ambassadors; chiefs of staff; the heads of the security services, MI5 and MI6. And obviously they can have an influence, if they choose to use it, over the names of all those put forward for the 31 public boards listed in 1977; or the 252 fringe bodies, which themselves employ 184,000 people and spend £2,367,000,000 a year.[5]

On the not unreasonable assumption that there are two or three hopefuls for every successful candidate for an honour or an appointment, the seven post-war prime ministers extended their influence over between 5,000 and 7,000 would-be ministers, lords, knights and chairmen.

This list excludes the prime minister's role in choosing archbishops, bishops and judges, which involves different considerations not dealt with here.

6 *Power over ministerial conduct*

In addition to their power to dismiss ministers, and in order to reinforce their authority, all new prime ministers issue a personal minute of procedure for ministers which lays down a whole range of requirements, governing everything from collective Cabinet responsibility to the need for No. 10 to authorise all broadcasts and the banning of articles in the press. Even memoirs are covered. These procedure minutes, which began as a guide to the conduct of government business, are never submitted in draft for Cabinet approval. The 1945 version issued by Mr Attlee, and now released under the thirty-year-rule, consisted of four pages and 23 paragraphs. The 1976 version ran to 27 printed pages, in 132 paragraphs, under 14 main sections and 51 sub-sections. A further minute, confined to travel, ran to six pages in 24 paragraphs, three sections and a schedule – making a total of 33 printed pages, 17 sections and 156 paragraphs. This minute is of considerable interest, in that Parliament, the public and the party are entitled to know what restrictions are placed upon ministers. It is, however, classified as confidential and hence the prime minister prevents any discussion of it.

The prime minister's power to secure compliance with these rules rests upon his or her power to dismiss those who breach them. However, as James Callaghan once made clear in a parliamentary answer, he regarded the application, or non-application, of the rules of collective Cabinet responsibility as being entirely within his own personal discretion.[6]

7 *Powers relating to the conduct of government business*

A prime minister's second greatest power, after patronage, lies in his or her complete personal control of the conduct of government business as it is carried out by ministers and officials. The prime minister determines which items of business are to be discussed in Cabinet and which are to be excluded. He or she has the power to set up Cabinet committees, appoint their members and keep their existence secret from the public, from Parliament, and even from other members of the Cabinet. There were 23 standing committees of the Cabinet and probably 150 *ad hoc* committees set up over the last five years. The prime minister has the power to circulate, or not to circulate, papers written by Cabinet ministers for Cabinet. He or she has the power to circulate, or to withhold, Cabinet committee papers from other members of the Cabinet who do not serve on that committee. He or she has the power to instruct the civil service on the conduct of its business, through the appointment of inter-departmental official committees, and to commission papers even on matters that primarily are the concern of a departmental minister.

From this it will be clear that the prime minister is able to use the government to bring forward the policies which he or she favours; and to stop those to which he or she is opposed. And to complete these powers he or she can refuse his or her consent to joint meetings of the Cabinet and the NEC to discuss matters of common concern, including the preparation of the next election manifesto. To this extent the conduct of government business can be said to reflect a personal and autocratic rather than a collective and democratic spirit.

8 *Powers over information*

A prime minister is also in a unique position to control the flow of information about the work of the government. Alone among ministers he or she has the power to inform Parliament, or the public, directly on any matter relating to the government's policy or activities which he or she believes it to be in the government's interest to have known. In addition he or she has the power to arrange for unofficial briefings of the press or trusted correspondents on any matter which he or she decides should be handled in that way; and under the 'lobby rules' the prime minister may decline to confirm or deny that any such briefings have taken place. He or she has the power to classify any documents to any level, and to establish a leak inquiry to be undertaken by a minister, a civil servant, or a police officer, into any suspected disclosure by a minister, or an official, of information which he or she, as prime minister, believes should not have been disclosed, and he or she may withhold the results of that inquiry from the Cabinet even when Cabinet ministers have been questioned. It also follows that his or her personal responsibility for the security services entitles him or her to have any person – including ministers – put under surveillance; and to withhold knowledge both of the fact of the surveillance, and its outcome, from anyone he or she chooses.

9 *Powers in international relations*

A prime minister may use the royal prerogative to secure the adherence of the United Kingdom to treaties which bind the UK Parliament, without any requirement for the formal ratification by Parliament of those treaties. He or she may also enter into binding commitments in respect of the European Communities – personally or through ministers – which have legal force in the United Kingdom without prior approval of Parliament or the Cabinet. He or she also enjoys special responsibilities for the conduct of the armed forces through the Secretary of State for Defence.

10 *Powers to terminate a Parliament or government*

The prerogative powers of the Crown, which have to be exercised with proper caution, because of the sensibilities of the monarch, also confer two final powers upon the prime minister. He or she can 'advise', and normally expect to secure, a dissolution of Parliament before the end of its natural life-span; and even in the absence of a defeat in the Commons. He or she can also terminate the life of the whole government by the simple procedure of tendering his or her own resignation to the sovereign, which automatically carries with it the resignation of all his or her colleagues. The prime minister is not constitutionally required to consult the Cabinet about his or her decision on either of these matters. But his or her real power flows from the ability to threaten to resign or to dissolve Parliament if the Cabinet will not support him or her. Thus votes of confidence, even within Cabinet, can achieve results when persuasion may have failed.

Prime ministerial powers and their use

As we have seen, the powers enjoyed by a prime minister are very wide indeed and can be used to exclude Parliament, the public and the party from the knowledge necessary for them to operate effectively. It is to the use of these powers that we now turn.

1 *Prime ministerial powers in an emergency*

It is essential for government to be able, in the national interest, to respond quickly and effectively to situations, at home or abroad, which require immediate decisive action, perhaps under the strictest secrecy. In such circumstances it may well be neither practicable nor desirable for that action to be delayed to allow for consultations, even within the Cabinet. For these purposes the prime minister must be accepted as the proper person to initiate such action, to arrange for it to be implemented, and to be ready to justify his or her action afterwards. But the existence of some situations which call for the exercise of his or her personal authority should not be used as an excuse for acting in this way when it is not strictly necessary to do so. It is obviously tempting for a prime minister to argue that all decisions he or she takes fall into this category of 'action in the national interest' and then require them to be supported as a matter of confidence. Not only is this unacceptable, it is often unnecessary: where decisions can be anticipated, a previous policy discussion should lead to guidelines being agreed in Cabinet beforehand.

2 *Prime ministerial power and the issue of consultation*

It is desirable that as many government policy decisions as possible should be reached after consultation with those whose interests are likely to be affected. Policies arrived at in this way are more likely to be effective, to be acceptable and to endure. Secrecy makes the consultation difficult if not impossible. It is therefore very important that the formulation of policy should not be shrouded in secrecy unless it is absolutely necessary; and where consultation does take place, those who are consulted must always include members of Parliament. Committees of the House are naturally angry if they discover that Bills they are discussing have been drafted to reflect unalterable agreements reached in bi-lateral discussions between the government and special interest groups. The same argument applies with particular force to Labour MPs and the Labour Party which, when Labour was in power, regularly experienced exclusion from the consultative process. Although some ministers made it their business to keep in close contact with the party, the party often thought that it was treated like an external pressure group and denied the special relationship with its ministerial colleagues which it believed it had a right to expect.

The tension arising from this discontent reached new levels during the 1977–9 'Lib-Lab pact' when Liberal MPs were brought into a formal consultative relationship with ministers, thus underlining the exclusion of the party and the Labour MPs. During the period when the pact was in force, ministers were expected to discuss their policy proposals with their Liberal counterparts before bringing them to colleagues. Neither

Labour MPs, even when organised in specialist groups, nor the NEC policy committees, ever enjoyed such rights. What is wanted is a permanent '*Lab*-Lab pact' whenever a Labour government is in power; and the institution of arrangements which would guarantee its effectiveness. This could best be achieved by developing greater accountability by the prime minister and ministers to back-bench MPs and the party. Such arrangements would in no way weaken the authority of the House of Commons, which would retain precisely the same rights to approve or disapprove government policies; just as the electorate would retain its power to re-elect or dismiss the government. But the policy presented in Parliament, and to the voters, would emerge from a very different consultative process – one that took greater account of the interdependence of the parliamentary leadership and the party which secures its election and sustains it in power.

3 Prime ministerial power: votes of confidence and appeals to party and personal loyalty

One of the unfortunate side-effects flowing from the excessive secrecy of government, and the centralisation of power within the Cabinet in the hands of the prime minister, is that the public, the House of Commons, Labour MPs and even the Cabinet often find themselves faced by *faits accomplis*. Some of these may involve a policy change of quite a fundamental character that should have been the subject of proper consultation. But if that consultation has not taken place, the only choice left is to accept what has happened, or to repudiate the decision and the prime minister who made it. Since no political party wants to repudiate its own elected leader, or to damage the party's interest by being seen to do so, there is a strong pressure to rally to what has been done. Prime ministers know this very well and may be tempted to make everything they do into a vote of confidence. This is inherently unsatisfactory because it personalises politics, substituting loyalty for the consideration of issues; and downgrades the role of MPs to that of 'lobby fodder'.

This problem can only be resolved if the personal power of the prime minister is diminished by giving others, including the Cabinet and Labour MPs, a greater say in the issues under discussion, before they have been decided and before any question of confidence arises. There will be circumstances in which a vote of confidence takes place, but they should be very much the exception and not the rule.

4 *Prime ministerial power and the party*

The attitude of the Labour Party towards its leader is always a complex one. Unlike the Conservative Party, whose leader is treated with elaborate personal respect and then disposed of as soon as he or she is thought to have failed, the Labour Party feels free to be critical of everything the leader says and does, but retains a fierce personal loyalty against all outside criticisms, and this will last until the leader dies or chooses to retire. Of these two attitudes, the Labour approach is much the better, but since Labour prime ministers depend so much upon that underlying loyalty, it must not be taken for granted, nor tested beyond what is reasonable, by trying to use it to reject policies the party wants, or to implement policies the party has rejected. The Common Market, incomes policy and *In Place of Strife* are examples where this has been tried and failed.

5 *Prime ministerial power, the parliamentary Labour Party, the National Executive Committee, annual conference and the trade unions*

In most of the discussion about the Labour Party conducted in the mass media, three supposed 'conflicts' are always highlighted. The first is the 'conflict' between the 'left wing' and the 'moderates' within the party; the second is the 'conflict' between the parliamentary party, on the one hand, and the NEC and annual conference on the other; the third 'conflict' involves the role of the trade unions. And to simplify the situation even more, the parliamentary party is seen as 'moderate' and the NEC and annual conference is said to be dominated by the 'left'. The trade union contribution to conference decisions is variously described according to how their votes are cast. If the trade unions vote with the 'moderates', their role is seen as being 'responsible' and 'democratic'. If they vote with the 'left', then the 'brute force of their block votes' is blamed for the outcome.

This presentation of events within the party has the merit of simplicity and the fact that it does not conform to reality is regarded by the media as irrelevant and – in so far as it spoils their political propaganda – dangerous too. The reality is, however, quite different and must be rescued from under the mass of half-truth and deliberate distortion with which it is overlaid.

(A) 'MODERATES' VERSUS 'LEFT WING' – A MISLEADING DESCRIPTION

First, the use of the adjectives 'moderate' and 'left wing' merits some examination. The Labour Party, being avowedly socialist in its aims, is itself left wing and so are all its members, as compared to the Conservatives and Liberals. Moreover, the term 'moderate' is equally confusing. By any world standard of socialism, the entire Labour Party is exceptionally moderate, offering, even in its supposedly 'full-blooded' manifestos in the past, the most modest proposals for changes in the structure of wealth and power, all to be achieved firmly within the framework of parliamentary democracy, complete with regular and free general elections. The main characteristics of the 'left wing' of the party are that it may be more analytical and philosophical in its approach, and more committed to carrying through the policies agreed at conference, once they have been endorsed by the electorate and a Labour government is in power. By contrast, some of the self-proclaimed 'moderates' have ended up in other political parties. Whatever else they turned out to be, they were not moderate socialists but committed Conservatives or Liberals. Thus the labelling now in general use is not very accurate in describing the wide spread of opinion within the party, and the spirit of tolerance to be found among people of differing views.

(B) THE PARLIAMENTARY LABOUR PARTY VERSUS THE PARTY?

The second 'conflict' is also most misleading. For, whatever may be said in the media, the attitude of the parliamentary party on the issues of the day may not differ as sharply from the attitude of the NEC and the conference as it is made to appear. The plain fact is that there is hardly ever a vote about policy among Labour MPs at meetings of the parliamentary party, and their collective view cannot be ascertained. In the five years from 1974 to 1979, for example, there were no votes at the parliamentary party meetings before the Cabinet decided to accept the renegotiation of Common Market terms; before key parts of the industrial policy were abandoned; before the cuts in public expenditure were approved; or before the 5 per cent pay limit was announced. In each case the Cabinet reached its view in private, announced it, and then called upon Labour MPs to support it as 'a matter of confidence'. Faced with the alternative of appearing to repudiate a Labour prime minister, or risking the defeat of a Labour government, Labour MPs gave their support to what had already been announced. It is anyone's guess whether they would have endorsed each, or any, of these policies if they had been asked before the Cabinet had reached its view and committed its public reputation to these policies. Certainly, in respect of some of these issues we know for a fact that the parliamentary party agreed with the NEC and conference and disagreed with the Cabinet. At no time from 1975 to 1979 did a majority of the parliamentary party vote for Cabinet policy in recommending the nation to accept the renegotiated terms for the EEC, nor for the legislation to hold direct elections. Nor can we be at all sure that the parliamentary party would have supported the cuts in public expenditure or the 5 per cent pay policy.

The real problem facing Labour MPs does not arise from pressure on them from the NEC, the annual conference or their own constituency activists. It stems directly from the excessive powers of the prime minister, who is able to secure compliance by the carrot and stick of patronage and threatened dissolutions. The remedy lies in the hands of Labour MPs alone. Unless they insist upon democracy within the parliamentary Labour Party, they can never reach a position in which their own view is both known and can be made effective in influencing their own leader, choosing their own Cabinet and insisting on prior consultations on matters of policy.

(c) THE TRADE UNIONS VERSUS THE NEC – AND WHY IT IS NOT TRUE

The role of the trade unions is also very different in practice from the public presentation of it. First, the trade unions already have the greatest say in determining the composition of the NEC. Out of 29 elected members of the NEC, the trade unions directly elect 12; and their votes are decisive in choosing the treasurer and the five members of the women's section, making 18 in all. Until 1981 the leader and deputy leader were elected by the parliamentary Labour Party. Now they are chosen by an electoral college in which the unions are strongly represented. This total of 20 compares with only seven constituency representatives, one from the socialist, cooperative and professional organisations and one young socialist. The supposed 'left wing' domination of the NEC by constituency activists does not stand up to a moment's examination.

Next, it should be made clear that without trade union support, no policy statement presented by the NEC has any chance of being endorsed. The 1974 manifesto policies for industry were overwhelmingly carried by conference, with trade union support; and the TUC economic and industrial policies in recent years have followed the lines first set out by the NEC; and were pressed upon the Labour Government by the TUC, even more strongly than by the NEC. Moreover, during the winter of 1978/9 it was the trade union membership, and not the NEC, which secured a modification of the 5 per cent pay policy.

Finally, it should be added that the relationship between the TUC and the Labour Government was much closer than the relationship between Labour ministers and either the NEC or the parliamentary Labour Party. Everyone in the party welcomed this close government – TUC contact and these contacts constituted the real extra-parliamentary role of the Labour movement. It is only against this factual background that the true position can be understood.

(d) THE REAL CAUSE OF TENSION – PRIME MINISTERIAL POWER

The tension within the party does not only stem from left wing versus moderate; or from Labour MPs or the unions versus the NEC and conference. It derives to a great extent from the tension that exists between the dominating power of the party leader, especially when he or she is prime minister, and the rest of the Labour movement, Labour MPs, the NEC, conference and the trade unions. Unless this power balance is redressed by the introduction of more democracy within the party and the movement, we shall never resolve the pressures which have built up, the nature of which it is so easy to misinterpret.

The Labour Party and its affiliated unions are united in wanting to make real socialist reforms through the agency of parliamentary democracy; and are quite open in spelling this out in resolutions and in manifestos. If – but only if – the electorate vote for a Labour government, the party expects its elected MPs to implement this policy. At present the main barrier to the realisation of that hope seems to be the power of the leader; and not Labour MPs as a body. The only possible criticism that can be levelled against Labour MPs is that they have accepted the situation which only they have the power to correct.

Unless this problem is dealt with by greater party democracy, and unless the pent-up pressure for economic, industrial and social change, now so evident inside the Labour movement, is able to be expressed in Parliament, there is a risk that it may seek expression outside the Labour Party and outside Parliament and thus damage the role of the Labour Party as the main democratic instrument of working people and their families. Indeed, there is an even greater danger. If the perspective of peaceful change, by democratic means, were to be blocked within the Labour Party, it would not just be the Labour Party but parliamentary democracy itself that might be undermined.

Towards a constitutional premiership

Having emphasised the immense concentration of power in the hands of the prime minister it is now necessary to consider ways and means by which the exercise of that power could be made more accountable to those in the country, in Parliament and in the party, over whom that power is held.

The problem is not that the power is grossly abused; if this were to happen, a prime minister would be overthrown by his or her Cabinet colleagues through a collective resignation or by Labour MPs through a withdrawal of support in the Commons. Either of these events would precipitate a change of leader; or a general election, in which case the decision of the voter would be final. The real problem does not lie in gross abuse, but in the full exercising of a power that has become so great that the fine balance of the Constitution is disturbed.

All constitutions and systems of government ultimately depend upon the goodwill and common sense of those occupying positions of responsibility; and require a degree of trust by those who are governed in those who govern them. Mechanistic solutions cannot replace the need for this common sense and this trust. But our history has taught us that even good kings were not good enough to make an absolute monarchy acceptable; and even good prime ministers can never be good enough to make the present concentration of power in their hands acceptable either. Some countervailing democratic influences need to be developed if we are to move towards a constitutional premiership more in keeping with the tenets of democracy. To these reforms I now turn.

1 An end to peerages

The abolition of the House of Lords, to which the Labour Party is firmly committed by an overwhelming conference vote, would dispense with the need to nominate peers, and the Labour Party does not support the idea of an elected second chamber. Nor do I.

2 The election of Cabinet ministers and the confirmation of the allocation of portfolios by Labour MPs

Were a system to be instituted under which all Cabinet ministers were elected by the parliamentary Labour Party, and the allocation of portfolios to all ministers were put to Labour MPs for approval before their nomination to the Crown was submitted, there would be a real sharing of power that would greatly strengthen the role of the government's supporters.

This would not diminish the power of the House of Commons as a whole over a government thus constructed. A majority of MPs would still have power to overthrow a government, if they wished.

3 The further development of the Commons select committee system

This should include the right to summon ministers and would open up the workings of government in a way that no other method could achieve. Effective select committees will probably do more to set up countervailing power to the power of the executive than any other single reform.

4 The institution of a parliamentary confirmation system for major public appointments

Departmental select committees should be able to recommend to the House whether or not ministerial appointments, chairmen of nationalised industries or of royal commissions, or even top ranking civil servants, should be confirmed by the Commons as a whole.

5 A Freedom of Information Act

Legislation conferring the statutory right of access to government papers, save those in a clearly defined narrow category involving defence and security or commercial or personal files, would greatly reduce the powers of the prime minister to the advantage of the public, Parliament and the party. The process of consultation would be revitalised by such a change and accountability would be much greater.

6 The return of the powers of law-making from Brussels to Parliament

Since so much of the law-making in Britain now flows from ministerial decisions taken at private meetings of the Council of Ministers in the European Communities without the express authorisation by the House of Commons, and since these powers are exercised by the prime minister through a combination of the royal prerogative and Section 2 of the 1972 European

Communities Act, effective means of restoring House of Commons power over the executive powers of the prime minister are needed to deal with this problem.

The European Communities (Amendment) Bill, introduced as a private member's measure in July 1979, shows how this could be done.[7]

7 *The strengthening of the powers of the parliamentary Labour Party*

In practice an examination of the ways and means of redressing the balance between the prime minister and the rest of the Constitution would reveal the need to strengthen the parliamentary Labour Party, and not to weaken it, as the media always suggest.

The parliamentary party has a very important role to play within the Labour Party of which it forms an integral part. Like all individual members of the party, Labour MPs have a responsibility to advocate, and to implement, the policies of the party as agreed at annual conference, and they have the opportunity to do so in the House of Commons. The party meeting, made up of all Labour MPs, should be seen as the main forum of debate within the parliamentary party; and the final authority on all matters concerning the day-to-day working of the party in the House of Commons, within the framework of conference policy. The parliamentary party should have the right, at all its meetings, to discuss all recommendations relating to the handling of parliamentary business, or to propose amendments of all kinds, which should in every case be put to party meetings for approval. Combined with the recommendations made above for the election of front-bench spokesmen, for the approval of the allocation of shadow portfolios and for a greater role for the subject groups of the parliamentary Labour Party, this measure would go a long way to redress the present imbalance in the power relationship between Labour MPs and the party leader.

There should also be regular meetings between the Parliamentary Committee and the NEC, which should have the last word on the manifesto, to discuss any matter relating to the work of the party that anybody may wish to raise.

These simple reforms should remain in force when a Labour government is in office.

Conclusion

These then are some of the reforms that could be instituted to redress the balance of power in favour of the public, Parliament and the party, and strengthen the nation at every level in its dealings with the prime minister of the day. The recommendations made involve the greater use of three tried and tested constitutional principles that have served to extend democratic accountability in the past. The first is greater disclosure; the second is the replacement of patronage by election or confirmation procedures; the third is the emphasis on truly collective decision-making as opposed to personal rule.

In arguing for this approach there is one factor to be taken into account that greatly strengthens the case. Not only has the power of the prime minister over the government greatly increased with the years, but the role of government itself has also greatly increased as the following figures reveal. Taking public expenditure over the fifty-year period 1925 to 1975 at constant 1975 prices, and taking 1925 as 100 per cent, central government's current expenditure has increased from £9,590 million to £37,195 million, i.e. to 388 per cent of the 1925 level in real terms.[8] During the same period central government's capital expenditure has risen from £559 million to £6,964 million, i.e. to 1,250 per cent of the 1925 level in real terms. Non-industrial civil service employment has risen in the same period from 114,000 to 517,000, an increase to 453 per cent on 1925.[9] The prime minister thus exercises greater personal power over a much more formidable array of state powers; and the case for greater accountability is, as a result, much stronger.

This growth of state power is necessary to protect the citizens against the even greater growth of extra-parliamentary centres of power – many of them now international – in finance and industry and in the international organisations, including the EEC, which now controls so much of our legislation, trade, economic and military policy. To seek a remedy to the problem by trying to reduce the role of government, absolutely, rather than by trying to bring it under greater democratic control, would only expose our people to greater domination by those extra-parliamentary forces from whom they have no means of redress at all. We need a strong government to protect us; and those who see that need must also be most vigilant in seeing that it is, itself, fully democratic in character.

The trend to centralisation of power is there for all to observe world-wide. We cannot allow it to grow in Britain, even in Downing Street, and least of all under Labour Party auspices. Strong leadership there must be, but it must be open, collective, and accountable, and must learn to exercise its necessary powers by persuasion and, above all, through the development of a constitutional premiership.

That then is the case for change, and it is a strong one. Nobody should suppose from this account that the only problem in British government lies in the excessive powers of the premiership, but it certainly rates as one of the major issues and merits serious public discussion. The more it is disclosed the clearer it will be that the dangers of an authoritarian system of government stem from the right in British politics, and from the media which supports an absolute premiership. It is the left, and left-centre, who want reform who are the true democrats, anxious to see political power shared more widely.

3

The Case for a Constitutional Civil Service

The argument in outline

In recent years, and especially now we are members of the EEC, the power, role, influence and authority of the senior levels of the civil service in Britain have grown to such an extent as to create the embryo of a corporate state. This threatens the workings of British democracy under which the people of this country are supposed to govern themselves through the Parliament they elect and the ministers who are accountable to it.

The main responsibility for allowing this to happen must be shared by Parliament, by ministers who have failed to speak out on this issue, and by successive prime ministers who have positively encouraged this trend to bureaucracy because it reinforces the power of their office. Major constitutional reforms are now urgently required. These must restore the authority of the House of Commons, secure effective ministerial control over the civil service and move towards a more constitutional type of premiership.

There are conflicts and tensions within our political system which receive a great deal of public attention. There are conflicts between the government of the day, whichever it is, and the opposition of the day; between the government and the people; between the front benches of all parties and the back benches of all parties; between the elected Parliament and other centres of power in society; between Britain and other foreign governments or foreign interests; and between class interests, as between capital and labour.

Each of these conflicts is familiar to political scientists and to the electorate as a whole. But there is another relationship which has received far less public attention, except in ministerial memoirs and some specialised writing, than its importance justifies. That is, the working relationship and the balance of power between ministers, elected to Parliament to implement the policy espoused by the majority, and the most senior permanent officials within government departments who have the major responsibility for public administration.

It is often argued that this relationship is one that should remain confidential and that it is not right to bring it out into the open. The reasons for maintaining secrecy are various. It is claimed, for example, that it is in the national interest to preserve secrecy. Certainly there are areas of government which it is in the national interest to keep confidential: for example, defence plans, security arrangements, budgetary decisions, position papers for international conferences, commercial arrangements and personal data. But the relationship in practice between different parts of the Constitution is a legitimate – indeed essential – subject for public discussion and understanding.

It is also argued that revelations about this relationship will undermine the confidence of those officials and ministers who have to work together. It is true that in any relationship confidence must be maintained, and that that confidence requires a degree of personal trust so that those involved will exercise proper discretion in what they reveal at the time or later. But to extend that argument, which rests upon common sense and the decencies of personal relationships, to argue that the nature of the relationship itself should be concealed, is to argue that the public has no right to know what goes on in its name. This is insupportable.

Ministerial memoirs or diaries are often criticised on the grounds that they undermine that relationship of confidence. I cannot share that view.

It may of course be embarrassing to be mentioned by name in such memoirs. But democracy must mean that a society can learn by experience; and if that experience and the lessons from it are to be concealed by secrecy, that learning process becomes much harder. The danger of memoirs seems to me to lie in quite a different direction. It is that the high drama that occurs during some of the great Whitehall battles is often so exciting that the clashes between individuals may blank out the real issues – reinforcing the false idea that it is the personalities that matter and not the constitutional issues. It is such gossip and malice that may undermine confidence, but not documented disclosure and proper analysis.

Civil servants sometimes argue that their special position makes it impossible for them to answer criticisms made of their conduct and it is therefore unfair to them to speak about their role. This argument, too, requires a proper response. Properly presented, the case against civil service power does not hinge upon the conduct of civil servants as individuals, but upon the power granted to them by the prime minister or other ministers. To that extent, civil servants do not need to justify the present arrangement – except in so far as they may wish to argue that the balance of power between the civil service and ministers is right; or that any failure should be attributed to the weakness or errors of ministers. As I hope to show, very senior civil servants have said just that in their own memoirs. Indeed, the power of the civil service to arrange for its view of policy to be transmitted discreetly to the media is every bit as great as is the power of ministers, and in the case of the Cabinet Office, the Treasury, the Foreign Office and the Home Office, this delicate briefing of top opinion formers is conducted on a regular basis. It is true that the most dramatic leaks which hit the headlines usually come from ministers in pursuit of their personal, political or departmental interests; and, in particular, from the prime minister of the day who, through No. 10, is responsible for 90 per cent of all the leaks which occur. But having said that, the editor of *The Times*, the *Financial Times*, the *Daily Telegraph* and the heavy Sundays and weeklies and their most trusted and senior correspondents are rarely left in any doubt as to where the mandarins stand on any major policy issue. The difference between ministerial leaks and official briefings is that ministers often have an interest in letting their own role be known, whereas senior officials have an equal interest in preserving their anonymity.

The civil service and prime ministerial power

My knowledge of the civil service derives entirely from my own personal observations as a citizen, as a member of Parliament and as a departmental minister. I have always been treated with great courtesy, both personally and in the handling of many thousands of constituency cases which have involved contact with the public service at various levels. There have been very few occasions when either my constituents or I have had any grounds for complaint about the conduct of individual civil servants. The public image of the faceless, humourless, unimaginative civil servant is a gross distortion of the truth. Like any big organisation, public administration has its weaknesses and its failures. But in general, in its conduct, its sense of responsibility, its dedication to the public welfare and its personal relations with the public, the civil service compares very well indeed with non-governmental organisations. Moreover, the degree of accountability in the public services is far greater than exists in the private sector through the operation of market forces.

All civil servants are Crown servants who see themselves in that capacity in their relationship with ministers. British governments are, in law, formed at the request of the Sovereign by an individual who is invited to form an administration, subject to his or her capacity to secure a parliamentary majority to support it. Thus, the prime minister of the day is the head of that administration and his or her personal authority is the only authority explicitly ceded by the Crown to an individual. The civil service accepts that authority and works under it and through it. All prime ministers then consolidate their authority over the civil service by personally assuming two key ministerial positions – that of the First Lord of the Treasury, which controls finance, and that of Minister for the Civil Service, which controls appointments. It is, thus, in the interests of the civil service to serve the prime minister of the day; and in the interests of the prime minister to have a strong civil service to support his or her personal authority. All the issues of importance concerning the role, power, influence and authority of the civil service thus take you right back to the alliance of mutual loyalty and support between No. 10 Downing Street and the mandarins. And nothing whatever can be done to change the present structure of power unless the nature of that alliance is changed by altering the power of the prime minister.[1]

Other ministers are, of course, appointed by the prime minister and require the formal approval of the Crown, but they hold their offices at the pleasure of the prime minister. So do the permanent secretaries, who enjoy a greater security of tenure and regard the Secretaries of State and departmental ministers they serve as birds of passage who, like them, are expected to work for the prime minister. If the prime minister retains real personal confidence in the ministers whom he or she appoints, then the permanent secretaries know it is in their interests to support them. But if the permanent officials have reason to believe that the prime minister has lost confidence in their departmental minister, it is in their interest to by-pass him and his policies. Moreover, the permanent secretaries' network within Whitehall, in which the Secretary of the Cabinet is a key figure, can work very effectively to undermine the prime minister's confidence in a minister whom the civil service dislikes or distrusts. This creates a situation in which the minister concerned can be slowed down, deflected, diverted, obstructed or, in the end, reshuffled or removed.

This should be clearly understood, because it places the main responsibility for making the necessary changes in the hands of the prime minister – and it makes intelligible the conduct of senior civil servants in their relationship with their minister. It also indicates that any reform of the work of the civil service would require a major change in the powers of the prime minister. Such a reform is unlikely to be welcome to any incumbent of that office, or to the senior civil service. But it could be secured by public pressure through Parliament or the political parties. The mandarins in modern Britain work as closely with the Emperor or Empress who governs from Downing Street as can ever have occurred in ancient China. Together they control the real levers of state power, many of which are so secret that most Cabinet ministers do not even know of their existence, let alone how they are being operated.

The role of the manifesto in a democracy

For the administrative class of the civil service the problems of government are necessarily seen from the top and from the inside where power resides. But for the electorate as a whole, the system is seen from below and from the outside. There are pressing needs to be met, injustices to be corrected and problems to be solved, and the ballot box is the main instrument for securing political change. From the voter's viewpoint, the agglomeration of state power at the top and the secrecy with which it is surrounded is often seen as a major barrier to industrial, economic, social and political advance.

The Labour movement was established to shift the balance of power in favour of working people and their families. Labour history can only be understood in those terms. First there was the struggle for free trade unions reflected in the campaigns against the Combination Acts, then the Chartist campaigns to extend the vote to working people, followed by the Suffragette movement to win the vote for women. Parallel with this came the establishment of the Labour Representation Committee, and then of the Labour Party, and in 1918 the adoption of a constitution with clear socialist objectives.

In each election since then the specific programme for the following Parliament has been embodied in a manifesto put before the electorate for endorsement, with a view to implementation if a mandate is given. Thus, once it has been adopted by the party conference and agreed by the party leadership, and endorsed by the electorate, the manifesto becomes the key link between the people and political power. It is the belief that real change can be made peacefully through the machinery of Parliament and the work of Labour ministers that makes the British Labour Party democratic; and explains why it has never adopted violent revolution as its instrument for social change. Therefore it is of central importance for the maintenance of confidence in our system of government that that process of social change can be made to work effectively and that the manifesto is taken seriously by members of Parliament, ministers and senior officials responsible for implementing it. For it is at the very moment when a successful party, with a mandate for its manifesto, sends its ministers into office that the role of the senior civil service becomes crucial.

Whitehall and consensus politics

How do the permanent secretaries view this process of party policy-making? It would be a mistake to suppose – as some socialists have suggested – that the senior ranks of the civil service are active Conservatives posing as impartial administrators. The issue is not their personal political views, nor their preferences for particular governments, though as citizens they are perfectly entitled to hold such views and to vote accordingly. The problem arises from the fact that the civil service sees itself as being above the party battle, with a political position of its own to defend against all-comers, including incoming governments armed with their philosophy and programme.

Civil service policy – and there is no other way to describe it – is an amalgam of views that have been developed over a long period. It draws some of its force from a deep commitment to the benefits of continuity and a fear that adversary politics may lead to sharp reversals by incoming governments of policies devised by their predecessors, which the civil service played a great part in developing. To that extent, the permanent secretaries could be expected to prefer consensus politics and to hope that such a consensus would remain the basis for all policy and administration.

As the term implies, consensus politics draws its inspiration from many sources in all political parties. The post-war consensus, which ended during the 1970s, was based upon the foundation laid by the Liberal Government of 1906 and especially the work of Lloyd George at the Treasury and Churchill and Beveridge at the Board of Trade. Consensus politics was institutionalised during the war-time coalition, in which Winston Churchill and Clement Attlee worked together. Despite the heated political debates of the 1950s and 1960s this broad consensus remained, in that the disagreements between the parties were contained within the framework of agreed objectives such as full employment and a welfare state. The differences were largely then confined to the question of which party was to be privileged to administer these policies.

The civil service laboured long and hard in support of this approach and helped to construct a top level corporate structure of committees and quangos, which brought together all those who could be persuaded to share their desire for the minimum of public controversy that is compatible with the two-and-a-half party system. Thus, when the senior civil servants see a new government come into power with a policy that goes outside that consensus, there is anxiety at the possible effect upon their own policy. Plans are laid that seek to contain this new surge of political power and divert ministerial energies into safer channels that do not disturb the even flow of established Whitehall policy.

The political views of senior permanent officials are not normally made public. Any minister quickly becomes aware of them by careful reading of the papers submitted to him by his own civil servants and in the flood of telegrams from our ambassadors abroad, which are widely circulated to ministers. Some retired civil servants are willing to express their own views on the governments which they have served, as the former Head of the Civil Service, Lord Armstrong, has done.[2] But it is rare for a leak of an actual government paper to take place. That is why, when it does, it merits very careful study.

In the spring of 1979 Sir Nicholas Henderson, the then British ambassador in Paris, sent a farewell despatch to the Foreign Office which was leaked to *The Economist*. It provides a classic insight into the mind of the Foreign Office and Whitehall, revealing views close to those expressed by the advocates of the Social Democratic Party in Britain; hostile to the trade unions, passionately committed to the EEC, and pessimistic about the future of Britain.[3]

Day after day, week after week, and month after month, the same analysis is fed to ministers and it would be surprising if it did not have an influence. Its influence is all the greater because all these papers and despatches are heavily classified and the public do not know what officials really think, cannot challenge their analysis and are continually assured that the mandarins are politically neutral, which they are not.

Civil service influence in practice

I have seen this process of civil service containment successfully practised against both Conservative and Labour governments over the last thirty years. The bold challenge of the 1964 Labour Government's 'new Britain' manifesto was gradually absorbed and finally defused by 20th July 1966, when the Treasury persuaded the then Chancellor to insist upon a package of economic measures that killed the national plan and instituted a statutory pay policy. It happened again when the 1970 Conservative Government was driven off its commitment to the free market philosophy developed at Selsdon Park and the then prime minister was persuaded to do a U-turn which took him back to the policies Macmillan had developed from 1962 to 1963, and that Wilson had been persuaded to follow from 1966 to 1970. It happened again after the referendum in 1975, when the Labour Government was persuaded to abandon its 1974 manifesto and to return to the policies of 1972–4, as pursued by Mr Heath. The same pressures are no doubt being applied to guide Mrs Thatcher back to the well-trodden paths followed on the advice of the civil service by Macmillan, Wilson and Heath.

It would, of course, be quite wrong to attribute all these policy changes to civil service pressures alone. All ministers must take responsibility for what they do and all are subject to a wide range of other pressures besides those which come from Whitehall. But it is not a coincidence that governments of both parties appear to end up with policies very similar to each other; and which are in every case a great deal more acceptable to Whitehall than were the manifestos upon which they were originally elected. It is also true that consensus or Whitehall policies, which have been pursued by governments of all parties for the last twenty years or more, have been accompanied by a steady decline in Britain's fortunes, which has now accelerated into a near catastrophic collapse of our industrial base. The governments which followed these policies – especially between 1964 and 1970, and 1974 and 1979 – have paid a heavy price in electoral terms, whilst those who furnished the briefing for the ministers concerned have continued in power, subject only to the normal wastage occasioned by retirement at sixty.

Whatever the future may hold for Mrs Thatcher's Government, the Social Democratic Party would appear to be dedicated to the pursuit of those same failed policies.

There has been no real examination of the role of the civil service during this period, or the methods it uses to secure ministerial compliance with its policies. Some of the techniques used by Whitehall to get its own way have emerged in ministerial memoirs, or other books and articles by those who have had first-hand experience of what goes on at the highest levels of Cabinet policy-making. Unfortunately, the revelations are usually so dramatic that they obscure the techniques themselves. Let me therefore list those methods broadly.

1 By briefing ministers

The document prepared by officials for presentation to incoming ministers after a general election is drawn up in two versions, one for each major party. (A similar brief is produced after a reshuffle.) This very important document has attracted no public interest. It is presented to a minister at the busiest moment of his life – when he enters his department and is at once bombarded by decisions to be made, the significance of which he cannot at that moment appreciate. The brief may thus be rapidly scanned and put aside for proper reading when the pressure eases, which it rarely does. In fact this brief repays the most careful scrutiny because from it can be deduced the department's policy, which officials hope the new minister will follow. It may be dressed up to look like a range of options for implementing the new government's manifesto, but beneath that presentational language it reveals the departmental view.

For example, in the 172-page Department of Energy brief for incoming Labour ministers in 1974, several of the 35 sections were marked 'Secret' or 'Confidential', including the following sentence: 'In principle it is desirable that all new orders for base load power stations should be nuclear.' In fact this policy was not followed by the Labour Government which ordered the DRAX B coal-fired station, but the brief correctly forecast both the sustained civil service opposition to the ordering of DRAX B, and also the decision of Mrs Thatcher's Government to revert to nuclear power using American reactors.

In October 1974 after the second general election I was reappointed to the Department of Industry and one of the briefing sheets in the package was headed 'For an incoming Labour minister – if not Mr Benn' – which indicated a premature hope of the reshuffle that occurred nine months later. It gave me a useful insight into the policy which the department hoped my successor would follow – as indeed he did. Academic research on the full set of briefs prepared by the civil service for ministers when they enter office and throughout their term would offer a more accurate explanation of policies followed and why, than a similar study of the manifestos upon which each government was elected.

2 *By setting the framework of policy*

The key to civil service influence lies in its power to limit the scope of policy-making. Lord Armstrong has spoken very frankly about this power:

> Obviously I had a great deal of influence. The biggest and most pervasive influence is in setting the framework within which questions of policy are raised. We, while I was at the Treasury, had a framework of the economy basically neo-Keynesian. We set the questions which we asked ministers to decide arising out of that framework and it would have been enormously difficult for any minister to change the framework, so to that extent we had great power.[4]

Thus ministers are continually guided to reach their decisions within that framework. Those ministers who seek to open up options beyond that framework are usually unable to get their proposals seriously considered.

3 *By the control of information*

The flow of necessary information to a minister on a certain subject can be made selective, restricted in other ways, delayed until it is too late or stopped altogether. Sir William Hayter, a distinguished former ambassador, acknowledged this aspect of civil service power in a letter to *The Times*, writing, 'The temptation to conceal from an unreasonable minister facts which might tend to confirm him in his unreason must have been very strong.'[5]

Geoffrey Moorhouse in *The Diplomats*, a study of the Foreign Office, gives a telling description of the renegotiations that preceded the EEC Referendum:

> Some of the home civil servants in the delegation from time to time quite deliberately kept their own departments in London ignorant of what was going on in Brussels for a delicately balanced day or two, or even for a few vital hours. This was not a betrayal of Whitehall; it simply meant that what Whitehall did not know Whitehall could not pass on.[6]

I can confirm this from my own experience in relation to a number of critical issues involving foreign policy, economic and industrial policy and civil nuclear policy. For example, when I was Secretary of State for Energy it came to light that in 1968 some 200 tons of uranium had disappeared en route by ship from Antwerp to Genoa. Most authorities are convinced it was hijacked to Israel despite the fact that it had been under the supervision of Euratom, the Common Market organisation which oversees nuclear fuel. When the loss became public I asked the United Kingdom Atomic Energy Authority, 'Was I told at the time?' (In 1968 I was also the minister responsible for energy.) No, I was not. Why not? On the grounds that we were not members of Euratom and it was not felt necessary to tell me. In fact, the danger of proliferation is one of the most sensitive areas in the handling of nuclear power and if fissile material such as uranium goes missing it is of prime national and international importance that the responsible minister should be told without delay.

Another example of vital information being withheld from the minister concerns the contract to purchase uranium from Namibia. In 1970, when I was the responsible minister, my civil servants authorised the British nuclear industry to obtain uranium from Rossing in Namibia, a country occupied by South Africa. The United Nations had declared this occupation illegal and the Labour Government insisted it was to be informed before any uranium contract was signed. The contracts were approved by Ministry of Technology officials. The Cabinet was not informed. I said in the House of Commons that I was misled.[7] One of the problems a minister faces is that his or her civil servants may have put something on record, so that it can be found when the file is checked, but they may not have drawn it to the minister's attention. Ministers require their departments to alert them specifically to major matters and in this case it did not happen.

There was a further instance in 1976, when a radiation leak occurred at Windscale, the plant for reprocessing radioactive waste. This was of vital political importance to me because precisely at that moment I was having to give my judgment to the Cabinet on the expansion of Windscale. When the leak was discovered, in one of the silos used to store old fuel elements, the first I heard of it was when it came out in the press. Yet the Health and Safety Executives' Nuclear Inspectorate and my department knew all about it.

There are many other examples where crucial information has been withheld by civil servants, in areas such as the breaking of oil sanctions against Rhodesia, the use of movements against sterling, the protection of Treasury control of British Petroleum and the campaign for pressure water reactors. Many other issues were dealt with in this way. To take just one example that involved a department other than my own, Defence: on one occasion the first draft of a defence White Paper came to the Cabinet showing a surprisingly large gap in the military balance between East and West. Questioning revealed that in calculating the military strength of the West the Ministry of Defence had left out the French armed forces. The reason given was that NATO did not exercise the same operational control over the French forces as applied to the rest of the alliance. In fact, of course, this crude misinformation was designed to win public support for a bigger defence budget by suggesting a more serious imbalance than existed. They were instructed to put the French back into the White Paper charts and they did.

4 *By the mobilisation of Whitehall*

It is also easy for the civil service to stop a minister by mobilising the whole range of internal forces against his policy. The senior civil servants are very strongly organised within Whitehall through a network of Cabinet committees under the general direction of the Cabinet Secretary, the most powerful figure of them all. The minutes of these committees are not circulated to ministers, who remain in general wholly ignorant about what is discussed, when, by whom, and with what effect. Civil servants as a whole accept this process as very natural and, since their own promotion depends upon the approval of their most senior colleagues, they tend to follow the lead given from above.

The normal method of mobilising Whitehall opposition is for officials to telephone their colleagues in other departments to report what a minister is proposing to do. This stimulates a flow of letters from other ministers (drafted for them by their officials) asking to be consulted, calling for inter-departmental committees to be set up, all in the hope that an unwelcome initiative can be nipped in the bud or transferred to the safety of an official examination.

Techniques used include the preparation of statistics based upon unverifiable assumptions such as an exaggeration of costs – used to delay the implementation of the health and safety legislation. There may be a warning that 'the lawyers advise that it would require legislation', followed by a second warning that 'the legislative time-table is so crowded that the measure is unlikely to get into the Queen's Speech in the foreseeable future'.

Ministers can be briefed against each other. To take one minor example, when Lord Brown (formerly Wilfred Brown of Glacier Metal) was Minister of State at the Board of Trade and wrote to me as Minister of Technology, my private secretary came to warn me that Lord Brown's letter had been written by him personally and did not reflect the views of the department. This warning was presumably to alert me to disregard it. Actually it served to remind me that the civil service did not expect ministers to go beyond the advice of their officials and had ways of preventing any such initiatives from being successful.

In October 1977 a very senior official at the Department of Industry minuted his Secretary of State to alert him to an initiative I was taking about the restructuring of the turbine generator industry. This minute was shown to me and it recommended a way of blocking my initiative and a draft that would do it. The minute then went on: 'If, however, you feel that you need to take a more active line in order to avoid being upstaged by Mr Benn, then the letter at E 5 would be appropriate.'

One of the most amusing examples occurred when my own permanent secretary in one department was violently opposed to a course of action I had decided to adopt. He knew that the matter would come up at a Cabinet committee attended both by me and by a junior minister in my own department whom he rightly thought was more sympathetic to his view. He therefore briefed this junior minister against my view. Unfortunately the junior minister concerned actually read out what he had been given and said that he ought to tell his colleagues that the permanent secretary did not agree with what the Secretary of State was advocating. Everyone looked rather embarrassed at this tactless revelation of what was going on.

5 *By the mobilisation of external pressure*

If ministers show signs of independence and require more pressure than can be generated internally, other resources may have to be brought into play. A telegram from an embassy abroad can be elicited to give a warning of the consequences that would flow from the pursuit of a certain course of action. NATO, the EEC or even the views of multinational companies or international bankers may be cited in support of a policy. In 1976 the IMF may actually have been informally encouraged to put pressure for public expenditure cuts upon the Labour Cabinet.[8]

These techniques can easily be reinforced by domestic pressures through the press. Nothing as crude as a direct appeal to the editor of *The Times*, the *Telegraph* or *The Economist* would be needed, since the mandarins and the media proprietors already share the same analysis, the same social values and the same interests, which at certain critical junctures can be very useful.

6 By the use of expertise

Most of my time in office has been spent in departments which have a high technical content – Post Office, Technology, Power, Industry and Energy. It is the task of ministers in such departments to interrogate their officials and the experts responsible until the political issues can be disentangled from the technical ones. Any lay minister will start at a disadvantage in dealing with such matters. It would be a mistake to suppose that senior officials are any more expert than an experienced minister. They may, however, seek to persuade a minister that the experts must be right and that such technical decisions are non-political. On one occasion in July 1966 I received a long minute in my Friday box advocating the expenditure of many tens of millions of pounds on two new scientific projects – the high flux beam reactor (HFBR) and the high magnetic field laboratory (HMFL). My permanent secretary had written 'I agree' and put his initials below. I laboured over the paper all weekend, and in the end decided to ask him to give me the reasons why this huge sum of money should be spent on these projects. When I did not receive a satisfactory answer I vetoed them. It was just a bounce and it had failed.

Nine years later a similar incident occurred. A paper was presented to me to put before the Cabinet committee recommending one of two courses of action on the fast-breeder reactor. Option 1 was to build the fast-breeder at a cost of about £2 billion. Option 2 was to pay about £1.5 billion for a watching brief which would allow us to be ready to build one later. Colleagues turned both options down, and the Cabinet Office which had masterminded the operation realised that it had over-egged the pudding.

Sir William Hayter in his letter to *The Times* argued that no weight should be attached to an election manifesto commitment on a particular type of nuclear reactor: 'And if expert opinion in this field is unanimous in favour of a particular course, is it likely that a minister, and one without any scientific qualifications, would be right and all the experts wrong?'[9]

This argument amounts to a declaration that democratic control cannot extend to technical matters and is only tolerable in the shrinking areas of policy that laymen can comprehend. It is a recipe for technocracy and the transfer of power to non-elected laymen in the persons of the mandarins.

7 *By the use of the CPRS*

One important innovation in Whitehall was the establishment of the Central Policy Review Staff which was intended to provide an opportunity for a broader, longer and more detached view of policy than could be obtained from departmental ministers or officials heavily pressed by the burden of day-to-day business. Though this idea of a Think Tank has certain superficial attractions, it has in the event turned out to be a very different body. Those recruited into it include both civil servants and outsiders, and it has in practice become a powerful lobby for the Cabinet Secretary, to whom it is responsible. The quality of its work reflects its small staffing. It is avowedly political in its opinions and the head of it sits in Cabinet committees with the status of a Cabinet minister able to circulate papers and to speak.

The CPRS should be put under a minister or disbanded altogether. Ministers should make time to be their own Think Tank and each government should see its own party colleagues outside government as the best agency for stimulating its thoughts about the future.

8 *By the use of patronage*

One extra source of power available to the civil service lies in its strategic command of patronage. Most public attention is focused upon the mere handful of appointments that are specifically in ministerial control. The use, or abuse, of the Honours List, and the charge of 'jobs for the boys' when a party colleague is given a major post, attract a great deal of press attention. But thousands of run-of-the-mill appointments to nationalised industries and quangos of one kind or another come from civil service lists and reflect civil service preferences, even if only because ministers are too busy to concern themselves with such appointments. Thus the civil service exercises an influence far beyond the confines of Whitehall, and can call upon the resources of its own appointees when it is necessary to do so.

The Common Market – buttress for bureaucracy

Britain's membership of the Common Market has had the most profound influence upon our whole Constitution and method of government. Much public attention has been paid to the philosophy embodied in the Treaty of Rome, to the unfair budgetary contribution and to the absurdities of the common agricultural policy. But the impact upon our own system of government has passed with very little comment. Yet British entry marked the most profound change in our system of government since 1066, or perhaps since the withdrawal of the Romans in AD 410.

We now have a written Constitution and a constitutional court; we are governed by ministers who legislate in secret, but can only enact legislation prepared by a Commission made up of politicians appointed to be civil servants who enjoy the powers of both breeds. Whitehall is now busy adapting itself to these new arrangements and doing so with zest. The Common Market is a mandarin's paradise. Not only has real power over many sectors of policy been transferred from London (where ministers work) to Brussels or Luxembourg (which they can only visit), but Parliament is now no longer sovereign and can thus be pushed into the background as far as the laws are concerned. If British legislation were to conflict with EEC legislation, the latter would be upheld by the European Court and enforced by the British courts whatever Parliament said.

Every item of EEC legislation automatically acquires the status of an Act of Parliament but is first negotiated by officials, often leaving ministers with a mere power to approve or disapprove the package as a whole. As a result, the infection of Common Market bureaucracy has spread back into the heart of Whitehall from the source of the virus in Brussels. The permanent secretaries who masterminded the preparatory work for all these activities through the Cabinet Office and the Foreign Office have now got a legitimate excuse to by-pass and override departmental ministers in the interests of coordination and the need to be good Europeans. Unless this process is stopped in its tracks, Britain could be governed by a Commission of permanent secretaries, with ministers able only to accept or reject what is put before them and the House of Commons a consultative assembly which can express its opinions but do little more.

It cannot be long before the British people realise that in the space of a generation this country has been transformed from being the centre of a world-wide empire to being a colony in someone else's European empire; heavily taxed, externally controlled and governed by a form of indirect rule on behalf of an imperial Commission on the continent. In saying this, we must acknowledge that a clear majority of the British Parliament voted for entry; and so did a clear majority of the electors in a national referendum. In the face of such an authoritative expression of British opinion, the civil service could legitimately argue that they were loyally implementing the decision reached. But it is not as simple as that.

Geoffrey Moorhouse explicitly identifies the role of the Foreign Office before the referendum. The following three quotations from *The Diplomats* are of the greatest public importance:

> There was absolute commitment to the work in hand, complete devotion to standing fast in the Market. The renegotiation of terms, quite obviously, would have failed without them. The result of the referendum might easily have gone the other way, too. There is a percentage of any national vote which expresses a gut reaction of many people who are beyond the immediate influence of evidence and argument; the crucial voters are those who can be swayed this way or that by the tides of political presentation right up to the moment of ballot. It would be difficult to overestimate the influence on that floating vote of the civil service alliance in Whitehall combined with the activity of the British delegation in Brussels.[10]

Later in the same chapter Moorhouse describes the way the civil service worked at that time:

> They saw it as legitimate and perfectly honourable practice to throw all their weight behind the emphasis on remaining

> in the Market, and to frustrate any attempts to turn the emphasis in the opposite direction. The codes of civil service say that at all times you support your own Minister in any conflict with another branch of government. That rule went overboard in Brussels.[11]

Finally, in the most revealing passage of all, Moorhouse says this:

> The diplomats have a concept of grand alliance which includes the integration of all things national. The economic fusion will be followed by the financial, and then the political. They do not doubt this for a moment: they see it as their job to help the process along.[12]

If this assessment is correct, some of the most senior civil servants – and especially those in the Foreign Office – are in the process of transferring their real allegiance from the United Kingdom to the European Community.

If so, the sooner the British people realise it the sooner they will understand what is happening to Britain and why.

The role of secrecy

Over everything described above, an official curtain of secrecy is supposed to be maintained. Why? Everyone who has worked in Whitehall as a minister or senior official knows very well what goes on and indeed may regard it as highly effective and praiseworthy. But the public at large are not officially permitted to know until thirty years later. True, the curtain of secrecy is regularly punctured by 'leaks' and they cannot usually be authenticated or traced. Memoirs are documented but they come too late to alter the course of events. Despite occasional revelations, the anonymity of most mandarins is preserved and the papers they write remain secret. In the meantime the public, who might have some influence on events by studying and challenging official briefs and putting forward alternatives, are kept in ignorance.

In whose interests is it that this secrecy should remain? It is in the interests both of weak ministers and strong civil servants, both of whom prefer to keep the public in the dark: weak ministers because they dare not invite challenges to their policy which they fear they could not answer; strong civil servants because they cannot be challenged as long as they remain anonymous.

Why ministers accept civil service power

It is sometimes said that a strong minister can always get his way with his department and that all criticisms made by ministers about the civil service are a confession of weakness and an excuse for failure, but the problem is much deeper than that. In the examples given here I am not seeking to allocate blame nor to make any excuses for failure, only to explain how the system actually works as I experienced it.

Why do ministers accept all this? Lord Armstrong was quoted as saying:

> We were very ready to explain it to anybody who was interested, but most ministers were not interested, were just prepared to take the questions as we offered them, which came out of that framework without going back into the preconceptions of them.[13]

That is another way of saying that many ministers are happy to take the line of least resistance. Some ministers are genuinely persuaded that what they are advised to do by their civil servants involves facing 'the harsh realities' and telling the people 'the truth however unpalatable it may be'. But whether the responsibility for allowing civil service power to be as great as it is lies with the prime minister, as I believe it does, with ministers who are partly responsible, or with a civil service which uses that power with such skill and effectiveness, the fact remains that the power is great and that its exercise raises questions of major public interest.

The corporate state – a new form of feudalism

Ministers who have held office have a responsibility to describe it as it is, to point to its weaknesses and dangers and to recommend political reforms that would reduce or remove those dangers. What we have constructed in Britain is the beginnings of a corporate state that more resembles feudalism than the democracy of which we often boast. Indeed the hierarchical character of the old feudalism which made its landlords into peers has been buttressed by adding bankers, industrialists, trade union leaders, ex-ministers and ex-permanent secretaries to the House of Lords, where they have powers to delay and effectively veto legislation from the elected Commons.

British corporatism, controlling a state function many times greater in real terms than it was fifty years ago, is, of course, quite different from that developed in Central Europe between the wars, which went fascist; and it is not at all the same as the corporate state set up by Stalin to build communism. British corporatism has come into being to sustain a fast declining mixed economy and to seek to revitalise capitalism within the framework of a European union committed to that same end; hoping for prosperity and superpower status. In this scenario of a British colony within a European super-state civil servants will be at the centre of a complex network of power structures representing industry, finance, the army, the security services, and possibly even the leaders of European labour unions, if they can be inveigled in to join the club as associate members.

There are millions of people who would not accept such a development. But if it is to be prevented, we must set ourselves new objectives and discuss them.

A strategy for reform

If we are to reopen the campaign for democracy, certain reforms must be considered urgently.

1 A Freedom of Information Act

There must be a Freedom of Information Act providing for a statutory right of access to knowledge about government and its workings, subject only to the accepted safeguards on information which it is in the national interest to keep secret.

2 *Stronger parliamentary control*

We need to develop select committees to probe into the heart of Whitehall policy-making, including finance, foreign policy, defence and the security services.

3 *A constitutional premiership*

The prime minister must be made much more accountable than he or she now is for the powers exercised and we must move towards a more genuine form of collective ministerial responsibility.

4 *More ministerial control over the civil service*

We need to ensure that ministers are able to secure compliance with the policies that they were elected to implement. Proposals to this end have been widely discussed and would certainly involve making the most senior officials in each department more responsible to the ministers whom they serve.

5 *The abolition of patronage*

Advertisement, open selection, election or parliamentary confirmation procedures should be used to cover all public appointments.

6 *The amendment of Section 2 of the European Communities Act*

We must restore full law-making and tax-gathering powers to the elected House of Commons and create a new basis for European cooperation by accepting that this must rest upon a willingness of fully self-governing states to work together.

The case for democracy

In considering these issues, we do not want to find new scapegoats or pile the blame upon ministers or civil servants who have let the system grow into what it is. What matters now is that we should examine what has happened to our system of government with fresh eyes and resolve to reintroduce constitutional democracy to Britain, so that policies in the future will reflect the aspirations of our own people and not just the interests of some mandarins, some ministers or some members of Parliament who now seem so strangely satisfied with the status quo. In a period of rapid technical change it is essential that the machinery of government at all levels should be capable of reflecting the desires of the people expressed through the ballot box more rapidly than is now the case. Indeed, it must, if we are to maintain the stability of our society.

4

Civil Liberties and the Security Services

The argument in outline

Freedom and democracy in Britain, and everywhere else, have always been won by struggle. Those who exercise political power, whether acquired by conquest, inheritance, revolution, or even by election, understandably want to keep it and will go to considerable lengths to think of reasons why they should. They may claim a divine right to rule derived from religion; a prescriptive right derived from the ownership of land or capital; a moral right derived from ideology; or simply argue that they possess special expertise. And when their power is threatened they may warn of exterior attack or disorder and use those threats to tighten their grip.

The present anxiety amongst those with power at the centre of corporate capitalism and state communism results from their failure to win the level of public support which they need to hold on to their power and the system which underpins it. Demands made for the wider sharing of that power by the mass of the people are everywhere rebutted. All ruling groups know how important it is to see that their arguments for staying in power are regularly presented through the means of mass communication. In medieval times a state church, through its bishops and priests, could be used for that purpose. Today it means influencing the mass media through its commentators or columnists who dominate the world of print, radio and TV. Those with power must be able to rely upon the media to construct a framework of conventional wisdom which supports the status quo by the selection of news and opinions either favourable to it, or only mildly critical.

Therefore anyone who campaigns for freedom or civil liberty must start by studying how public opinion is influenced.

The establishment view of Britain

The British media largely reflect the view of the British establishment. At home we are told that British workers, under the influence of strong and irresponsible trade unions, have kept British productivity so low and wages so high that jobs must go, and that living standards and public services must be cut back in a new spirit of economic realism. We are also told that the country is now under a growing threat of attack or invasion by the Soviet Union which requires our weakened economy to carry a still heavier burden of defence expenditure, and it makes it necessary for the United States to site a new generation of cruise nuclear missiles on airfields which they occupy in Britain.

Through the media, the establishment then goes on to identify all those who oppose such policies and resist job losses, wage cuts, educational or health economies, or rearmament, as militants, extremists or subversives, who represent a threat to law, order and freedom. This analysis, buttressed by endless news stories about rising levels of violence, falling moral standards and the risk of anarchy and chaos, is then used to justify tighter and tighter security at every level. We are told we need expanded and better paid military and police forces, and a bigger and more elaborate secret intelligence network able to maintain a comprehensive surveillance of all persons who are, or might be at some later stage, engaged in activities that threaten our freedom. Through the British media the establishment makes out a picture of the situation confronting the British people designed to condition us all into accepting the policies that flow from its own one-sided analysis.

The establishment view of the 'free world'

However, when it comes to the coverage of the world scene, the British establishment media often have a totally different analysis to offer.

Any black person in Southern Africa who, denied freedom through the ballot box, is driven even to consider using force to win the liberties we declare we would defend by force, is then branded a terrorist, probably a Marxist and almost certainly under direct Russian control. Thus it was that, throughout the period of Ian Smith's white dictatorship, the African majority in Rhodesia were represented as Marxist terrorists who had no real support – until an internationally supervised election revealed that Ian Smith's dictatorship was supported only by the white settlers, and was swept away.

Similarly, the Shah of Iran was held up for years in the British media as a model of what an enlightened monarch could do to raise the living standards of his country. No mention was made of the fact that he was put back on his throne by the American Central Intelligence Agency, and armed to the teeth by the West, including Britain, so that he could hold his own people down and thus enable British and American oil companies to exploit, at great profit, the Iranian energy resources needed for Western capitalism to survive. The dictatorship in Chile was also set up by the USA and is now being sold arms to keep itself in power by a British Government that daily protests its deep commitment to political liberty. Nor is there any British establishment support for those who throughout Latin America are fighting for freedom. The struggle there is being conducted by a courageous combination of trade unionists, socialists, and a growing number of progressive Catholic priests who are living their theology in struggles to help the poor, the homeless, and the landless. Yet their oppressors are never systematically criticised by the British Government, nor are the dictatorships in South Korea, Taiwan, the Philippines or Thailand, all of which are part of the anti-communist alliance.

Underpinning these alliances is a loose network of intelligence activities, allowing an exchange of information about any progressive or democratic movement which might challenge power structures anywhere, upon which the status quo throughout the capitalist world depends for its security.

The establishment view of the communist world

When it comes to the coverage of the communist countries, it is Russia which is singled out for attack. Marxism may be constantly denigrated and attacked at home but that is no bar to British media approval abroad, in countries which it is in the interests of the British establishment to support because they are anti-Russian. Marxist Yugoslavia, though run by the Communist Party without free elections in the Western sense, gets a good press because in 1948 Tito broke with Stalin and the country is seen as a useful bridgehead for Western influence in Eastern Europe. Communist China, denounced in extreme language ten years ago, is now almost an ally, to whom Britain may sell arms, just because China's hostility to the USSR appears to be strong and growing, and it can be relied on if a war with the USSR took place.

In Poland the strikers were described as heroic dissidents struggling for freedom. And when Polish trade unionists demanded political reform and access to the Polish media to present their case, they were praised by the same British leader writers who use their columns to denounce any British trade unionist who demands the same rights for British Leyland workers.[1] It is the Soviet Union which the establishment sees as the world enemy we must be prepared to fight, and that determines its policy on most international issues.

Towards a new analysis

How then can we make sense of such hypocrisy and reconcile the contradictions of the British establishment position? Only by understanding that the establishment is not interested in freedom at all; it is engaged in a naked national power struggle.

Corporate capitalism in the West, state communism in the East, racism in Africa and military dictatorships in the Third World have one thing in common. They are all centralised systems with too much power at the top. They are all increasingly dominated by their military and security chiefs. They all maintain tight secrecy around their most sensitive operations. They all control, or greatly influence, directly or indirectly, what the media in their own countries say. And they all, including Britain, fall short of the highest standards of a truly open self-governing democratic society.

To say this is not to blur the real differences which exist between the various political systems. For these differences are of fundamental importance if each country is examined on its own internal record. The fact that the people in Britain and some capitalist countries can still speak up, organise, and vote their own governments out of power is of immense significance when compared to the fact that in the Soviet Union and the communist countries, or the military dictatorships with which we are allied, that right has not been ceded. But it is not true to say that civil liberties are any greater in South Africa, Chile, Brazil or China, than they are in the USSR, Poland, Hungary or Czechoslovakia – for they are not. Indeed, in any objective assessment of human rights, communist countries are no worse than some of those nations whom the West is now embracing as friends of freedom, and arming on those grounds. Nor was there any moral justification for the American war in Vietnam, or the British and French attack upon Egypt at the time of Suez, which might not be used by the Russians in support of their interventions in Hungary, Czechoslovakia and Afghanistan. All those actions were indefensible.

Nor indeed can any security service, operating the tightest secrecy, in any country credibly argue that it works to higher moral standards than any other. It may, but since we are not allowed to know, the case must go unproved.

It is against this type of analysis that we have to examine the state of civil liberties in Britain and the operations of our own military, police and security services.

The official view of state security

The official version of what the security services in Britain are, and what they do, and why we need them is very straightforward, and could be described roughly like this:

'Britain is a democracy, birthplace of the Mother of Parliaments, the bastion of personal liberty, and a leader of the free world. To protect this freedom from our foreign enemies, i.e. the Russians and their satellites, we need strong armed forces, the latest nuclear weapons, the NATO Alliance, extensive civil defence and an effective military intelligence. To protect ourselves from subversion and terrorism at home we need a strong police force, including the Special Patrol Group, the Special Branch, and those military intelligence units who work with them against the IRA, the PLO, the Angry Brigade or any group likely to disrupt our lives or take away our liberty to think and act freely. To perform these tasks the intelligence work has to be carried out in secret. But no one who is not an enemy spy, a terrorist, or a violent revolutionary, need fear the role of the security services. They are only interested in espionage, terrorism, subversion, and major crime, and these they will keep under regular surveillance. They will track down, expose and bring the offenders to justice, so that the rest of us can enjoy our liberty undisturbed.'

This is the 'official version' in outline.

In a world where military aggression, coups d'état, hijacking and violence are commonplace, all much publicised in the media, solid citizens are reassured to hear that behind our servicemen and the bobby on the beat, and backing them up, we have secret services that are 'discreet, self-effacing, courageous, vigilant'. There is enough truth in the dangers to convince the majority of people that all these elaborate security systems are justified; and there is a marked reluctance to criticise these services. Those who should speak up about excesses rationalise their silence by convincing themselves that the only people who might suffer would be a minority of foreigners, native trouble makers or militants, and these sort of people are asking for trouble anyway and hence are not deserving of much sympathy.

There is also another powerful reason for not speaking up. Anyone who does comment unfavourably upon the activities of the security services knows that he or she will immediately attract their attention, and this alone will lead to a security file being opened on them, with all the risks that that involves. Yet we know that we should raise questions on these matters; for the operations of the military, police and security services may develop in a way that will threaten the very freedom they purport to defend.

My experience

My first direct experience of the security services occurred just after I had been demobilised from the navy and had returned to university. I was invited by my old public school headmaster to go and see him, and was introduced to a certain colonel who was in plain clothes, and asked me if I would like a job.

I asked him what the job was and he said that he was not in a position to tell me, but he mentioned a salary of around £1,000 a year, which was more than twice as much as I later received as a BBC producer. If I was interested, he said, he would take me to see someone else who would explain what this involved.

I thought for a moment, and then said that in any case I would not be able to undertake such a job as I wanted to work within the Labour movement, was on the list of Labour parliamentary candidates, and hoped one day to get elected to the House of Commons. Expecting that this reply would end the interview, I was very surprised to hear him say: 'Oh, that is no problem. You could do both jobs.' I knew enough to know that an office of profit under the Crown, i.e. a paid government job, automatically disqualified anyone from election to Parliament. The real reason for his interest in recruiting me may very well have been that he knew precisely what I wanted to do *before* he approached me and, indeed, that must have been *why* he made the approach.

I reported all this to my father who said very clearly: 'Whatever you do, don't get mixed up in that sort of business.' And I sent a message back confirming my refusal.

As a result of saying 'No' so definitely, I was never taken to meet the man who would have explained it all. But that was not the end of the colonel. A few years later, after I had been elected to Parliament, he wrote and asked to come and see me again, this time at the House of Commons. He then repeated his invitation to do some work for the Foreign Office and said that if I wanted to know more about it I should ask a certain Labour MP, whom he named, who had served as a minister in the

1945–51 Labour Government. I thanked him courteously and declined once more.

It was many years later that I came across the name of the colonel again in a newspaper story about the security services. I cannot help wondering how many other people in the Labour Party, in Parliament, in the trade unions or outside, were recruited on the same basis and are still on the government pay-roll, unknown to all the colleagues with whom they work.

The security services and the Labour movement

The security services, or at least an element within them, regard those who work within the Labour movement, especially its socialist activists, as being a security risk for that reason alone. Conservatives would not be so classified.[2]

This interpretation of a security risk has never been publicly discussed by ministers, although if it is as widespread as I believe it to be, it raises major issues of public policy and civil liberties. For it means that the security services, far from being limited in their work to the discovery of direct external and internal threats to our internal democracy, are also active indirectly as the upholders of the status quo in our society and are treating socialists who wish to change that status quo by democratic means as potential enemies of that democracy.

In the long run this is the biggest threat to political freedom from the state. In the short run it is used to justify a degree of surveillance of certain organisations and individuals in Britain which goes far beyond what is publicly admitted.

The methods used include the widespread interception of communications, the extensive tapping of telephones, and the maintenance of a bar upon employment for people in both government and sensitive industrial work against whom no conceivable charge of treason or subversion would stand up for one moment in any court of law, nor would it command public support if it had to be justified publicly. Hence the secrecy.

The trade unions are of course a special target for surveillance by the security services. The evidence recently published by the Post Office Engineering Union must be taken seriously in this context.[3] There is no room for doubt that active trade unionists do have their telephone calls regularly intercepted, and this surveillance is redoubled during industrial disputes, as in the miners' strikes in 1972 and 1974.[4] I was present on one social occasion when a former Labour prime minister indicated this quite clearly.

Twice, as a minister, I was told categorically that candidates I had proposed for major public appointments were not acceptable on security grounds. The two men concerned were senior members of the General Council of the TUC, active in the Labour Party, and each was then playing a key role in supporting the policies of the then Labour Government. In each case it took a letter from me to the prime minister personally, and in one case a request for a meeting with him, to discuss the matter, to have these objections overruled. Had I not done so, those men would have remained disqualified from public service on security grounds.

Ministers who have direct responsibility for the work of the security services, if asked about the way they exercise their responsibilities, always insist that their control is direct, personal and complete. I very much doubt whether this is the case. If it is so, the Labour ministers must have authorised the incidents of which I have personal knowledge, and this they certainly should not have done. But in my view it is much more likely that the security services do not inform the ministers of what is going on, or cover up their activities in phrases designed to secure acquiescence.

The government reaction to pressures by labour

All this surveillance is stepped up during industrial disputes and the military are brought in to advise ministers. Certainly my own direct observation of the potential role of the services during the oil tanker drivers' dispute in 1978/9 suggested strongly that the armed forces saw themselves as preparing a military operation against trade union adversaries which required, for its success, a detailed knowledge of what the 'enemy' was planning. I shall never forget the experience of that winter. As Energy minister, I had a statutory responsibility to maintain supplies. I kept in close contact with the Transport and General

Workers' Union, whose members were involved in the dispute and who alone could actually guarantee the maintenance of essential services, which in any case they had no wish to disrupt. A regular round of meetings to assess pay claims, to prepare for an emergency, and to meet the employers and the union, certainly gave me a remarkable insight into the attitude of the British establishment at its highest military and civilian level towards the trade unions – an attitude of deep hostility and suspicion, which led it to plan its counter measures with something of the same anxious precision that must have been in evidence between the fall of France and the Battle of Britain in 1940.

It was also apparent to me that Britain could get far better emergency supplies with trade union cooperation than would have been possible if all the resources of the armed forces had been brought into play.

The government reaction to pressures by capital

How different it is when pressure is brought to bear on government by the forces of capital. In 1976 when there was a run on the pound, in which the City of London and the banks were playing a leading part, there was no evidence whatever that the security services were interested in the activities of those who were speculating in our currency, against our clear national interest.[5]

Moreover, the attacks upon the British national interest from capital received far less public attention, if reported at all. The unions, by contrast, were often presented as a group holding the nation to ransom. It is impossible to escape the conclusion that the British establishment and its permanent intelligence services see capital, both national and international, as a natural ally in its unending conflict with the organisations of working people who produce the wealth in this country.

One very small incident in my experience illustrated this double standard. There is a modest exchange scheme in operation in the civil service under which civil servants may be seconded for a period to industry. Such an exchange with business management can obviously be of mutual advantage.

But when an exceptionally bright young civil servant, whom I knew well, made arrangements to go on attachment to a trade union and then sought official permission to do so, he was told that 'it would harm his civil service career'. And he was left in no doubt of the reason: the trade unions were, in general, felt to be in some vague way subversive.

Some former civil servants have moved into the trade union and the Labour movements, motivated by a preference for serving a cause in which they deeply believe, and which they serve loyally. I should be surprised if a few others have not been deliberately planted within our movement in the past to carry on their surveillance from the inside, maybe on the basis of some personal approach similar to the one made to me.

The idea that Labour is an alien hostile force is deeply embedded in the minds of at least some top people in the civil and military establishment in Britain. This is in part a product of the segregated educational background, upbringing, conditioning and class origins of most senior public servants. Their political beliefs are, and must remain, their own private affair, and their right to hold them as citizens in a democracy must be maintained in all circumstances. But it is quite another thing if they incorporate their own political attitudes into the work they do as military or civil servants and construct policies or administrative strategies to reflect them as part of their supposedly non-political role in serving the governments of the day, half of which since the war have been Labour.

Civil service ignorance about the Labour and socialist movement

In this connection there are other aspects which should concern us. One is the extraordinary ignorance there is amongst the upper echelons of the civil service, including the security services, about the trade union movement, and socialism in its many forms. I will give two examples to illustrate this. In 1974, within a few days of arriving at the Department of Industry, a major firm which had for some time been in deep financial difficulty, informed me of its imminent collapse. I called a meeting attended by the most senior officials to consider how we should respond. One of them was a deputy secretary who had had a senior position as an industrial policy adviser for some years and the following conversation took place during the meeting. 'You had better get on to the Confed at once,' I told him. 'The what?' he asked. 'The CSEU,' I answered. 'I am afraid you have an advantage over me, Secretary of State. I do not know of it.' 'The Confederation of Shipbuilding and Engineering Unions, whose headquarters are in Walworth Road,' I explained. He had never heard of it. Here was a man responsible for policy-making at the highest levels in the government service, who had not even heard of the Confed. It was, I fear, not an untypical experience.

On another occasion the International Secretary of the Labour Party invited me, as a member of the Labour Party National Executive, to attend a meeting with a delegation from the Socialist International of which the Labour Party, the SPD in Germany, and all the world's democratic socialists, are members. Its headquarters were then in London, its Secretary General a respected former British trade union official. Embarrassed and anxious, my civil service private secretary informed me that in no circumstances could I attend. When I expressed surprise at this statement, it turned out that he had been told officially that the Socialist International was the same as the International Socialists – now the Socialist Workers' Party, and a Trotskyite organisation.

If Whitehall really did not know the difference between the Socialist International and the International Socialists, then something very fundamental must be wrong. These examples, insignificant as they may appear, should remind us that some of those who advise ministers, and run the security services, are not necessarily very well informed about the Labour and socialist movement, here or abroad.

Looked at one way, these deficiencies of political understanding may serve to disabuse us of the idea that the security services are all-knowing in their work, for they are not. No doubt they employ a number of intellectuals who can advise them from their academic knowledge of the differences between the myriad of ideological tendencies that are marshalled under the heading Socialism – which are as numerous as the religious creeds which call themselves Christian. But looked at another way, it is alarming to reflect upon the poor quality of the advice fed to ministers. My former teacher, Professor Sir John Wheeler-Bennett, the historian and founder member of the Royal Institute of International Affairs at Chatham House in London, once told me a story that confirmed this view. He went to see Trotsky in Mexico City in 1939 just before the Russian dissident was murdered by the Soviet secret police. After their discussions, Trotsky gave him a number of his books, and Wheeler-Bennett took them with him when he crossed into America. The border officials there, though very suspicious, and after asking a lot of questions, allowed Wheeler-Bennett in.

Later on, he joined the British War-time Mission in Washington and a friendly American colleague showed him the report that had been submitted on him by those same border officials. It read something like this: 'Mr Wheeler-Bennett entered the USA on his return from a visit to the Russian revolutionary Leon Trotsky, and his suitcase was full of Communist propaganda. When asked about this, Mr Wheeler-Bennett told us that Mr Trotsky was opposed to Joseph Stalin. Wheeler-Bennett is clearly not a man to be trusted.'

International intelligence

With intelligence like that it is not surprising that the US and British governments should have allowed themselves to be so misled on so many occasions about events in so many parts of the world. They are kept out of touch with reality.

The US-UK intelligence links are exceptionally close, no doubt deriving from war-time work on the atomic bomb, and maintained and extended ever since to cover joint defence interests. These links amount to a virtually complete supervision of British security by their American counterparts, in return for which the British government are no doubt supposed to have access to such intelligence information as the US authorities are ready to disclose.[6] It would appear that the US-UK intelligence communities often operate together well below the level at which British ministers are allowed to know what is happening. These close links were not of much value in forecasting events in Iran, where both the US and the UK had a massive intelligence operation, and great influence with the Shah. Our embassy in Teheran was little short of ecstatic in their praise of the Shah, and the briefings I received from our officials there when I went on a ministerial visit in 1976 were equally laudatory. They were all wrong, and I learned more about what was going on, and what was likely to happen, from Iranian students who lobbied me at public meetings in Britain, and who sent me their literature, than from all the official briefings.

Not that the intelligence services ignored these same students. I am sure they were all under continued surveillance by MI5, MI6, the Special Branch, the CIA, the FBI and SAVAK, the former Iranian intelligence service, with whom I assume US and UK intelligence worked very closely.

The risk of error increased by secrecy

There is another aspect of security work which needs to be examined most carefully, and that is the possibility of a simple error being harder to correct because of rigid secrecy.

One incident that came to my attention underlines the dangers. A very senior scientist with whom I worked closely over a number of years had, earlier in his government career, been engaged in the development of weapons. He told me that during that period one of his junior scientists had been invited to meet an attaché from the Soviet Embassy, and had quite properly gone at once to his superior – my old colleague – and sought advice as to what he should do. He was instructed to accept the invitation and then report the whole conversation, including what the Russian had asked him about, back to his superiors when he had had the meeting. This the young man did conscientiously.

Later this young man came up before a promotion board upon which my senior scientist colleague was a member. The board was told that the young man was not suitable for promotion because 'he had had contacts with the Soviet Embassy'. Had the senior scientist concerned not known about the episode personally and been able to establish to the satisfaction of the board that this man was acting throughout under official instructions, the young man's career would have been ruined.

This is one of the dangers which arise from the very nature of secret vetting, in which the suspected person is denied knowledge of the information held on file about him and therefore cannot query its authenticity even when it may be inaccurate. It is not easy to see how this problem can be resolved while protecting sensitive sources, but it is obvious that secrecy protects mistakes, and that where malicious misinformation is fed into a security file there may thus be no way of preventing a grave miscarriage of justice.

The effect of the emergency in Northern Ireland on civil liberties in the United Kingdom

The emergency in Northern Ireland, with the immense effort that has gone into the development of the intelligence counter measures, has added a new dimension to the problem of reconciling security with democratic rights. An enormous amount of money and effort has been poured into the technology of surveillance and security, and an apparatus has been set up which, improperly used, would resemble that of a police state. At no stage was the policy to be followed by this intelligence system ever brought to the attention of the Cabinet or any Cabinet committee of which I was a member. What should concern us is the possible effect this system could have on security practices in the rest of the United Kingdom.

On one occasion I was considering, with ministerial colleagues, the implications for civil liberties of an extension of nuclear power for the generation of electricity, following the publication of the Flowers Report on nuclear power and the environment. Nuclear processes involve the handling of exceptionally dangerous materials, not least plutonium, which, if it fell into the hands of terrorists, could lead to a direct threat to our national survival. It fell to me, as Energy Secretary, to satisfy myself that the security arrangements were strengthened to obviate the risk of such a disaster occurring. Among the measures I put before Parliament was a Bill that authorised the arming of the Atomic Energy Authority constabulary. This was only one of a number of measures details of which, for obvious reasons, should not be disclosed. But in a ministerial discussion about these measures I expressed the anxiety that we might be paying too high a price in civil liberties for the provision of electricity by nuclear, as against other means.

The response I got surprised me: 'Why worry? We have done all that in Northern Ireland.'

The real price of high technology

The real anxiety is not that Britain will consciously adopt the methods of a police state but that we might slide into them almost casually as a result of seeking protection against the non-political hazards of high technology.

The price that we may already be paying for security is far greater than most people appreciate, and extends right across the whole of society. For with the sophisticated methods of surveillance, and the capacity to computerise and correlate all the information known about an individual, the files could go on growing until there is a shadow profile containing political, educational, medical, financial and strictly personal data about anyone who might ever criticise the policies of the establishment, or any of their allies, whoever they might be.

Government black-listing could then be extended – unknown to those affected – to exclude a wide range of people from any possibility of holding responsible positions. The trade unions now have evidence that employers already operate such a system in industry. A fully fledged government vetting system – like the German Berufsverbot[7] – would inevitably mean that only the obsequious and the obedient could hope to get appointed to the civil service or to executive positions in the public service or private industry. Such people would have 'earned' their success by having nothing whatever on their records to show that they attended radical meetings, read socialist literature, or took part in any public campaign, or indeed ever thought for themselves.

A nation managed by those who could survive all these tests would soon find itself run by the mediocre, conspicuous only for their lack of curiosity or public-spiritedness, and hence likely to be completely unaware of the rich inheritance of genius and talent which is the greatest asset a democracy can nourish. This very anxiety was in fact once put to me by a permanent secretary who saw the dangers of this for the civil service, and I think he was right.

In such a society the degree of protection afforded to democracy might seem formidable, but in reality it would long ago have throttled the life out of what it was intended to safeguard. And because this protective mechanism would itself be operating behind the tightest screen of secrecy, there would be no accountability from our 'protectors' to those they claimed to protect. Thus, immune from effective criticism, they would be free to control the rest of us, turning on any who dared to criticise them as 'enemies of the people', a charge that the media would amplify and broadcast, no doubt tipped off to do so by journalists friendly to the intelligence establishment.

These fears are not as fantastic as they might appear. George Orwell's nightmare of *1984* is not rooted in any one political ideology, and can come as easily from the right as from the left, or from the centre. The police state could as easily come about as a result of attempts to prop up monetarism or mixed economy capitalism as to protect communism or fascism, since all use the same justification and the same technology which is now at the disposal of all societies. In a sense this has already started.

You do not have to blur the essential differences between those societies whose people can remove their governments by using the ballot box and those for whom that remedy is not available, to appreciate the threat that a technologically sophisticated security system can pose to human dignity in both. No democrat accepts the arguments of the Soviet government that the potential threat to the USSR justifies their continual refusal to allow public criticism or campaigns against their political leaders and the policies they pursue, or the denial of full trade union rights to organise in defence of living standards or of free speech. In the guise of the dictatorship of the proletariat, a new class of communist rulers has taken power, and has buttressed that power with the technology of repression. To say this is not to call for a return of the Czar or to the cold war, or an escalating nuclear arms race, which can only increase insecurity and feed the very fears upon which the arguments for repression rest. Nor does this involve a repudiation of socialism. It is, by contrast, to assert that socialism and democracy are indivisible.

But if we reject the Soviet arguments for tight security to control the pressure for change, we cannot ourselves accept uncritically the calls that are made in the West for tightening our security apparatus at the expense of our freedom of thought and action. The truth is that the very same factors which have strangled political freedom at birth in the post-revolutionary communist countries are now being called in aid to persuade us to give up some of our freedom in order – so we are told – to protect ourselves.

The campaign for peace

The greatest threat to our security and our liberties lies in nuclear war and the psychology involved in preparing for it. An exchange of nuclear weapons would mean the end of civilisation as we have built it up. Every nation touched by it would descend to barbarism for the survivors, as broken-backed societies tried to re-establish the means of life. All hopes for freedom and democracy or living standards consistent with human dignity would disappear.

The first demand, therefore, must be for detente and co-operation between East and West, based on their common interest in survival and our belief that evolutionary change towards democracy can only develop as a result of scaling down the arms race, and diverting resources towards peaceful development. Such peace campaigns, especially if they meet with a positive response in Britain, will in themselves attract the close attention of the defence and security establishment because they will reduce public support for the massive budgets upon which that establishment depends for its existence, its power and its legitimacy.

Those who campaign for peace, or seek out and maintain personal communications with the people in countries now branded as our enemies in order to discuss detente, will also find themselves under surveillance and scrutiny, and must expect to be denounced in the media, and may risk their own prospects of certain kinds of employment or promotion.

Since peace is indivisible from social justice at home and abroad, such a policy for detente and cooperation is inextricably linked with campaigns for economic, trading and foreign policies that recognise the rights of all people to enjoy the freedom to which we aspire. Steady and uncompromising support for human rights and social and economic justice in other countries will strengthen and underpin our demands for the same rights at home. This combined campaign for peace and human rights is so strong that the security establishment cannot defeat it.

The real answer to state oppression in communist countries does not lie in escalating the size of our armed forces; if we do that, the oppressors will proclaim our action to be a threat to their national survival and use it, in turn, as an excuse for tighter internal security. The solution lies in widening contacts and moral support for those in such countries who are themselves campaigning for freedom. The excesses of Soviet military control over Eastern Europe which make the Warsaw Pact under the Brezhnev doctrine so oppressive cannot be eased by a new arms drive to which the Kremlin will respond in kind, but only by adopting policies that might lead the Russians to recognise that their own security ultimately depends upon having, as neighbours, peoples who want internal freedom without becoming hostile to the independence of the USSR. Eastern Europe is not as monolithic as we are led to believe.

To those who say that all these arguments are naïve there are some very straightforward answers.

First, nuclear arms technology and its accompanying domestic security arrangements are already eroding our domestic democracy and liberty in a fundamental way without a shot being fired.

Second, if such weapons are really intended for use, that means the end of every freedom we are allegedly defending, and if they are not for use, they are a monumental waste of human resources that should be used for human betterment.

Third, that to reject the nuclear arms race as a valid defence strategy is not to be pacifist but to face the harsh reality that human survival must be the central objective of any credible defence policy.

There is no point in countering aggression with threats to obliterate the aggressors, because this can only lead to the destruction of both aggressor and victim. Collective resistance must be organised on the ground.[8] Experience since 1945 proves beyond question that the best defence against oppression is guerilla warfare and civil resistance. These have been successful in the liberation of so many colonies of former European empires, and offer us the most practicable defence strategy in the event of any threat to our independence by new predatory imperialists who might have designs upon our territory or those of our allies. A determined resistance at home would prevent conquest and eject attackers far more effectively. And the morale necessary for that sort of resistance depends upon the freedom and democracy to sustain it being safeguarded at home.

The campaign for democracy and self-government in Britain

The analysis I have set out presents security and freedom as being indissolubly linked world-wide. But it is also clear that any nation which seeks to develop a policy embodying these aims must first secure the right to do so by working for democratic self-government, moving towards a real world government in the long term. It is in that context that we have to examine the extent to which our own democracy in Britain today allows us the right to demand such policies and be sure that they are implemented.

We boast so often about our democracy that we have not noticed the erosion of our rights that has occurred in recent years. We have surrendered our power to make our own laws and impose our own taxation, to the EEC; the right to determine questions of peace and war, to our own military alliances; the right to decide our economic policy, to the IMF; and the right to develop our own industrial strategy, as a result of the operations of the multinational corporations.

The exercise of all the central powers of a modern British government lies in the hands of a prime minister. As we have seen, he or she presides over a huge civil service and military establishment which holds the interests of capital to be virtually synonymous with the national interests – which they are not – and which interconnects at official level with the establishments of the EEC, the IMF, NATO and the multinationals, not to mention the security services of countries whose policies are also linked to the interests of capital. This governing British establishment has its domestic power base embedded in the London triangle of Whitehall, the City, and Fleet Street, each of which sense their common interest in this new status quo and support each other through the instruments of policy and influence which they have at their disposal.

Even the Cabinet was never told by Mr Attlee that he had authorised the building of a British atomic bomb, nor did the elected House of Commons vote the money for it, since the cost was concealed under headings in the estimates for public expenditure presented to Parliament.[9]

This same exclusion of Cabinet and parliamentary control has existed ever since. Press reports since the May 1979 election suggest that the nuclear weapons decisions of the 1974–9 Labour Government were all similarly concealed from both Cabinet and Parliament.[10] So are the budgets and policies and international links of the security services in Britain, in Northern Ireland and world-wide.

In the regions and localities, the police are insulated from any real control by the elected representatives of the people who live in those areas, and the chief constables are now free to act as if they controlled police forces which are a law unto themselves. Essential legal safeguards such as habeas corpus, juries picked at random, and unanimous verdicts have been chipped away one by one.

And over this whole system of government there is a massive shield of official secrecy, made more effective by a quiescent and cooperative media posing as 'fearless' and independent while the steady flow of accurate information about policy, essential for real democratic accountability and political liberty, is successfully contained by those who exercise power.

To reverse these trends will take time. We need:

1 An analysis of the dangers to the security of the state, external and internal.

2 A study of the technology now available and the use to which it is being put in other comparable countries.

3 To consider the case for publishing every year all information that could be published without endangering security, including:

- i The budget and staffing of the security services.
- ii The names of those in charge of them – as in the USA.
- iii The guidelines issued to those services relating to their objectives and methods.
- iv The numbers of dossiers in existence relating to political activities.
- v A report on the reasons for collecting these dossiers and an account of what happens to the information acquired for inclusion in them.
- vi An annual report on the total number of interceptions of communications by telephone or mail.
- vii The full list of foreign security services with which UK security services have arrangements for reciprocal exchange of information, or with which they work.

4 To argue the case for a special House of Commons select committee, meeting, when necessary, in secret, composed exclusively of privy councillors empowered to question both the responsible ministers and security chiefs on the whole range of their policy and activities – to report annually to Parliament in a form which can be published.

5 To press for an appeals procedure for citizens reporting to the select committee on matters concerning their own records only.

6 To have the same rights to information for citizens about records and files kept on them as are enjoyed by US citizens under contemporary US legislation.[11]

7 To secure the introduction of a 'Security Services Annual Act' under which, as with the Army and the Airforce Acts of earlier years, Parliament gains the ultimate control of the security services.

5

The Democratic Control of Science and Technology

Science and technology are often presented as serving to liberate mankind from superstition and fear, and as offering us a source of unending power for the benefit of humanity. If they are not democratically controlled, however, they can threaten the liberties and the survival of the human race. Unless we can quickly fashion new forms of accountability, science and technology used in war could turn out to be the greatest curse in human history. President Carter's Secretary for Defence, Mr Harold Brown, has been reported as saying that a nuclear exchange between the Soviet Union and the United States would cost the deaths of 265 million people. With great precision he divided the numbers into 165 million Americans and 100 million Russians.[1] Against that background we must look at some of the problems that are posed by the scientific and technical revolution.

Science as a liberator

We must consider briefly the main stages by which science and technology have reached their present state of importance. In the pre-scientific age, the exercise of power was based upon strength, conquest, land ownership, and the control of communications by having a horseman who would carry messages backwards and forwards quickly. Power was also exercised by the manipulation of mystical beliefs to encourage ignorant people to propitiate the gods of nature by ritual and by sacrifice;

this mystery was used as an instrument of popular control. Into that world, before science in its modern sense was born, came some revolutionary theological ideas, which in the Western world we think of as primarily Christian ideas. Once we preach the idea that all men and women are brothers and sisters, we release into the argument a view of society that runs counter to the interest of those who hold political power. Out of the idea of monotheism, of one God over the whole of society and brotherhood under God, comes the idea of solidarity. This has played a large part in developing modern trade unions and democracy – the moral right of people to govern themselves because they are brothers and sisters. Although the organised church may not have advocated these ideas, because the organised church has very often preached obedience and told the poor to be patient and that they would be rewarded in the next world, there was released into society before science developed a different moral view of how society should be organised.

As science developed it became seen as a liberator. People were taught to study the laws of nature instead of the laws of God. Religion was demystified by science, humanity acquired the self-confidence to handle its own affairs, the authority of the Church was threatened and the religious pillars upon which state power rested were undermined. Modern education was founded and science developed as a radical force. In that sense science still claims to be a liberator.

The process did not end there. Out of science came the foundation of modern technology (although of course technology preceded science in the sense that the development of practical solutions to practical problems goes back to the beginning of the history of mankind). It is certainly true, however, that a liberated science played a significant part in transforming the nature of production, and that in its turn began serious political discussions about what state structure was required to allow this liberation of production to take place. Two hundred years ago the Scottish philosopher Adam Smith, in his *Wealth of Nations*, argued strongly that it was necessary to end the old feudal system and develop a capitalist society which would free the entrepreneur to produce new power structures so that technology could realise its full potential. For the common man, therefore, who did not own a factory, the transfer of power from the feudal landlord to the entrepreneur who used technology became the experience of the nineteenth century. A new religion evolved, no longer based upon the ideas of the early church, but the religion of profit and loss – that which was profitable was good, and that which made a loss was bad. Today a new apostle, Milton Friedman, is redeveloping the ideas of Adam Smith in order to justify a renewal of the capitalist ethic.

This market force religion, just like the old medieval church, underpins the structure of power in Western society. Education becomes to some extent the servant of a new system, producing people in the quantities and with the qualifications that that system requires. But that is not the end of the story because science also became in the nineteenth century the basis for social studies. There is no doubt that the following quotation from *Das Kapital* by Karl Marx was a very significant development of social science:

> Technology discloses man's mode of dealing with nature, the process of production by which he sustains his life, and thereby lays bare the formation of his social relations and the mental conceptions that flow from them.[2]

Marx was clearly the first serious student of the structure of society and of the economy on a scientific basis. There were other socialists besides Karl Marx who demystified capitalism in the way science demystified religion. They gave a new confidence to men and women to understand how their society worked, threatened the religion of market forces, and laid some theoretical foundation for trade unionism, which was initially just a defence mechanism. They also helped clear the way for political democracy in the sense that their work gave to those who studied socialist ideas a fresh impetus to replace a power structure based upon capital by a power structure based upon the ballot box.

Science and the new feudalism

In recent years, however, science and technology have come to be seen as the servants of the modern establishment. The growth of capital and its deployment in an international context have led to an enormous demand for research and development and for engineering skills of various kinds. In this way capital has paid for and controlled a great deal of the development of the scientific and engineering communities. Labour too, concerned directly in the process of production, has extended its interests into areas previously seen as the professional reserve of the scientists and engineers, and the government has also become involved.

For these reasons it is no exaggeration to say that the struggle for control of science and technology has moved into the centre of the political debate. On one side of the world we have corporate capitalism, increasingly dominated by enormous international companies. On the other side we have state communism, where the entire output of science and technology has been harnessed to the purposes of a state communist system. Both in the state communist societies and in the corporate capitalist societies, power has become more centralised than Adam Smith would ever have regarded as desirable. In a sense we are now living in a world where feudalism is being re-created through the great corporations which command science and technology, and have very little to do with the *laissez faire*, free enterprise, competitive system which laid the foundation of capitalism itself. In all systems of government, science and engineering are an integral part of the administration, the educational system, industry and the military. In this sense scientific and technical expertise has become the new religion, replacing to some extent profit and loss. If you are a Ph.D. or a Nobel Prizewinner, this is what society is invited to worship. There is a conflict now between the technocracy that comes from science and engineering and the democracy that stems from the ballot box, or the voting machine.

Six principles of science

Against this background we can begin to identify some of the crucial issues. First we must compare the principles upon which science and to some extent engineering rest with the principles upon which we believe that democratic self-government rests, and then see how these two traditions interact.

To a layman it seems that the scientific tradition derives from six main principles:

First, an insistence upon maintaining a rigorous regime of accurate scholarship.

Second, a practice of subjecting hypotheses arising from research to the critical scrutiny of the scientific community which then judges those results by the highest possible standards.

Third, a determination to defend and entrench academic freedom to protect scientists from improper external pressures which might lead them to abandon their research or, worse still, to corrupt their results to suit the powers that be.

Fourth, an acceptance of the importance of dissent within the scientific tradition, allowing scientists to seek to establish new hypotheses, even though these may run counter to the conventional scientific wisdom of the day. This is how innovation develops.

Fifth, the maintenance of an output which overrides political, theological or ideological divisions between nations. In this sense, scientists see themselves as non-political.

And sixth, the assertion of the importance, in science at any rate, of publishing results so that the whole world may benefit from the new knowledge as it is acquired.

These characteristics of science give it authority and make it a valued part of the rich tradition that we have inherited from the past, and which we need in full measure in order to develop society in the future for the widest possible benefit of its people.

Science and democracy

How do these traditions and principles contrast with the ideas that lie at the root of what we would call modern parliamentary democracy? If we look at the democratic tradition we find that, in Britain, the idea of democracy is based not upon the sovereignty of Parliament, let alone the sovereignty of government, but upon the sovereignty of the people as a whole, who have a moral right to govern themselves. By exercising their vote, they *lend* their sovereign powers to members of Parliament, to be used on their behalf for the duration of a single Parliament. These powers must be returned intact to the electorate, to whom they belong, to lend again to another Parliament at a subsequent election. That is the basis upon which the democratic argument rests. It means that every man and woman over the age of eighteen is entitled to vote for his or her representative in Parliament. It means that the consent of Parliament is required before any Act can be passed laying down new laws or imposing new taxation. It means that members of Parliament must be able to change the law, armed with the power they have from the people, and it must mean that ministers or civil servants can only act under the law and they are accountable to Parliament for everything they do and hence through Parliament to the electors as a whole. The final safeguard, and in some ways the most important aspect of democracy, is its destructive role: in the end the people can dismiss ministers without bloodshed, and replace them by others. From a minister's point of view, there is some advantage in being removed peacefully rather than being removed by bloodshed. It is ultimately the destructive power of democracy that gives it its vitality, because ministers who know they can be dismissed are obliged to listen; in this way the capacity to dismiss changes the relationship between those who govern and those who are governed.

Ten questions for scientists

If that is the scientific tradition on the one hand, and the democratic tradition on the other, how should ministers responsible for technical decisions approach those scientists, industrialists and engineers who come to them with projects that they wish to see supported? When I was Minister of Technology[3] I gave a great deal of thought to what a layman could do when confronted with a highly complex project such as Concorde, or a nuclear programme. How should the layman approach the expert in order to assess whether the project should proceed or not? In the late 1960s I drafted a series of questions designed to indicate that the role of the elected representative and the minister is not to seek to reproduce the expertise, which he or she could not do, but to see that the expert is subjected to a rigorous cross-examination on behalf of the people. These ten questions formed the basis for that process.

First, the minister must ask the technologist: Would your project, if carried through, promise benefits to the community, and if so, what are the benefits, how will they be distributed and to whom and when will they accrue?

Second, what disadvantages would you expect might flow from your work? Who would experience them? What, if any, remedies would correct them? Is the technology for correcting them sufficiently advanced for the remedies to be available when the disadvantages begin to accrue?

Third, what demands would the development of your project make upon our resources of skilled manpower, and are these resources likely to be available?

Fourth, is there a cheaper, a simpler, a less sophisticated way of achieving at least a part of your objective and if so, what would it be, and what proportion of your total objective would have to be sacrificed if we adopted it?

Fifth, what new skills would have to be acquired by people who would be called upon to use the product or project which you are recommending, and how could these skills be created?

Sixth, what skills would be rendered obsolete by the development that you propose, and how serious a problem would the obsolescence of these skills create for the people who have them?

Seventh, is the work upon which you are engaged being done, or has it been done, or has it been started and stopped in other parts of the world, and what experience is available from abroad that might help us to assess your own proposal?

Eighth, if what you propose is not done, what disadvantages or penalties do you believe will accrue to the community, and what alternative projects might be considered?

Ninth, if your proposition is accepted, what other work in the form of supporting systems should be set in hand simultaneously, either to cope with the consequences or to prepare for the next stage and what would the next stage be?

And tenth, a final and very important question: If an initial decision to proceed is made, for how long will the option to stop remain open, and how reversible will this decision be at progressive stages beyond there?

Accountability and nuclear power

That is the framework against which we should now turn to concrete cases. First, one which is of interest all over the Western world, the role of civil nuclear power: having been responsible for the British atomic energy programme for eight years, I have been deeply involved in the issues which this raises.[4] Nuclear power began in Britain as a by-product of work on the atomic bomb, and the decision to go for a civil nuclear programme was taken in 1957 after the Suez war had for the first time reminded the West, and particularly Britain and France, that it could not necessarily rely for ever upon unlimited supplies of cheap oil. The 1957 programme was the first proper civil nuclear project in the world, and indeed by 1970 Britain had generated more electricity by nuclear power than any other country including the United States. It was a small programme but it was ahead of others. Since then of course the Americans and the Russians and the French and the Germans have long overtaken us.

But certain issues had to be faced arising from the questionnaire cited above. First of all, what is the true economic cost of nuclear power? Does it include, for example, paying for the research and development that has lain behind the nuclear programme? Does it include the cost of decommissioning nuclear plant and of safeguarding what remains? How do we compare the benefits of what would now be perhaps £5 billion to build a fast-breeder reactor, with what we could gain by spending £5 billion in insulating everybody's roof? If we spend £5 billion on a fast-breeder reactor, we wait ten years and end up with electricity, which is all a fast-breeder reactor gives you.

If we start insulating people's homes, we get our first benefit tomorrow when the first home is finished, and it is a cumulative benefit.

Next, we have to confront the difficult question of nuclear safety. We need not accept the alarmist arguments against nuclear power, because the nuclear scientists will quite properly say that hundreds of thousands of people have died in the mines, where safety has been at a very low standard; they die in oil rigs; they die because they are electrocuted; they die because they are gassed by mistake; they die in accidents; and by comparison the safety record of nuclear power operations has so far been outstandingly good. Having said that, one must also recognise that in dealing with issues of safety in terms of nuclear power, mankind is facing a unique problem. We are leaving the problems for future generations to cope with, without being sure that they will be able to handle them. We must take account of the long-term difficulties that may arise from an incapacity to control systems, either by accident or by war, or by some other cause of the kind that occurred at Harrisburg.[5] We must also bear in mind that we have not yet found a visible large-scale method of dealing with nuclear waste. A heavy responsibility falls upon those who have to decide these matters.

Next there is the problem of proliferation. It is misleading to say that there are nuclear safeguards. There is only a rough and ready monitoring system, so that if somebody is found to be breaking the rules, as in the case of Pakistan, it becomes a political problem. There are no guaranteed safeguards when dealing with the distribution of nuclear technology.[6] There is the problem of civil liberties. There is the problem of getting information; even when I was in office, there were occasions when I was not informed of matters that should have been brought to my attention as the minister responsible for nuclear power.[7]

There are many commercial and indeed scientific pressures in favour of a big nuclear power programme. The older I get the more sceptical I become about nuclear power. The division between Catholic and Protestant is as nothing to the arguments between the pressure water school, the gas-cooled school and the high temperature school. In the end we have to be agnostics. We want electricity and we want to know how to generate it safely and efficiently, without worshipping in one of the great temples created by the nuclear establishment.

If we turn from civil nuclear power, which is after all the classic case of beating swords into ploughshares, to military nuclear power, the situation is still graver. One of the greatest threats to the maintenance and development of democracy derives from the growing power of the domestic military establishments all over the world. These military establishments, armed with a terrifying array of technology and a vast security apparatus, are now firmly entrenched in both East and West and have their counterparts amongst the dictatorships of the Third World. In America what President Eisenhower called 'the Military-Industrial Complex' has long had a big influence on government policy – as we saw in Vietnam and Chile. President Reagan appointed a general, Alexander Haig, as his Secretary of State. Russia has an equally powerful military establishment, which may well have demanded the invasion of Afghanistan and may have argued for intervention in Poland. The arms race, which seems likely to escalate again, immensely strengthens these military establishments in both the United States and the Soviet Union, where they command much of the research work done and much of the output of the productive industries. Each justifies its own, by reference to the existence of the other. And in this sense the domestic military propaganda in East and West actually reinforces its opposite number and helps to bully the political leaders and the people in both countries into funding more and more arms expenditure.

Moreover, since nuclear weapons are genuinely dangerous to develop, produce, store, handle and deploy, that fact alone becomes an additional argument for increasing domestic security and surveillance at the expense of civil liberties and the democratic process. The media, which in all parts of the world are much influenced by the governments of the day, use all these points to drown the voices of those courageous dissidents who are opposed to what is happening. In the renewed cold war atmosphere that is being deliberately stimulated, domestic critics can then be denounced almost as if they were agents of the enemy. Their harassment can be justified by arguments based upon the overriding need for national security. Unless this process of militarisation is halted and reversed, the risk of nuclear war will inevitably increase. Whatever the outcome of such a war, one thing is certain. In the return to barbarism that will follow it, no democratic institutions will survive anyway.

Popular pressure, therefore, to interrogate and to control all military establishments – their strategy, budgets and weaponry – is now urgently needed.

Science and civil liberties

The more complex the technology the more vulnerable it is to disruption. Where an industrial, communication or transport system can be disrupted there will be close surveillance of those who work in these areas. At this point technology offers the complete answer, with surveillance through a computerised police system. The problem is that there is no effective democratic control over this type of police activity. This is a threat to the democratic process because, in a democracy, there must be genuine debate between people of different opinions.

If science is to develop, human genius must be able to break out of the framework of conventional wisdom. The quality of life cannot only be measured by the number of cars, the number of television sets, how easily we can move abroad for our holidays in the Mediterranean. The quality of life essentially depends upon the capacity of the human mind to bring itself to bear upon the problems of our time. If we are not careful, we may drift into a police state accidentally as a result of even the most harmless applications of technical solutions.

The role of scientists in a democracy

Technology because of its brilliant success has opened up choices which demand political decisions and a clear statement of objectives. Objectives must be evaluated through the political process. For democratic socialists the priorities must include the question of how we mobilise resources to meet human need;

the democratic control of industry, much of which is multinational and has entirely escaped accountability to anybody; the democratic control of finance, the military and the administration. Above all, we must allow the free flow of information, end secrecy and give everyone access to an education that will enable them to contribute to the decisions which affect their lives.

Scientists and engineers have an important part to play. They must not mystify, for that establishes a new religion. They must not oversimplify, because that misleads and deceives. Their role is to clarify the choices available to society. To offer leadership through education, but not to dominate through expertise or power. Decisions, in a democratic society, must ultimately be made by the people as a whole.

6

The Case for a Free Press

A mature democracy depends for its success upon being able to receive news and comment, selected and presented from a variety of social and political perspectives. This need is not met by having a proliferation of news sources which all observe the political scene from much the same viewpoint. If a variety of perspectives are not provided, the public information function becomes debased into a mere propaganda machine. The news that is circulated becomes an instrument for propaganda rather than a service of information.

The fate of democracy rests with the voters who can make and unmake governments and bring effective pressure to bear throughout the lifetime of each Parliament. Since public opinion, in a free society, also exercises a considerable influence over the conduct of all organisations, the factors which shape it and express it greatly affect the development of society itself. This being so, the conditions governing the supply of information to citizens and to the public at large, upon which their judgments are formed, become of central concern to all those who are determined to uphold democracy. Any tendency to censor the output of necessary information, distort the news or suppress views, must be seen as a threat to freedom. In short, democracy depends upon the establishment and maintenance of a genuinely free mass media.

Yet in Britain we do not have a free press, nor an unbiased broadcasting system.

The power of the media

Seven multinational companies or wealthy families own all the mass circulation newspapers in Britain (for full details see Appendix A). Generally speaking, they use their papers to campaign single-mindedly in defence of their commercial interests and the political policies which will protect them. These proprietors also own most local newspapers, and each in their own locality pursues the same editorial policy to a greater or lesser extent.

Similarly, the broadcasting authorities, although governed by statutes or charters which are intended to maintain some fairness and balance, have allowed their news bulletins gradually to become outlets for the perspective of the British establishment and the middle classes. The same, with some honourable exceptions, has happened to their current affairs programmes. That is to say, the broadcasting companies, like the press, are openly hostile to the interests of working people, including the Labour and trade union movement, to democratic socialism and to any movement such as the Campaign for Nuclear Disarmament whose ideas might otherwise gain wider support and challenge the status quo. This bias has now been carefully studied and analysed, documented and published.[1] We now know that the sense of unfairness felt for so long by so many people on the left is not imaginary but is real, proven and cannot be denied.

The power of the mass media, and the uniformity of view, though not of style, which they project, was most dramatically demonstrated during the Common Market Referendum in June 1975. Every daily and Sunday newspaper except the *Morning Star* came out editorially in favour of Britain's membership, and denounced all those who warned that Britain's interests would be gravely damaged if we remained within the EEC.

The most sustained campaign of all has been against the trade union movement, which has been identified as a virtual enemy of Britain, and whose supposedly undue influence is used to explain all Britain's economic and industrial problems. The careful monitoring of BBC and ITV broadcasts carried out by the Glasgow University Media Group has established the nature and extent of the anti-union bias, and has identified the techniques and language used for that purpose.[2] These techniques are much more subtly applied in Britain than in the straightforward and blatant propaganda of totalitarian societies where old-fashioned denunciation and outright suppression are thought to be sufficient. A cleverer use is made of language, presentation, and misrepresentation, and the methods can be applied equally against any cause or organised group, and not just against the Labour movement.

But the power of the media extends far beyond anti-union bias. The press and broadcasting authorities keep up a skilful campaign of fear designed to support cold war policies and continually emphasise crime and disorder, to buttress the case for making law and order a key issue. They also denigrate and belittle those who stand up for alternative approaches and policies. These strategies require the distortion of views, as well as news, so that what is said is presented in a way that makes it either unintelligible or threatening. They also fail the simple test of balanced reporting, which is that everyone whose views are described should be able to accept that description as fair, whatever comments may be made on those views by others.

The media thus have immense power, the power to decide what to report as news, and what is not news and therefore should not be reported. They have the power to decide how news is to be covered, who is to be invited to comment, and who is not to be invited. Above all, they have the power, and use it, to neglect issues, and emphasise personalities, to the point that certain groups, such as the Social Democrats, can be given massive and favourable coverage, while many others, the minority communities or political groups such as the Ecologists, can be ignored or denounced, even though they have considerable public support. The use of adjectives or descriptive phrases to isolate a viewpoint unacceptable to the editor is so regular a practice as to pass almost unnoticed.

The press and the broadcasters can also build up a certain viewpoint by a sustained campaign after which they can commission a public opinion poll to capture, by carefully phrased questions, public support for that position. They then use the poll to claim this to be 'public opinion', and so give bogus authenticity to the editorials which created the view in the first place. This is one more way in which the media are gradually ceasing to be an information service, and more and more are becoming openly propagandist in tone and content and getting ever more strident in language and emphasis.

Those who work for the media are to a large extent the victims of the propaganda machines for which they work. Journalists, producers, cameramen, print-workers and other media employees are locked into the same economic crisis that has gripped the society upon which they report. They can suffer agonies of anxiety about their job security. They can be bought and sold like cattle when the newspapers for which they work change hands from one multinational to another – as *The Times*, the *Sunday Times* and the *Observer* staffs have learned. But it is not only the newspaper staffs who have an interest in these proprietorial battles.

The readers, and the public, are entitled to know which multinational combines are gaining control of the nation's information services, and what are the interests which they serve. Moreover, it is clear that greater power over the nation's affairs can be acquired by newspaper purchase than by election to Parliament, and the would-be newspaper owners are deeply interested in acquiring that power from which they can never be ejected by the electoral system. As far as the staffs are concerned, they soon get to know the editorial lines so well and are so conscious of what is expected of them that many effectively pre-censor their own stories, knowing that their job is to write within narrow guidelines of what is expected of them, without having to be reminded of it by constant editorial directive. Within this band of media people there are courageous journalists prepared to stand up against the prevailing line and risk all in the defence of what they believe to be right in a programme or a paper, or turn to the union for collective support. But in general the media proprietors and top level directorate find it easy to impose their will on the outlets in print, radio or TV which they own or control.

The threat to democracy

The effect of this system, the way it operates in practice, is serious in a democracy because it deprives the community as a whole of the range and calibre of information, analysis and opinions which it needs if it is to overcome its problems, resolve its conflicts and control its future.

Those who question the system and seek greater fairness in news coverage and a wider range of perspectives are met by two arguments. First, it is said that we have a press the public wish to buy and that, if it was not good, they would not buy it. This is an argument that could be equally applied to the USSR media since Russians also buy their establishment's controlled press. Our argument must be that, although Western commercial media are not government-controlled or censored to anything like the same degree, we also lack a choice. Variety does not lie in multiple presentations of the same position but in reporting and discussing from a range of different political perspectives.

The second argument is that any change would involve subordination to state control of the media at the expense of our basic freedoms. This viewpoint has no basis whatsoever in fact, since no one is advocating state control of the media. We are saying that the control by private proprietors, many of them now multinational in character with many other commercial and financial interests, has not given this country the press which a democracy needs.

The public have very little say in the press on offer to them because, contrary to popular belief, newspapers do not depend for their financial viability upon the money paid by readers alone. They are dependent upon advertising, which is an allowable business expense for tax purposes. This tax allowance rests upon the operation of the tax system passed by Parliament which relieves those companies which advertise in the press of much of the real cost of the advertising they do, and deprives the Treasury of the money it would receive if advertising expenses were paid out of the profits of the companies which engaged in it.[3] So the press is itself, with official government support, an industry dependent for its survival upon the present system of tax law. If advertising was not tax deductible, the Inland

Revenue would receive substantial sums each year which could, under different arrangements, be made to sustain a wholly different, but equally independent, newspaper industry. This is something we must consider later. First, however, I want to look briefly at the role played by the media in sustaining the post-war British political consensus.

The post-war consensus

The reforms of the 1945 Labour Government drew their inspiration from all three political parties. First, there was Harold Macmillan's book *The Middle Way*, published in 1938, in which he called for a planned economy to get rid of unemployment. Harold Macmillan is now controversial again because his book advocated policies well to the left of the 1979 Labour manifesto. Macmillan said the great problem of unemployment in the 1930s had to be dealt with by planning and influenced the strategy of the 1945 Labour Government, of which he was not of course a member.

The second influence came from the Liberal, Lord Beveridge, who had worked for Churchill at the Board of Trade in 1909, had invented labour exchanges and was there when Lloyd George was developing the national insurance policy. Beveridge had written the two great books of the war, *Full Employment in a Free Society*, based on Keynesian economics, and *Social Insurance and Allied Services*, known as the Beveridge Report.

The third contribution came from various Labour sources ranging from the unions to the Fabian Society and these elements laid the basis of an economic policy known as 'Butskellism' which was to last into the 1970s. There was consensus. A centre party has in effect been in power for most of the time since the war. What is now being advocated by the Social Democrats has in fact been the policy of successive British governments despite various attempts to break it. Wilson intended to break the consensus in 1964 with the National Plan, but it lasted eighteen months before a return to the traditional Stop-Go method of managing the economy. Mr Heath tried to break the consensus with his Selsdon Park policy but he too quickly retreated. Then in 1974 Labour was again elected with a more radical policy based on planning agreements and government intervention in profitable industry, but by the summer of 1975 that too had folded. So we could argue that from 1951 to 1979, for twenty-eight years, the country has been governed by a body of people who shared a great deal of agreed doctrine. As a result media coverage of politics in that period was straightforward. The media were absolutely safe if they stayed in the parliamentary arena, because then there were only marginal differences on economic policy between the two main parties. There was a solid body of similar opinion on both front benches. Leaders of all three main parties were within hailing distance of each other all the time and, partly because there were few fundamental political differences, 'Yah-boo' politics became very popular. If you did not really disagree with someone on the other side, you insulted him. Therefore, media coverage of politics could be contained within certain clear limits.

Since 1979 the consensus has fundamentally broken down. It has broken down because, after years of decline, we are in a situation where the crust of consensus at the top no longer corresponds to the experience of a large number of people. All the high hopes of Harold Macmillan in the 1950s, that we not only had never had it so good but that we would never have it bad again, have changed. Whether the forecasts of three or four million unemployed are right or not, the fact is we are in deep trouble. So politics is now reassessing itself. Nobody disagrees that the old politics are not working, but three broad types of remedy are competing for public attention: monetarism, corporatism and democratic socialism.[4]

The problem confronting the media is how to present the issues. How are the British people, faced with this hair-raising crisis, to be informed about the meaning and the nature of the alternatives?

The media and consensus

Contrary to the general view, Labour Party policy today is not to the left of what it was. Nor is there anything new in the recognition that Marx had a part to play in the party. In 1948 the Labour Party republished *The Communist Manifesto*, yet the media today have succeeded in turning the word Marxist into a term of abuse. In doing so, the media have deprived us of one of the great sources of socialist analysis. Why is it we can have an objective hour-long documentary programme on Buddhism in China but we cannot have the same sort of coverage of the various strains of opinion within British politics, including the left of the Labour Party? There is a very interesting debate going on in the Labour Party and it should be covered seriously and not in terms of personalities or in terms of the prejudices of the interviewer or producer. The Religious Affairs Department of the BBC broadcast a well-balanced interview with two Mormons in which they were treated very fairly. Why is it that the BBC Religious Affairs Department is able to handle events in a more balanced way than the Current Affairs Department?

The consensus media – the *Sunday Times*, the *Observer*, the *Guardian*, the *Daily Mirror* and the BBC – are natural spokesmen for the centre party. Their editors and leading figures do not consider themselves conservatives, but most of them are equally unable to support a Labour Party which is challenging some of the assumptions which have awarded them a comfortable lifestyle. This is perfectly understandable, but what is not understandable or acceptable is the apparent inability to make sure that each of the political alternatives on offer is fairly represented to the British people. The test of fairness is that the presentation must seem fair to the person whose point of view is being presented. If a journalist wants to argue later that that person is entirely wrong, that is fine. But everyone hearing their own point of view projected should be able to say, 'Yes, that's what I am trying to say.' This does not happen.

Most strikes are presented as disruptive. Why do workers always 'demand' and 'threaten' and management always 'offer' and 'plead'? We never hear of workers 'offering' to work for less than the inflation rate and 'pleading' to be allowed to keep their jobs; we never hear of managers 'demanding' that workers work for less and threatening to sack them if they do not.[5] It is above all a matter of professionalism. One of the questions which journalists in general – and the governors of the BBC in particular – ought to be asking themselves is: how do we help a nation in trouble to understand fairly and clearly the political alternatives that people are trying to put before them?

In this context the role of a public corporation such as the BBC is particularly important. Most people in the mainstream of the Labour Party – and I count myself as one – are merely advocating policies that have been approved by huge majorities at successive party conferences, yet they do not feel their views are fairly represented. They feel that the BBC is an instrument being used by the centre against the left – and it is no answer to be told that Mrs Thatcher does not like the BBC either.

The role of the BBC and the consensus media is similar to the role of the medieval church and our task is to try to re-establish the right of dissent. Just as dissenters had to struggle – against bitter resistance – for the right to be heard, so we are struggling for the right to put our socialist point of view fairly and consistently before the people of Britain. We want it to be presented without labels such as 'extremist' or 'far left', which are used as a sort of government health warning to alert readers and listeners to disregard what they are about to read or hear.

At the moment there is a 'Five Mile Act' under which, if a point of view does not fit into the consensus, then it is isolated.[6] When it is granted access to the public it is usually only for the purpose of ridicule, or when it is carefully dressed in words like 'left wing', 'Marxist' or 'extremist' to indicate that it is not to be taken seriously. As a result the public find it hard to understand what is happening. When people do not understand, they become frightened and more receptive to an authoritarian solution. And it is the centre – and not the left – who are offering an authoritarian solution. As I hope will be clear from this book, the left is offering open government and industrial democracy to give people a chance to take control of the events which shape their lives; the monetarists simply believe we should be thrown to market forces.

The truly authoritarian party in Britain is the Social Democratic Party. They are the corporatists. They believe that political decisions should be restricted to small numbers of important, unaccountable persons meeting behind the closed doors of Downing Street, or at the headquarters of the EEC

Commission in Brussels; they want to keep us trapped in a defence policy where the president of the United States or the generals in the Pentagon have more say over the nuclear weapons on British soil than any elected British politician. Why are the SDP and its spokesmen not subject to a media scrutiny at least as rigorous as those of the Tory and Labour parties?

The media and the Social Democrats

The Social Democrats have been the beneficiaries of the greatest display of media support ever given to any group of MPs in recent history. Their every move was chronicled in detail, their every statement was reported respectfully and in full, their characters received unfailingly favourable mention, and any discrepancies or gaps in their policies were excused or conveniently ignored in a way that no other movement's policies have been treated. In personal appearances before they defected, the Social Democrats were rarely cross-examined upon the morality of remaining in a Labour Shadow Cabinet or National Executive Committee which made them privy to Labour's inner strategies, at the very moment when they were preparing to leave. When the long-awaited break came, its timing apparently planned so as to give the media a chance to prepare programmes for simultaneous broadcasting, the new Social Democrats were launched upon their venture with a fanfare of publicity that rivalled the coverage accorded to the American space programme or a royal tour.

One commercial TV programme, 'TV Eye', at a cost that must have run into tens of thousands of pounds, commissioned a top advertising agency to prepare a party political broadcast to advocate the policies of the Social Democrats. It commissioned a public opinion poll, and took a bus with specially painted Social Democratic markings to marginal constituencies and fixed a specially printed poster to a huge hoarding in London. In front of it the psephologist, David Butler, was interviewed about the prospects of this supposed new party.[7] The fact that not one of the Social Democrat MPs was prepared even to follow Dick Taverne's more honourable precedent of testing their new allegiance at once at the polls in their own constituencies received no comment. A decent veil of collusive secrecy remained to cover the fact that the Social Democrats are seeking to build their public support around two of the most unpopular policies in Britain, support for the further integration of the UK into a full Common Market federation, and the acceptance of American cruise missiles and perhaps even the neutron bomb on bases in this country.

No one who followed the saga of the SDP launch on BBC and ITV can have failed to conclude that both broadcasting organisations had abandoned the pretence of impartiality or balanced coverage of British politics. They had not kept an objective distance. They had become active participants in the creation of the new party, and one of its most powerful assets. It was the media's willingness to give themselves up to this purpose that enabled the new group of barely more than a dozen MPs, with no policy or agreed programme, to establish themselves as the 'biggest' party in Britain within a month.

This is the power of the media, and those who say that the SDP's growth was possible because people 'wanted' this new party, with no policies, are refusing to face the real truth: that the media now control political life in a most frightening way and are able to create and destroy parties and people. The BBC and ITV may protest as hard as they like that the coverage they gave was dictated by news value, rather than by political sympathy, but whose news value? News value is what the media decide it to be, and the truth is they decided to give this party and not, say, the Campaign for Nuclear Disarmament, which is far more significant, the kind of mass coverage that it got.

Some of us recall the coverage given when the dissenting MPs were on the left rather than the right of the party. When Nye Bevan led a group of over fifty Labour MPs in opposition to the parliamentary leadership, the BBC maintained a constant line of attack upon them, and went so far as to ration appearances by Bevanite MPs, even on non-political programmes, so as to be sure that they had no more than their minimal share of radio time.[8] The fact we must face is that the BBC and ITV are now active participants in the political debates upon which the nation is engaged, and no longer impartial commentators upon those events.

Rhodesia and the Cold War

In their coverage of foreign affairs, too, the newspapers and the broadcasting authorities have for long openly editorialised in support of establishment policies.

During the long-drawn-out Rhodesian war, Ian Smith, who was in rebellion against the British Crown, was treated with immense respect as the man seeking to maintain civilised standards. Robert Mugabe, whose overwhelming electoral support was always there, and known to be there by many of those reporting during this period, but could not be established because Ian Smith would not permit a free election, was projected as a Marxist terrorist, whose violent methods would undermine freedom. No wonder then that British listeners and viewers were surprised by the election results when they came, and cannot now get used to seeing this 'terrorist' honoured as a major international leader.[9]

The Rhodesian war should be a warning to those who may be tempted to believe what the media now tell us about world affairs more widely, and East–West relations in particular. It is abundantly clear that the coverage given is heavily biased in the direction of cold war policies. Programme after programme, day after day, is prepared and broadcast to provide justification for the build-up of nuclear weapons so ardently advocated by the military leaders in America and Britain. The broadcasters are the voice of the British establishment, and the role they play is comparable to that played by the established churches in support of the feudal kings who ruled Britain centuries ago.

Those of us who seek to open up this closed system had better recognise that we have a real battle on our hands. For a start the BBC and ITV will not allow the scripts or video recordings of the programmes they have already broadcast to millions of viewers to be released for public scrutiny, even by academics. Whereas one copy of every slim volume of poetry published that may sell only a few hundred has to be deposited by law in the British Library, the governors of the BBC and the IBA will not permit words and pictures that have been heard and seen by millions to be analysed at all. Moreover, they are so sensitive to criticism that they hardly ever permit adverse comments on themselves to be reported even in their own news programmes, and they would not allow their academic critics, such as the Glasgow University Media Group, to have their findings explained and discussed on the air.[10] But despite these Canute-like efforts to stem the tide of criticism and divert the pressure for reform, the subject of media bias, and the key role of the broadcasters in perpetuating it, has become a major public issue and cannot for much longer be suppressed. One reason for the progress now being made is technical, for with video recorders citizens and researchers can keep their own recordings of BBC and ITV broadcasts and illustrate their arguments with evidence that was previously unavailable.

The Tory press

So far I have concentrated mainly on the consensus media, those newspapers and broadcasting companies which pride – and perhaps delude – themselves on their independence and rigorous pursuit of the truth. Certainly we must concede that the quality of the information put out by this section of the media is higher than that offered to the vast majority of the British public who rely for information upon such newspapers as the *Daily Telegraph*, the *Sun*, the *Daily Mail*, the *Express* and the *News of the World*. I have not dwelt on these publications because by and large they make less pretence to offer their readers anything other than crude propaganda in support of the class interests of the people who own them. The late Lord Beaverbrook, who owned the *Daily Express*, the *Sunday Express* and the *Evening Standard*, was at least frank on this subject. He told the 1949 Royal Commission on the Press, 'I run the paper purely for the purpose of making political propaganda, and with no other motive.'[11]

Because they are less subtle than the consensus press, they may be said to be less insidious, yet we must acknowledge that they have been responsible for misinforming entire generations of working people about the events which have shaped our lives. At least as dangerous as the misinformation have been the insistence on presenting important issues as if they are simply a conflict between personalities, and the obsession with trivia.

Most of the so-called popular press have refused to address themselves to what is actually happening. For the vast majority of adults in Britain their newspaper is the only written account of what is happening in the world that they are likely to see. These people have been betrayed by the insistence of the popular press on remorselessly trivialising and personalising all the great and complex issues of our day to a level where they almost defy comprehension.

The irony is that, despite the difference in style and content between the 'popular' newspapers and the liberal media, they mainly subscribe to the same consensus.[12] At the end of the day readers of *The Times* and the *Guardian* are being fed a diet of consensus politics similar to that being offered to *News of the World* and *Daily Mail* readers. The fundamental criticism of the British newspapers is not that they necessarily support the policies of the Conservative Party, but that they support conservative policies whether carried out by a Conservative or a Labour government. So, for example, all national newspapers except the *Morning Star* support the principle of public spending cuts as a solution to our economic crisis (though they differ over the degree); they all support incomes policies (though most journalists reject the application of such policies to discussions of their own incomes); they all supported the Vietnam war (though they varied in the degree of atrocity they were prepared to condone); they all supported the Common Market during the 1975 Referendum; with the exception of the *Daily Mirror* since August 1978, they all support the British presence in Northern Ireland; they all supported Mr Callaghan against Mr Foot for the Labour Party leadership in 1976 and in the 1980 leadership contest all (with the exception of the *Daily Star*) supported Mr Healey against Mr Foot.

A Labour daily?

It is not necessary to disagree with the consensus opinion on any of these issues to recognise that this state of affairs is unhealthy in a society that aspires to democracy. It is sometimes argued that if there is a demand for an alternative point of view, there is nothing to stop those who are unsatisfied with our national newspapers from establishing their own. It has, for example, been suggested that the Labour movement should put funds into a new national daily paper, but the cost of establishing new national papers is enormous. Moreover, the omens for the success of such a paper are not good. With the exception of the *Daily Star*, and the *Sun* which grew out of the *Daily Herald*, no new popular national newspaper has been successfully established in Britain since the *Sunday Express* in 1918 and that cost £2 million at the prices then prevailing before it broke even.[13] What is more, to be successful a newspaper does not depend simply upon attracting readers. It has to attract advertisers and a paper with a predominantly working class readership could not easily do this. It is sometimes alleged that the *Daily Herald* died because not enough people wanted to read it. This is false. When it folded the *Herald* was still selling far more copies than *The Times*, the *Guardian* and the *Financial Times* added together. It died because its readers were too poor to make them a worthwhile target for advertisers.[14] We also forget that many British national papers already make big losses and are only sustained by the ability of their proprietors to write off those losses against taxes on profits in another area of their business empire. Sir James Goldsmith is said to have lost up to £12 million in his attempt to launch a national news magazine.[15] That should be a warning to anyone who may be seduced by the undeniable attractions of a Labour movement newspaper.

Even if it were possible to break the consensus by setting up a Labour movement newspaper, it would fall a long way short of a solution to the problems posed by a national news media almost entirely in the grip of an outdated and sterile consensus. As far as newspapers are concerned, the root of the problem lies in the way they are owned and controlled.

As I have already mentioned, seven multinational corporations or large family concerns control most of the written information available to the people of Britain. The only national daily or Sunday papers not owned either by a multinational corporation or by a wealthy individual are the *Guardian* and the *Morning Star*, the two least ready to follow the establishment line. With these exceptions, all national newspapers and most local papers are controlled by men who seem uniquely unsuitable to comment upon or comprehend the events which shape the lives of ordinary people. This is not to suggest that the proprietors form some sort of dark conspiracy which consciously aims to deny the truth about the world to people who read their newspapers. Proprietors vary in the degree to which they impose their own views on the newspapers they own. What is suggested, however, is that it is inconceivable that men whose backgrounds and all the other circumstances of their lives make them conservatives would wish to be associated with publications propagating a consistently different point of view from their own. They do not have to tolerate such a state of affairs.

If the Labour Party wins office at the next election, it will do so in the face of a sustained press campaign against it. The Red scare is not a new development. It has been a feature of media coverage in every general election campaign for the last sixty years. In 1924 the *Daily Mail* came up with the Zinoviev letter, allegedly sent by the President of the Third Communist International to the British Communist Party outlining plans for creating civil strife in the event of the Labour victory. Although the letter was probably a forgery it became the inspiration for headlines such as 'Civil War Plot by Socialist Masters' (*Daily Mail*, 25th October 1924) and 'Vote British, Not Bolshie' (*Daily Mirror*, 29th October 1924).[16] In the 1945 election massive publicity was given to Churchill's smear that Labour's programme would require a 'Gestapo' to enforce it.[17] Nothing changes. In the 1979 general election the *Daily Express* was publishing lists of allegedly Marxist Labour candidates under the headline 'Labour's Danger Men'; and comparing the Labour and Communist Party manifestos under the headline 'The Red Face of Labour'.[18] In the light of what has gone before, who can doubt that a wave of media-induced hysteria and disinformation would greet a Labour government committed to withdrawal from the Common Market and nuclear disarmament? The establishment of a free press will, therefore, have to be a priority in the plans of a future Labour government.

Some proposals for reform

Reform of the media has only recently come to be taken seriously. The Glasgow University Media Group, the Campaign for Press Freedom, the Minority Press Group and academics such as James Curran at the Polytechnic of Central London have produced a wealth of carefully researched analysis and proposals for reform which would reward serious study. At the time of writing the Labour Party National Executive Committee has a working party considering what must be done to obtain a media responsive to the needs of a twentieth-century democracy rather than an arm of the British establishment. I do not wish to anticipate the proposals of the working party, but in the interests of stimulating debate on this important subject I set out below some of the possibilities for reform which are now being discussed in the Labour Party and elsewhere.

1 An Open Press Authority

This has been suggested by James Curran and Jean Seaton in their book *Power Without Responsibility.*[19] This would be a public agency accountable to Parliament and it would aim to extend the freedom to publish. The OPA objectives would include the following:

i Provision of a launch fund, raised partly from a tax on media advertising expenditure, to assist new publications.
ii Grants to assist publications that have failed to attract significant advertising.
iii A National Print Corporation to extend modern printing facilities to a wide range of publications.
iv A guarantee of distribution for minority publications through a new wholesale organisation.

2 Anti-monopoly legislation

Consideration will have to be given to legislation to break up the huge newspaper monopolies; existing monopoly legislation has proved wholly ineffective for this purpose. Such legislation should also prohibit or severely limit investment by newspaper chains in television and commercial radio.

3 *Reform of the wholesale trade*

Wholesale and retail distribution of British newspapers and magazines is dominated by just three companies: W. H. Smith, John Menzies and Surridge Dawson. In many areas one or other of these companies has a complete monopoly. The result is that non-consensus publications have great difficulty in reaching the news stands. The French have solved this problem by imposing a legal obligation on wholesalers and retailers to carry, on request, all lawful publications excluding pornography. Publishers have to pay a handling charge on all returns. As a result the French public have access to a far more diverse range of political views than we do in Britain. The French example should be studied.[20]

4 *The right of reply*

Where a newspaper or magazine has published a report about an individual or group which seriously distorts the truth, the person or organisation offended should have the right to set the record straight in the columns of that newspaper. The reply should be allotted adequate space and prominence and it should appear as soon as possible after the original story. It should be made legally enforceable. The Campaign for Press Freedom has set out the case for a right of reply in an excellent pamphlet.[21]

5 *Broadcasting*

i Instead of being composed of the 'great and the good', worthy citizens chosen for their alleged impartiality, the boards of the BBC and the Independent Broadcasting Authority should contain representatives of a wide spectrum of opinion and interest groups.

ii The proceedings of the two boards of governors and all internal directives on policy should be publicly available.

iii The IBA should be given a legal obligation when awarding franchises, to give preference to non-profit-making applicants such as cooperatives; at present most franchises go to companies more concerned with profits than quality.

iv The BBC is too big. It should be broken up into separate independent units for television, radio and the overseas service.

v The BBC licence fee, which places the Corporation at the mercy of the government, should be abolished and replaced by a grant awarded by Parliament five years in advance.

vi The Fourth Channel, as presently constituted, is controlled by the IBA and will buy in programmes from commercial companies. It should be reconstituted as a separate, publicly financed cooperative which would act as a 'publisher' of programmes made by freelance and independent production groups.

6 *Satellite Broadcasting*

By the mid-1980s satellite communication systems will make it feasible for American or European commercial television to be relayed into Britain. The result could be a diversion of advertising revenue away from existing publicly regulated services and an end of any chance of creating and maintaining public service broadcasting. As a matter of urgency Britain must contact other European governments with a view to placing under international control all companies using satellites for this purpose.

Conclusion

These are some of the ways in which the British media could be developed to serve democracy rather than a consensus which has long been overtaken by events. I list these suggestions simply as a basis for consideration in an area where, until recently, there has been very little positive discussion. The free flow of information is the life blood of democracy and the present ownership structure and organisation of our media is incompatible with democracy. At a time of crisis, such as we now face, it is important that people should be able to choose freely between the various alternatives that political parties are seeking to put before them. To do that they need to be properly informed. That should be the role of the media in a democracy.

THE WAY AHEAD

7

The Moral Basis for Democratic Socialism

When Jesus was asked by one of the Scribes, 'Which is the first commandment of all?' St Mark's Gospel records his answer thus:

> The first . . . is, . . . The Lord our God is one Lord:
>
> And thou shalt love the Lord thy God with all thy heart, and with all thy soul, and with all thy mind, and with all thy strength: this is the first commandment.
>
> And the second is like, namely this, *Thou shalt love thy neighbour as thyself. There is none other commandment greater than these.*[1]

Any student of the teachings of the historical Jesus – and I lay claim to be such a student and no more – must take that passage as his starting point in the search for their revolutionary consequences. Few would question the use of the word 'revolutionary' to describe the effect upon an individual when he or she interprets this commandment in social sense.

Historically many churches appear to have been, and to remain, more concerned with the task of preaching personal salvation than with the social imperatives spelled out in Jesus's reply. Generations of churchmen have formulated creeds and liturgies, discussed the mystical aspects of theology and worked within ecclesiastical hierarchies to interpret the word of God for the faithful, supported by various disciplines designed to secure their compliance.

It has also been true that ecclesiastical and temporal power have often been fused into a combined establishment to secure the submission of the people to the authoritarian demands of church and state. In such situations the social imperatives relating to our obligations to practise neighbourly love were shrunk into a vague and generalised injunction directed to the rich and powerful to express their love by being good and kind; and to the poor to return that love by being patient and submissive. Both rich and poor, powerful and weak, were then reassured by the church that in the world to come each would have their just reward and all suffering and injustice would be swept away for all eternity.

Not surprisingly, this interpretation of the teachings of Jesus did not commend itself to the poor and the disinherited who saw through this argument and rejected the role allocated to them in this world – of accepting injustice. Thus, outside the established churches, and in parallel with them, the practical commandment to practise true neighbourly love based upon an acceptance of our common humanity acquired an impetus of its own.

This radical interpretation of the teachings of Jesus spread wherever the Bible was available for study – and no doubt explains why the authorities were so anxious to keep it out of the hands of the laity. In this way the message reached and influenced a far wider audience – including those for whom social action was much more relevant and meaningful than the call to personal salvation.

The secularisation of the Christian ethic

The radical interpretation of the message of brotherhood and the resulting anti-establishment agitation has surfaced time and again throughout our history. Wycliffe and the Lollards were engaged in it.[2] So was the Reverend John Ball whose support for the Peasants' Revolt cost him his life in 1381.

The belief in the 'priesthood of all believers', which lies at the root of Congregationalism, or the Quakers' 'inner light' were – and remain – profoundly revolutionary in their impact upon the hierarchies of the church itself. Nor was this revolutionary agitation confined to the church. The divine right of kings claimed by Charles I as a defence of his powers was overthrown along with the King himself and in the ensuing revolution a furious debate began about the legitimacy of the organs of both church and state power. The Levellers asserted that, 'The relation of master and servant has no doubt in the New Testament: in Christ there is neither bond nor free.'[3] Gerard Winstanley went further and defined the Creator not as God but as 'Reason' and on that basis rejected the historical justification for the doctrine that 'one branch of mankind should rule over another'.[4]

In this way a bridge was constructed that carried the message of brotherhood and sisterhood from Christianity to secular humanism, a bridge that carried the ethics across but left the creeds behind. Across the bridge there is now a growing two-way traffic of people and ideas. Christians involved in political action cross it. Humanists use it to go back to the teachings of Jesus and study them. In a theological sense there is a great divide between the Christians on one side and the humanists on the other. But it is impossible to escape the conclusion that over that bridge revolutionary ideas deriving from the Bible and the carpenter of Nazareth have spread to influence hundreds of millions of people for whom the need for neighbourly love within a common humanity is more immediately apparent than the value of mysticism, liturgies and creeds.

The political effect of preaching brotherhood

Along this route many Christian values have travelled until they became embedded in our society as 'sacred' human rights that ought to be upheld in our political life. The American colonists proclaimed them in their Declaration of Independence in 1776:

> We hold these Truths to be self-evident, that all Men are created equal, that they are endowed by their Creator with certain inalienable Rights, that among these are Life, Liberty and the Pursuit of Happiness.

There are many other examples. Environmentalists and ecologists assert that we are all stewards of the earth, on behalf of our brothers and sisters and our children and grandchildren, for whose right to live free from pollution we are morally responsible and politically accountable. They are revolutionaries too in their hostility to exploitation of the planet and its people by feudalism, capitalism or any temporal authority. The deeply held conviction that conscience is above the law, because conscience is God-given and laws are made by men and women, is also highly revolutionary – and those who struggled to assert it and those who died to secure it are the true founders of our civil liberties, including the right to worship in our own way and to hold dissenting political views.

Perhaps the greatest inheritance that this country has derived from the teachings of Jesus has been the heritage of democracy itself and the political ideas that are associated with it. If we are 'our brother's and our sister's keeper', then 'an injury to one is an injury to all' and from that premiss derive most of our contemporary ideas about solidarity and the moral responsibilities of trade unions. The right of each man or woman to vote in elections also stems from their right to be treated as fully human and equal in the sight of God. So too does the pressure for social justice and greater equality which the ballot box allows the electors to exercise through their vote. So does the internationalism which is part and parcel of socialism which has never accepted any divine authority for nationalism at the expense of others. All this was beautifully summed up in the words of the Great Charter in 1842.[5]

This is why so many democratic socialists in this country look back to the teachings of Jesus as a major and continuing source of political inspiration over centuries of thought and effort. For many Christians such openly secular interpretations of the teachings of Jesus may seem to separate completely those who hold them from the creeds of Christian faith. It is argued that without the acceptance of a personal God whose Fatherhood is ever present the brotherhood and sisterhood of men and women loses its meaning and the teachings of Christ degenerate into mere ethics. In order to consider that argument it is necessary to look back into history and consider how, in the past, Christianity came to terms with the then equally threatening challenge of the natural sciences.

How Christianity adjusted to the natural sciences

In past centuries the faith of a Christian would have been defined in such a way as to require him or her to deny the validity of all scientific enquiry into the nature of the universe or the origins of man if they conflicted with the Book of Genesis. Galileo fell foul of the church. Darwin was denounced for his *Origin of Species* and so were all those who challenged the most literal interpretation of the words of the Old Testament. Indeed Darwin was forced to admit in 1870:

> My theology is simply a muddle. I cannot look upon the universe as the result of blind chance. Yet I see no evidence of beneficent design or indeed design of any kind in the details.[6]

Darwin became an agnostic, but he was buried in Westminster Abbey and today few would find difficulty in reconciling his theories of evolution with their Christian faith. Scientists who study the working of nature are now accepted as they are without being seen as heretics. Today Christian Fundamentalism remains a respected viewpoint, and since Fundamentalists no longer have the political power to persecute science, science has no interest in discrediting Fundamentalism. They co-exist in peace. That struggle is over. It was a struggle against the church and not against the teachings of Jesus.

The challenge of socialism and Marxism to the church

But how should Christians respond to the challenge of completely secular socialism and Marxism which for over a century have consciously disconnected their view of brotherhood and sisterhood from the church and its creeds and mysteries? Such socialists believe that the continuing denial of our common humanity does not derive solely, or even primarily, from the sinful conduct of individuals but is institutionalised in the structures of economic, industrial and political power which

Christian churches may support, sustain and even bless, while turning a blind eye to the injustices that continue unchecked. Socialists argue that neighbourly love must be sought in this world and not postponed until the next one. They do not believe that priestly injunctions restricted to matters of personal conduct, 'Be good' or 'Be Kind', are any substitute whatsoever for the fundamental reforms that require collective political action. The socialist interpretation of the parable of the Good Samaritan would cast many churches and churchmen in the role of the priest and the Levite who passed by on the other side; and would identify the socialist position with that of the Good Samaritan who was less concerned with the personal salvation of the traveller who was stripped and beaten than with his immediate need for medical treatment, accommodation and food in this world, here and now. Unless Christians can respond institutionally and politically to that socialist challenge their faith can become an escape from reality and indeed an escape from the challenge posed by Jesus himself. In a world characterised by brutal repression and exploitation under regimes of all kinds, Christian escapism is no more acceptable than it was on the road to Jericho.

The Christian response to Marxism

How should Christians answer this challenge? It is just not good enough to declare a holy war on socialism and Marxism on the grounds that they are atheistical. That is how, historically, the Catholics treated the Protestants and the Protestants treated the Catholics – burning each other at the stake. Yet that is the approach advocated by many Christian anti-communist crusaders and it lies behind the harassment of Marxists in many Western capitalist countries including Britain; and in all countries living under anti-communist military dictatorships.

But before adopting such a position it is necessary to consider other interpretations of the true meaning of Marxism. Dr Nathaniel Micklem, former principal of Mansfield College, Oxford, had this to say in his book *A Religion of Agnostics*:

> Though he disguised his moral indignation under cover of scientific terminology, it was in response to the call of a higher and more lasting justice that Karl Marx repudiated the 'bourgeois' inequality of his day.[7]

This view was echoed by Ivan Svitak in his speech at Charles University during the Prague Spring of 1968:

> Marx was not, and is not, and never will be, the inventor and theoretician of totalitarian dictatorship that he appears today, when the original meaning of his work – true humanism – has been given a thoroughly Byzantine and Asian twist. Marx strove for a wider humanism than that of the bourgeois democracies that he knew and for wider civil rights, not for the setting-up of the dictatorship of one class and one political party. What is today thought to be the Marxist theory of the State and the Marxist social science imply an ideological forgery, a false contemporary conception, as wrong as the idea that the orbits of heavenly bodies are circular.[8]

Milan Machovec in his book *A Marxist Looks at Jesus* carried this argument a stage further and assessed the relationship between Jesus's teaching and Marx's writing:

> You can corrupt the heritage, overlay what is best in it, or push it into the background, but those who seek it out tomorrow will find life and new hope beneath the layers of dirt and the petrified outlines – simply because they are attuned to it. Thus in Christianity the dogmatised image of Jesus Christ has never been able thoroughly to banish the image of the man, Jesus of Nazareth.[9]

This interpretation merits very serious consideration. If such a view prevails, a century from now the writings of Marx may be seen as no more threatening to the teachings of Jesus than the writings of Darwin are thought to be today.

This is not to suggest a political concordat between the hierarchies of the Vatican, the Kremlin and Lambeth Palace –

with all their historical experience of centralised organisation and bureaucracy, such an agreement could pose the greatest threat to freedom of conscience the world has ever seen. But as the ecumenical movement gathers momentum it should extend the range of its dialogue to embrace socialists and Marxists as well as Catholics, Protestants, Jews, Buddhists and Muslims. There is one compelling reason why it must. The technology of destruction, in modern weapons and the rocketry to deliver them, now requires us all to open our hearts and minds to the inescapable need for neighbourly love on a global scale; we must build the social, political and economic institutions that can express that love, bringing together those who now marshal themselves under different banners of religious and political faith. A holy war with atom bombs could end the human family for ever.

A personal view

I say this as a socialist whose political commitment owes much more to the teachings of Jesus – without the mysteries within which they are presented – than to the writings of Marx whose analysis seems to lack an understanding of the deeper needs of humanity.

But untold numbers of people all over the world – and I am one of them – are now claiming the right to study all the sources of insight which they find meaningful, and reach their own personal conclusions about their significance, free from the threat of excommunication for failing to satisfy the tenets of faith laid down by any church or any party. My brand of socialism derives from Christian teaching. I was confirmed as an Anglican, but as I have got older the mystery, the ritual and the organisation of the church have been less interesting to me. As the link between the Labour Party and socialism is so tenuous I sometimes wonder whether the same may not be true of the link between Christian teaching and the churches.

The political debate in Britain

My object is to analyse the political debate now in progress in this country, upon which our future will depend. We do not know what the outcome will be but we must try to identify some of the issues and choices.

First we must do some excavation, because there are four levels at which politics is discussed. The level most beloved of the media is of course the level of personalities – Are you in favour of Mrs T or Mr F? Most political coverage is one huge festival of personalities. This is utterly irrelevant to the real political purpose. We must dig deeper.

If we go below the level of personalities we come to policy, and that is more important – What shall we do? What are the issues? The only qualification we need make about resting our attitude to politics on policy is that policy changes. And events change. Therefore we cannot attach ourselves to a political policy. Remember the exchange between Lloyd George and Clemenceau where Lloyd George said how much he admired the continuity of French policy despite so many changes of government; Clemenceau replied that he admired Britain for its continuity of government with so many changes of policy.

Below policy, at a more fundamental level, we are talking about the structure of decision-making – Is it democratic or is it dictatorial? Here we are beginning to reach something more like bedrock, because if we look at the divisions and arguments in the world today they are very much about who has power, how they got it, how they got rid of it, as well as how they exercise it, and who they are. But of course the real bedrock, the granite foundation upon which politics rests, is values – What is life about? Why are we here? What are our obligations to our fellow men and women? Christians concerned with values (and this is the point of entry of the churches into the political arena) must examine structures, policies and personalities in terms of the extent to which they reflect Christian values.

The world today

Having said that, if we look at the here and now of the world in which we live, it is a deeply unjust world where there is a grave inequality of wealth and power, and people dying of starvation; where there is a massive and unprecedented arms race and the capacity to destroy humanity is now vested in those who have nuclear weapons on a scale that is beyond any possible military justification.

There are competing theologies and ideologies which are part of this process. There are a number of authoritarian governments about, who justify their authority on a different basis according to their history and their ideological position. There is profound insecurity in the world, both national and personal. There is no doubt whatever that the Russians are scared stiff that the West will ally with China, just as the West is very scared of the Soviet Union.

There is rapid technical change where humanity now re-equips itself with a new set of tools about every decade, instead of moving painfully from the stone age to the bronze age, and gradually to the age of early mechanisation. It is inevitable that the re-tooling of society will bring about a change in the power structure. If we have people working as craftsmen, power is obviously decentralised. In a nuclear power station, power is centralised because of the dangers involved.

The mass media are immensely powerful in every country, and have largely replaced the role of the churches as the main instruments by which people receive their values. In the old days the priest climbed into his pulpit every Sunday and told us what we should think; now we have a pundit on every television channel every day who tells us what is acceptable to the establishment of the country in which he or she is performing. In the Soviet Union of course the press is state-controlled. In Britain the press is owned mainly by seven multinational corporations or wealthy families. They own most local papers as well, and what they say is virtually identical, with one or two exceptions.[10]

If we look at the Western countries, loosely called the capitalist countries, the problems are easy to identify. At the time of writing, there are 2.6 million people out of work in Britain. That figure leaves out of account women who do not bother to register for work, older unskilled workers, and people on 'job opportunity schemes' which are really devices to keep the figure down. It leaves out of account the firms that are working short time, where people are living on unemployment levels of income but officially registered as employed. The Trades Union

Congress reckons there are 3.5 million people now who are truthfully unemployed, and, on the assumption that many of those out of work have dependants, we must reckon that far more people are living in homes where the breadwinner is dependent upon some form of social benefit. Then there are about 9 million old people who are also on social benefit.

The results of mass unemployment are far-reaching. It particularly affects women, because when there are few jobs on the market we are often told that women ought to go back to the home and leave room for the men. Unemployment strikes at blacks more sharply than whites and provides an open forum for the National Front. If a black man has a job then he is said to have stolen a white man's job; if he has no job, he is called a scrounger on the welfare state. Race relations are now under heavy pressure.

The £3,000 million that ought to be financing the public services is now going on the dole.[11] We are therefore seeing a very serious cut in public services and increasingly the problem is being presented in terms of law and order. In some areas of Liverpool there is over 40 per cent unemployment; youngsters of nineteen and twenty, who have never worked since they left school, appear to have no prospect of working. Not a lot of imagination is needed to realise that vandalism grows among unemployed young people. My fear is that the Northern Ireland situation could well reproduce itself here in circumstances deriving from unemployment. When he was the Minister of State in Northern Ireland, I remember Stan Orme telling a story of a firm in Londonderry which the management announced it would close – and the following day the shop stewards arrived with automatic weapons. It would be a great mistake to think that what is happening in Northern Ireland is solely a theological argument between the Pope and Ian Paisley. There has been a long period of chronic unemployment in Northern Ireland.

When a society gets frightened – as we are today – there is always a swing to the right. This can lead to a real military threat. The Cold War becomes a diversion from the situation at home. It is the same on both sides of the Iron Curtain. The Russians are saying that the Poles are enemies of socialism, implying that they are all CIA agents. In this country anyone who criticises the government is very easily branded as a communist, as a Marxist, as somebody who is in some way disloyal to society.

The establishment view and its origins

If we read the *Daily Mail*, the *Daily Mirror*, the *Sun*, the *Express*, the *Telegraph* or most local newspapers, there is a marvellous consensus view about what is wrong – lazy workers, incompetent managers, industrial wreckers, and a decline in moral values. This is the standard editorial which is to be found in almost every newspaper every day, including those that are alleged to support the Labour Party. It is a supreme form of scapegoatism, in which the establishment has found something wrong with the people it governs. We have all heard examples of people who are governed trying to change their governors; but this is the first example where the governors are trying to change the people they govern. We can change a government but we cannot have an election that changes the electorate. Yet what is really being said is that the electorate is rotten; that it has gone wrong; that it cannot design things, produce things, will not work, and so on. This is, of course, leading to a new form of authoritarianism. We speak of Britain – but we could easily say the same of Eastern Europe where the Soviet government, building itself on the dictatorship of the proletariat, has found that it just cannot get people to do what they are told. They then attribute their difficulties to falling moral standards, a failure to believe in socialism. This authoritarianism seems to be the dominant new force in the world. Yet it is an inevitable consequence of capitalism.

This has been clear since the beginning of the industrial revolution. Then it became apparent that neither feudalism nor the seventeenth-century change in the balance of power away from the monarchy and towards the gentry in Parliament was capable of permitting new technology to be developed. Adam Smith, the first great philosopher of capitalism, said that in order to develop technology the entrepreneur has got to operate in conditions of *laissez faire*.[12] To see the political implications of what Adam Smith said, we must turn to a pamphlet written by Edmund Burke in 1795, on the political consequences of capitalism:

> Labour is . . . a commodity, and as such an article of trade . . . When any commodity is carried to the market it is not the necessity of the vendor, but the necessity of the purchaser that raises the price. The extreme want of the seller has rather (by the nature of things, with which we shall in vain contend) the direct contrary operation . . . The impossibility of the subsistence of a man who carried his labour to the market is totally beside the question in this way of viewing it. The only question is, what is it worth to the buyer?[13]

That was Edmund Burke interpreting Adam Smith.

The demand for equality

Of course that led to a counter pressure, and ultimately to the Chartist declaration of 1842:

> Labour must no longer be the common prey of masters and rulers. Intelligence has beamed upon the mind of the bondsman, and he has been convinced that all wealth, comfort and produce, everything valuable, useful and elegant, have sprung from the palm of his hand. He feels that his cottage is empty, his back thinly clad, his children breadless, himself hopeless, his mind harassed, his body punished. But undue riches and luxury and gorgeous plenty might be heaped in the palaces of the taskmasters and flooded in the granaries of the oppressors. Nature, God and Reason have condemned this inequality and in the thunder of the people's voice it must perish for ever.

That is the re-emergence in one sense of the religious challenge to the inhumanity of *laissez faire*. Then, of course, it was the industrial revolution, the spread of the franchise first to the middle class, and then to the working class, that led to the *cri de coeur* from Walter Bagehot. In 1867, the year of the North America Act, Bagehot wrote of the franchise:

> In plain English, what I fear is that both political parties would bid for the support of the working man, and both of them would promise to do as he likes if he will only tell them what it is. But as he now holds the casting vote on our affairs, both parties would beg and pray to give that vote to him. I can conceive of nothing more corrupting, or worse, for a set of poor ignorant people than that two combinations of well taught and rich men [the Conservatives and the Liberals] should constantly offer to defer their decision and compete for the office of executing it. *Vox populi* would be *vox diaboli* if worked in that manner.[14]

Here we have Bagehot saying, if this Chartist idea gets going the voice of the devil will come to us through the people.

How democracy undermines capitalism

In other words, we are forced to conclude that, in order to operate effectively, capitalism, as seen by Bagehot and Adam Smith, requires more inequality than free trade unionism and democracy based on the ballot box will permit. That is to say that the unions will put such a pressure on profit margins that capitalism becomes deadlocked. If people who have no money to buy schools or hospitals can vote for schools and hospitals, by electing a candidate who promises to give them a health service and a decent educational system, a second pressure is put on profit margins and capitalism cannot cope. This is the point we have reached in Britain today. There is a log-jam, and because of this we have low investment, bad industrial relations, a long-term decline in British industry, and now the world slump and the fear of war.

The alternatives

If this analysis is correct, the political argument in Britain now is therefore about how to clear the log-jam. We have to agree with Mrs Thatcher in saying there is a log-jam. Even if we do not agree with her solution, she has at least turned her mind to the problem. Her answer – and it got a full endorsement in the 1979 general election – is that in order to make capitalism work again we have to adopt monetarism, which is basically the rebirth of Adam Smith. The Tories say, 'We have to weaken the unions by unemployment, so that union pressure on wages is reduced. We have to cut public expenditure and then capitalism will spring back into life phoenix-like from the ashes.' That is the monetarist solution.

The second solution is what we might call the corporatist solution, which says that monetarism is too disruptive of the social fabric, and that we cannot be sure it will be safe to live in a country where there are three million unemployed, as there may well soon be. The corporatist solution involves recreating a sort of feudal society, in which the big industrialists will meet with the big trade union leaders to discuss how we can get a rational solution to our problems and impose it from above. The corporatist solution involves dealing with the unions, not by creating high unemployment which lowers their wages, but by imposing a statutory prices and incomes policy. It deals with the problem of British democracy getting out of control by tying the British political system to a Common Market where the Commission, the Council of Ministers and the Treaty of Rome provide a natural discipline on any tendency, in any member country, for people to vote themselves more than is permissible by the dictates of the free movement of capital and labour. The corporatist solution – upon which George Brown, Ted Heath and maybe David Steel and Roy Jenkins would all agree – is for stronger state power. Stronger state power will enforce a rational solution to this log-jam. It will discipline everybody. There will be more intervention in industry; more intervention in the unions; society will be contained within a new structure.

The beauty of corporatism is that it can be attached to various political philosophies. For example, Stalin's Russia was corporatist on the justification that a dictatorship of the proletariat must by definition be acting in the interests of the working class. Mussolini was also a corporatist in that he wanted to revitalise capitalism by a corporate state. Franco's Spain was also corporatist.

The third solution is democratic socialism. This too recognises that there is a log-jam. It recognises that we have to have some discipline in order to run a society, but says we will by-pass the deadlock of market forces and go for direct investment in industry and the services, and try to get democratic self-discipline to clear the log-jam. In effect democratic socialism says we can no longer worship the idea that market forces are the solution to our problems because it is immoral to do so.

Democratic socialism and Christianity

The roots of democratic socialism are connected with the teachings of Jesus. There are many quotations which illustrate this. I cite one or two here in order simply to identify my own political credentials as a socialist. H. G. Wells, an atheist, wrote a marvellous passage about Jesus:

> In what he plainly said is it any wonder that all who were rich and prosperous felt a horror of strange things, a swimming of their world at his teaching? He was dragging out all the little private reservations they had made from social service into the light of a universal religious life. He was like some terrible moral huntsman, digging mankind out of the snug burrows in which they had lived hitherto. In the white blaze of this kingdom of his there was to be no property, no privilege, no pride, no precedence; no motive indeed and no reward but love.[15]

No one would argue that a whole political tradition rests upon an acceptance of the reading by H. G. Wells of the Christian message, but where in the New Testament do we find any authority for the class structure? In Gerard Winstanley's famous pamphlet of 1649, we find this interesting slippage from a theological justification for equality into a humanistic one:

> In the beginning of time the great Creator, Reason, made the Earth to be a Common Treasury, to preserve beasts, birds,

> fishes and man, the law that was to govern this Creation. For Man had domination given to him over the beasts, birds and fishes, but not one word was spoken in the beginning that one branch of Mankind should rule over another.[16]

That is not a theological statement, but it shows the enormous impact that Christianity had upon the humanistic tradition. Then we go to Robert Owen, a British industrialist, who was the first socialist. He said:

> From the principle of individual interests have arisen all the divisions of mankind – the endless errors and mischiefs of class, sect, party, and of national antipathies, creating the angry and malevolent possessions, and all the crimes and misery with which the human race have hitherto been afflicted.[17]

And Keir Hardie, a founder of the Labour Party, in his Christmas message in 1897, said:

> When I think of the thousands of white-livered poltroons who take the Christ's name in vain, and yet do not see His image being crucified in every hungry child, I cannot think of peace. I have known as a child what hunger means, and the scars of those days are with me still, and rankle in my spirit, and unfit me in many ways for the work to be done. If the spiritually-proud and pride-blinded professors of Christianity could only be made to feel and see that the Christ is here present with us and that they are laying on the stripes and binding the brow afresh with thorns, and making him shed tears of blood in a million homes, surely this world would be made more fit for his Kingdom.[18]

Now that is very violent language, but it indicates the moral fuelling – the Christian fuelling – behind the ideas of socialism.

Why Christians must speak out

Saying this involves arguing that the church should perform a more prophetic role, and not see itself primarily in administrative or managerial terms. If the church sees our problems at the level of values and institutions, then it must condemn state communism, fascism, dictatorship, and the worship of money and power.

Christians in Britain must speak up loud and clear against monetarism and militarism which now directly threaten our lives. Monetarism, or the use of profit and loss as the main criterion for judging human activity, is a cancer eating into our society. Monetarism elevates money into an object to be worshipped. All moral values, or many of them, are subordinated to the religion of the market place, where those with wealth enjoy economic and political power, and then use it to advance their own narrow and selfish interests regardless of the consequences for the rest of society. Militarism poses a threat to the survival of humanity itself, as the nuclear arms race gobbles up scarce resources of money and skills, both needed to relieve poverty, and of course it also makes war more likely.

Militarism and monetarism have both concentrated power in the hands of the few who control the deadly war machines in both East and West. How can bishops and priests and pastors stand aside from these great moral issues on the grounds that they should not get involved in politics? No one is suggesting that the churches as such should come out in favour of one political party or another. But with honourable exceptions, many religious leaders have not spoken up on the greatest questions of our day. It is not enough to plead for moderation, or to ask the rich to be good and the poor to be patient. And ritualised religion, or appeals to individuals to seek personal salvation or to await justice in the world to come, are not an adequate response. A clear moral challenge to evil ideas is needed. If this is not forthcoming, other voices will emerge and become dominant, as occurred in Germany before the war. Already in America we are witnessing the growth of religious primitivism among some born-again Christians who have virtually sanctified nationalism, monetarism and militarism. On a visit to America in December 1980 I saw a television programme which consisted of a sermon, punctuated by appeals for nuclear rearmament. It showed where the nuclear submarines were, and how they should be increased in order to cover all Russian cities, and denounced any form of state intervention to help poverty or anything else on the grounds that this was making a free market economy unworkable.

The best of the Christian tradition of social action has always been revolutionary, democratic and humane, in challenging wealth, power, privilege and injustice, whether under kings, conquerors or commissars. The liberation theology now preached in Latin America shows how Christians can integrate their faith with social action, and support working people and their families against all the forces that oppress them.

Britain too now needs a liberation theology, which encourages Christians to intervene directly in society, and help people. This would enable people to return to use the skills and the support that the churches could give them in their struggles. If that were done, Christian teaching would reach out to touch the lives and raise the hopes, and influence the hearts and minds of millions of people who now feel isolated, powerless and threatened, and many of whom are near to despair.

The future involves the churches in a very big decision. As organisations, are they to remain secure under state protection? After all, the churches historically have been able to come to terms with powers of all kinds – fascism in Spain, Portugal and much of Latin America; feudalism in pre-revolutionary China; Nazism in pre-war Germany; communism in Poland; multinational capitalism in America.

Are Christians to go out and bear the message of brotherhood? That involves enormous controversy. The churches should play an essential role in the public debate, and in the struggle for freedom and democracy. In Britain today Christians have a key role in determining the final outcome of the argument about the future pattern of power. They cannot stand aside and ask someone to tell them how it is going to finish, because how it finishes depends so much on what Christians and the churches do meanwhile.

8

The Way Ahead

Britain's present decline is not inevitable. A more hopeful future is possible, if we can take control of it. It is true that the world scene and the prospects for Britain, as we enter the 1980s, are darker than for many years past. All the governments in East and West are seriously concerned about their own external security; and all are also faced with internal problems which they are not confident they can resolve. Expenditure on arms and nuclear weapons is escalating sharply, while the gap between rich and poor is widening, and human rights continue to be denied all over the world. The Western economies are in the grip of a deepening slump, as grave as we experienced in the 1930s. But this is a man-made slump and we do not have to accept it.

The true cost of unemployment

It is against that background that we, in Britain, have to consider the prospects for this country.

We are an old and experienced self-governing nation, rich in skill and talent – and in natural resources. We also have a tradition of respect for decent human values and fair play; and a proper suspicion of those who abuse the power they possess. Why then do we tolerate the criminal waste associated with the present levels of unemployment? School leavers find their prospects blighted; men and women in their prime are thrown upon the scrap-heap; older people are driven into early and permanent unemployability.

But the damage does not end there. Unemployment cuts back the income of everyone living in households where the breadwinner is out of work. Thus inequalities of wealth and income widen and real poverty is beginning to be a serious social evil once again. All this at a time when the technical means to produce plenty for all are at hand.

Unemployment pay is money diverted from the schools and health services we desperately need and which are now short of cash. The pressure has begun to drive women who want to work back into the home to make more work for men; suspicion and fear are being generated between different communities, with all the risks which that involves. We know that vandalism and violence can be born of despair and that, in turn, brings forth demands for 'law and order politics'; but what we need is 'law and order and work and social justice' if we are to safeguard the fabric of society. We cannot ask the police, or the Army, to fill the gap left by the failures of economic, industrial and social policy; and if they tried to do so it could lead to unacceptable levels of authoritarianism.

The state as the life support system of the economy

We are now paying the price for eighty years of failure by British capitalism. Profits were not recycled into re-equipment on the scale necessary to sustain our industry against international competition. They went into secondary banking, into land and even overseas to equip our competitors. Our experience has been that competition does not restrain prices when monopolies, many of them international, are able by their size and power to repeal the laws of supply and demand in respect of their own prices. Our experience has shown that market forces cannot provide steady growth and certainly cannot cope with rapid technological or political change.

Contrary to popular belief, the experience of the last eighty years or more has shown that the people of this country have – with the exception of the 1979 general election – consistently voted for policies involving greater government intervention in the economy. What is more, in the past all governments – Liberal, Labour and Conservative – have accepted the need for government intervention to make good the requirements that capitalism is unable or unwilling to fulfil.

We could go back to 1900 when the National Physical Laboratory was set up by a Conservative government because industry would not do its own research. We could go back to 1903 when Joseph Chamberlain called for Protection.[1] In 1916 the Department of Scientific and Industrial Research was set up because British capitalism had not done adequate research in chemicals, and we were being defeated by German industry that had. We could go back to Lloyd George's insurance scheme and the 'distressed area' policy introduced in the 1930s. We can look at all the post-war measures, a formidable list which it is easy to mock. They include grants, loans and subsidies to invest, to re-equip, to relocate, to train and retrain, for research and development, for export promotion, to halt closures, to finance expansion, to restrain prices, to sustain jobs, to create jobs, to promote mergers and to help small businesses. A mass of money has gone in and of course it has created millions of jobs.[2] In addition there have been endless tax reliefs for industry, even to the point of financing the businessman's London flat, his suit, his car and his dinner in the West End. The Honours List has been used, liberally, to assist in these matters, and so has the Queen's Award to Industry.

Who benefits from the system? We would all suffer if it collapsed but the people who pressed for it most were the industrialists. I have sat many times beside my television set and watched City bankers at big dinners denouncing public intervention. I have seen the very same men in my office the following morning, when I was Minister of Technology or Secretary of State for Industry or for Energy, pleading for cash. The truth is that the state has always acted as a life support system for our economy. Now the Tories are trying to switch off that life support system. What is more, they are trying to switch it off at a time when the world economy is in deep recession.

This is all happening in a world in which the energy shortage is now so serious that prices may rise and tip the world economy back into real slump. It is happening on the eve of the biggest acceleration of technical change the world has seen for many years, with the microchip cutting a swathe through administrative work and modernisation transforming the factories. Moreover, it is happening when we have an expanding labour force.

As a result there will be more redundancies. There will be lost production and lost trade. There will be greater costs. There will be a decline in the quality of hospitals, schools and other public services. There will be lower productivity as men seek to protect themselves by work sharing. There will be emigration of our skilled people. Others are already beginning to recruit, if they can, from this country. To accelerate the process of decline, as the Tory Government are doing, is to cause immeasurable damage because it is eroding the manufacturing base upon which we must depend when the oil has run out in twenty-five years.

The government have a choice. First, they can carry on, braced for confrontation, protesting that everything will come right after a transition period. However, they have found that as this strategy is applied, support has grown for policies designed to reduce the hardship and the suffering and to bring people back into productive empoyment. The many who are suffering under the government's policy far exceed the few who are getting rich from the sale of public assets.

The government's second option is to seek political security in consensus, but this will not work because the damage is now too great to be undone by a reversion to the policies of the past.

Mrs Thatcher's Government face another, more fundamental problem. They began by defending capitalism on the grounds that it underpins parliamentary democracy. They now discover that parliamentary democracy, with the exercise of the vote, steadily erodes capitalism by demanding policies of intervention. So if they wish to stick to capitalism they will eventually have to challenge the desires of our people expressed through parliamentary democracy. That is the problem that confronts them.

The dangers of de-industrialisation

British industry is now caught in a rapidly accelerating downward spiral of de-industrialisation which is doing more lasting damage to our manufacturing capacity than the war-time air-raids. We struggled then to keep our factories open and working, because we knew our survival as a nation required it. It is just as important to keep them working today and it is the plain duty of any government to prevent the destruction of the nation's industrial base.

Severance pay is only an anaesthetic to dull the pain of dismissal. When that money is spent the job has gone for ever, both for the men or women concerned and for their children and those who follow on. What future is there for us all if we accept that those who want to live by selling their labour are forced instead to sell their jobs, their skill and their birthright to work? Unless we plan properly, we shall see the microchip, which could open up immense possibilities for human betterment, introduced to cut out hundreds of thousands of clerical jobs without providing more jobs or more leisure.

How then are we supposed to live through this period of deliberate de-industrialisation? And what are we to do after it has taken place? The answer we are getting is clear and very dangerous.

The misuse of the oil revenues

As a nation we are now living on the unexpected, and strictly temporary, legacy of the oil revenues. Within five years of the first oil being landed from the Argyll field, in June 1975, we became virtually self-sufficient. Britain is thus completely insulated from the payment in foreign currency for the oil we need at the greatly increased – and rising – OPEC prices. Instead of spending that money to re-equip our industrial base and to sustain our economy and living standards when the oil runs out, we are now using it to finance tax cuts for the wealthiest section of the community; and to pay for a veritable flood of manufactured imports, made cheaper by a strong oil-backed pound sterling, which is accelerating our de-industrialisation. Unless the present policy is changed, every barrel of oil we bring ashore will help to export jobs. Then, when the oil reserves have been exhausted, we shall be left with such a narrow industrial base that it will not be strong enough to sustain our population and there will be a real danger of chronic large-scale unemployment and/or emigration. Meanwhile, those who can afford to do so can move their capital abroad without any exchange control.

The scapegoats for decline

How are these issues and problems explained to the British people? Day after day, and night after night, and month after month, all Britain's problems are laid at the door of familiar scapegoats. We are told that 'lazy workers, militant shop stewards, incompetent managers, extravagant public services, and extremists, are responsible for what has happened and are daily taking us nearer to anarchy and chaos'. But this simply will not do as an explanation for what is happening, and why.

For a start, it is not true. British workers, in general, work for longer hours, with less pay, and poorer public services, than their European counterparts; and our production problems stem from persistently low investment levels in the past and a failure to introduce democracy at the place of work. This has certainly been true at British Leyland, for example. Yet, despite all those problems, workers at British Leyland still succeed in producing £3-billion-worth of vehicles each year, and in exporting £1-billion-worth of them; thus contributing enormously to the real wealth of the nation. The task of production is an exceptionally difficult one for all those engaged in it, and it is strange that British Leyland should be attacked so violently, and so consistently, especially since most of the attacks come from people who are much better paid, for doing much less difficult work, and many of whom may well be unable to mend a puncture on their own bicycle, let alone manufacture, sell and maintain sophisticated engineering products.

By contrast, anyone who could afford to put £10,000 into gold sovereigns or Kruger rands in January 1973 would by 1980 find them worth well over £100,000. This represents a capital gain of £90,000 without having had to do a hand's turn of work to earn it.[3] Compare that to the wages of a car worker, steel worker or miner over the same period, who might now be faced with redundancy on the grounds that his productivity was too low. And speculation like this is also an insult to many thousands of small businessmen who have to struggle so hard for a living. Any child can see that these are the economics of the madhouse.

The contradictions we must resolve

But the contradictions go far deeper than that. How can anyone explain the logic of an economic system which permits unmet human need to co-exist with unemployed people, able and anxious to meet it, whilst unused financial resources are diverted into speculation that does not add one penny to our real wealth? What is to be said to an unemployed building worker who lives in a town where there are sub-standard houses, schools, hospitals or old factories that he has the skill to repair or rebuild, while so many of the nation's savings are exported to re-equip our competitors or invested for capital gains in land? The inescapable fact is that the economic system we have in Britain, and the monetarist philosophy by which it is guided, has not provided, and cannot provide, a way to harness our skills, to develop our resources, so that we can meet our needs and all share in the benefit that would bring.

Lessons from the 1930s

This is not a new problem. The inter-war years were cursed by a similar slump that had similar consequences. In 1933 three million men and women were out of work in Britain. How did we recover? It was not the monetarism of Ramsay MacDonald, nor the pre-Keynesian job creation schemes of Roosevelt's New Deal, which brought back full employment. It was rearmament and war which got our economy going again.

No one who remembers the rusting hulk of the half-finished Cunard liner in John Brown's shipyard needs to be reminded that it was the warship building programme that brought our yards back to life. So it was with steel, and coal, and engineering, and vehicles as the orders for guns and tanks and aircraft poured out from the War Office, the Admiralty and the Air Ministry before 1939 – all financed by the taxpayer. All that rearmament, which gave us full employment, was public expenditure and it was largely self-financing, as dole payments tailed off, and those who had received them began to pay taxation from their new wages into the Treasury, and were producing real goods and services. The challenge to this generation is how to get back to full employment without rearmament and without a war that would destroy humanity.

An alternative strategy for Britain

How are we to do it? Our problems are much more political than they are economic. No democratic society can govern itself without a broadly agreed analysis of what is wrong and how to correct it. The post-war policies have broken down irretrievably and there is no prospect of reviving them. The politics of monetarism now being applied cannot possibly win national support because they are destructive, divisive and completely lacking in any moral content or moral appeal. We must discuss the alternative strategy, and examine it carefully, free from misrepresentation. There are eight objectives we should set ourselves.

1 Full employment

We must resolve to restore full employment as a major national policy objective, and any government must also accept responsibility for finding the means to achieve it.[4]

2 Re-equipment

We must consciously commit the lion's share of our national oil and other industrial revenues to the modernisation, expansion and diversification of our manufacturing industry. Where public money is used there must be full public accountability and new forms of public ownership that are very different from existing nationalised industries – decentralised, democratic and sensitive to the people they are intended to serve.

3 Planned trade and payments

We must plan our trade in manufactures and our international payments to protect our industries (whilst they are being re-equipped) from destruction either by excessive growth, by imports or by currency speculation.

4 *Industrial democracy*

We must move steadily towards industrial democracy by accepting the principle of joint determination of economic, industrial and social policy at the national level, in both the major public and private corporations, and at the place of work. Elected trade union representatives of professional managers and skilled and unskilled workers should exercise an absolutely equal influence and control with those appointed by the providers of public or private capital.

5 *Expanding the public services*

We must expand our educational, health, housing and environmental services to meet pressing social needs, to improve the quality of life, to prepare for the future and to increase employment, both directly and in the industries that supply the equipment for those services. In future, public expenditure will have to be a source of dynamism in every industrialised society, without a wasteful use of the world's scarce raw materials.

6 *A return to self-government*

We must regain for the British electorate, through the House of Commons, full control of all law-making and tax-gathering powers now ceded to the European Communities. This will regain for us the legal right to rebuild our industries, plan our trade, and once more buy the cheapest food available on world markets. Britain should take the lead in arguing for a wider and looser association of fully self-governing nations in Europe, willing to cooperate but without the bureaucracy, rigidity and waste which necessarily forms part of the Common Market as it was established.

7 *A fairer society*

We must create a much fairer, more open, more democratic and more tolerant society in Britain, which is still riddled with patronage, privilege, inequality and unaccountable power.

8 The right to be heard

We must find better ways of communicating with each other about the real issues and the real choices, free from personalities, trivialities, distortion and abuse. The right to free speech must be accompanied by the right to be heard, to permit a genuine national dialogue about the future in which all can take part.

Where will the money come from?

The question most frequently asked about Labour's economic programme is, can we afford it? Where will the money come from to build more homes, hospitals, schools? Will it necessarily mean higher rates of income tax? The answer is that huge sums of money presently being squandered are available for productive investment. We lose about £14 billion a year in wasted production due to unemployment.[5] We pay about £3 billion a year to people on the dole.[6] About £9 billion a year accumulates in pension and insurance funds, which are the workers' savings, and a further £4 billion accumulates in bank deposits.[7] On top of this we spend about £1 billion more on defence, proportionately, than other West European countries.[8] Altogether that comes to £31,000 million – £31 billion available to re-equip our industries, to expand our health, housing, education and other public services. What we are discussing is the reallocation of this enormous sum of money, much of which now goes into gold and currency speculation, works of art, rearmament, land or investment abroad, where it helps to re-equip our competitors. If we could channel these funds into our industry and public services, this country could solve its problems. There is nothing wild or extreme about this. It is practical common sense. If the Labour Party is allowed to get this message across to the people, they will understand that what we are saying makes sense.

The international dimension

Though each of these proposals is moderate in itself, taken together they constitute an agenda for radical and democratic reforms that are long overdue. Clearly explained, fairly reported, advocated with sincerity and patience, but resolutely carried through, this reform programme would command widespread support extending far beyond the confines of the Labour Party to fair-minded people in all parties, and in none. Indeed, it would have to command such support, for without a real and solid majority these policies could not be implemented, nor negotiated internationally as they would have to be.

Such a programme, however, is likely to win wide international support. Many people in the Western world are now equally imprisoned by the monetarist philosophy, which appears to contemplate, without concern, the acceptance of enormous damage to the public welfare. Britain would do the human race a favour if we were the first to proclaim that the monetarist emperor has no clothes. The reforms outlined above would not only help safeguard the interests of our people, but would also reflect the aspirations of hundred of millions throughout the developing countries who are now calling for a new world economic order. Such a new economic order, which allowed us to plan the use of our limited resources of food, energy and other raw materials, could benefit us all, reduce international conflicts and help to make the United Nations more effective as an instrument for development as well as peace-keeping.

Our future is in our own hands

The world economic situation, and Britain's own problems, are not inevitable nor pre-ordained. They are the result of abdicating social responsibility and control in favour of market forces. We should reject all mechanistic projections that suggest an inescapable fate for humanity, as if we are somehow condemned to observe what is happening as mere spectators. To accept that would be to deny our own humanity, our capacity, our genius and our own history.

As far as economic policy goes, the people of the world will not bow the knee for much longer to the authority of the International Monetary Fund. Nor will the British people ever adopt the *Financial Times* Share Index as its new Book of Common Prayer. Men and women may risk imprisonment, or lay down their lives for their beliefs, but they will not willingly cooperate with policies that are against their own real interests, nor abandon their moral responsibilities to their fellow citizens just to keep the Public Sector Borrowing Requirement down. As the Archbishop of Canterbury said recently, 'People do not give their lives to get the money supply under control.'[9]

The Creator did not make us to worship a new monetarist mammon whose high priests are now attempting to dictate to us what we should believe, what we should think and what we should do. Humanity deserves a wider vision than that. We were all born free, to live out our lives in useful ways for the improvement of the human condition and for the enrichment of life for the human family, in peace. It is the task of statesmen to make that possible. And it is the belief that common effort may succeed that keeps so many hopes alive. As that message spreads – and it is spreading – the support for it will grow. For it is the essential message of democracy.

9

The Trade Unions in the 1980s

The argument in outline

The trade union movement has experienced a century of external influence upon successive governments, including forty years of consensus politics in which it became an active participant at the highest level of decision-making. Lately it has seen that consensus transformed into a kind of corporatism, which was not in the interests of labour, and then rejected because a declining British capitalism can no longer afford to maintain full employment and the welfare state. Today monetarist policies are being implemented through a major assault upon the role of the trade union movement, in which the government and some sections of the media are both involved.

In meeting this challenge, the trade unions are making both a defensive and a constructive response which will extend their role, politicise them, and lead to pressure for major reforms. What is required is a new constitutional settlement with labour to lay the foundations for a new consensus markedly more favourable to working people, and to which they are entitled by virtue of their contribution to our society and the simple claims of social justice.

For over a century the trade union movement has occupied a growing role within our society. In its beginnings it can be traced back to the extension of the franchise to working people; and the use made of those votes by trade unions to secure from successive governments legislation favourable to the interests of the workers, including the easement of legal restraints upon trade unionism itself. Indeed, it was dependence upon the votes of working people which encouraged the 1906 Liberal Government to lay the foundations of the welfare state. Over the years the bargaining power of the unions, plus the moral challenge posed by socialism, the patient social planning associated with the Fabians, the emergence of Keynesianism, and the growing electoral strength of the Labour Party, which the unions had established, all helped to ameliorate the harshness of market forces.

It was not only Liberal and Labour politicians who contributed to this process. The tragic experiences of the pre-war slump made a deep impression upon some Conservatives too. Harold Macmillan, for example, was shocked by his experiences of unemployment when he served as MP for Stockton-on-Tees before the war. His book, *The Middle Way*, was quite explicit in calling for a planned economy:

> Such a correlation of all the factors in our economic life as will bring about the full employment of our resources and a dependable stability in the more prosperous conditions which we hope to create . . . such a wise governance of the economic system as will eliminate or control the trade cycle.[1]

Churchill's war-time coalition embraced all these ideas and the 1945 Labour Government under Mr Attlee implemented many of the proposals which had emanated from Keynes and Beveridge, who were both essentially radical Liberals.[2] Attlee's social and socialist revolution, carried through with trade union support, can thus be seen to be a part of a long process of change. Harold Macmillan's premiership marked the high water mark of consensus politics and he moved his party firmly away from its earlier ideological commitment to *laissez faire*, towards a mild form of economic planning through the establishment of the National Economic Development Council within which the trade union leaders were invited to play a role.[3] Macmillan's election victory of 1959 confirmed the public acceptability of that approach, and was made possible by the apparent success of the mixed economy. But it was not only the Conservative leadership that had shifted its position.

The Conservative victory in 1959 greatly strengthened the

school of social democratic revisionism within the Labour Party, which had argued for some time that a reformed capitalism could in fact meet all the legitimate aspirations of labour and urged the Labour Party to rid itself of its commitment to a programme of socialist transformation. This ideological commitment to consensus politics attracted adherents from all parties, from capital as well as labour, and became an article of faith within the establishment. Those trade union leaders who espoused it used their influence, and their votes, to contain and defeat the unrepentant socialists within the movement and the party. Both the trade unions and the Labour Party became markedly less political and less aware of their need for each other.

Meanwhile, the membership of the trade union movement continued its steady growth; and trade union leaders were invited to join more and more boards and quangos of all kinds, and their views were sought and respected as an accepted part of the national consensus. Since the general election of 1979 that process has been halted.

The breakdown of consensus and the emergence of corporatism

One factor which played a major part in the breakdown of consensus was the relatively poor performance of British industry in comparison with its major international competitors. The post-war boom, upon which full employment in Britain had rested, began to run out of steam as the economies of Germany, Japan and Italy recovered. Long-term weaknesses in the British economy, attributable to a failure to reinvest the nation's savings in the nation's industries, and the parallel failure to establish labour as an equal partner at the place of work, emerged more clearly.

Moreover, full employment was seen by the owners of capital as having had the effect of greatly strengthening the bargaining power of labour. Recurrent balance of payments problems were met by policies of stop-go, which interrupted the flow of investment, without weakening labour's bargaining power. This in its turn led to a series of incomes policy initiatives which, under various names, were devised to contain the bargaining power of the unions. Industrialists, the City, the civil service and the establishment increasingly blamed all the problems of the economy on to the trade unions, and the media hammered this explanation home on every possible occasion, virtually ignoring all other explanations.

It was, in fact, Mr Wilson's Government which, in 1969, first attempted to limit the power of unions by legislation.[4] That attempt failed but, in failing, it so damaged the relations between the Labour Government and rank and file trade unionists that it played a decisive role in Labour's defeat at the polls in 1970. The next, Conservative Government, under Mr Heath, returned to the attack on the unions in earnest, with its own Industrial Relations Act and a rigid statutory incomes policy. The confrontation which followed led to the defeat of the Heath government; and the return of a Labour Government which itself foundered on its own rigid pay policy after the 1978/9 winter of discontent.

It is important to understand why consensus politics failed. Beginning as the finest flowering of liberal capitalism, built upon the illusion that real conflicts of interest could be wished away by high public expenditure on jobs and welfare under managed capitalism, consensus politics finally succeeded in elevating fudging to the highest level of statesmanship. It brought the top people together in an endless huddle, which began, no doubt, from the highest motives and ended in a series of desperate attempts to fend off the insistent demands of labour whose interests were not being met, by an economic system which was incapable of doing so. As public support for consensus politics weakened, those in all parties who believed in it became more and more authoritarian in their thinking and, almost unconsciously, began to construct the nucleus of a corporate state.

The main policy elements of this embryonic corporatism consisted of a permanent statutory incomes policy; legislation to restrict and centralise the power of trade unions; an interventionist industrial policy; and a move to restructure capitalism within a federal Europe. It was hoped that the package might be reinforced by adopting proportional representation, which would insulate a form of 'national government' from effective challenge. In the event, these views, though espoused by a formidable body of high-ranking public figures, suffer from one serious defect. They do not and, by definition, cannot command a popular majority. Though the City and industrialists may have welcomed the idea of controlling the trade unions, they concluded that the price was too high since it involved the maintenance of near full employment and the welfare state.

The trade unions tried to make the system work but could accept neither legislation directed against themselves nor statutory controls over wages. Finally they came to recognise that, even with their own cooperation, this system, far from achieving economic expansion and moving steadily towards greater equality, led to stagnation and a widening gap in wealth and income between the owners of capital and those who live by selling their labour. Disillusionment with consensus corporatism came when the Western industrialised economies moved into slump. Weakened by three-quarters of a century of under-investment and hindered by an oil-strong pound sterling, Britain saw its competitive position crumble under a triple hammering from cheap EEC manufactured imports, expensive EEC agricultural products and a huge annual Common Market tax demand.

It was against this background that Mrs Thatcher's Government came to power in May 1979.

Monetarism, the media and the unions

Mrs Thatcher's Government rejected the inheritance of Churchill, Macmillan, Eden and Heath, and resolved to tackle what they believed to be the root cause of the problem – the low level of profitability in Britain – by using monetarist methods.

The Thatcher Government's first priority is therefore to restore profit margins. This requires cuts in real living standards for the majority of working people, and cuts in those public services of health, education and housing upon which working people depend, so as to reduce public expenditure. It is argued that greater profits will be earned and the taxation of them will be reduced so that the real return to the owners of capital will be substantially increased, supposedly encouraging them to invest more – though why they should want to invest when unemployment is cutting demand has never been explained.

In truth, all the sophisticated arguments about money supply are irrelevant. What we are getting is a political strategy designed to bring about a fundamental and irreversible shift in the balance of wealth and power in favour of the owners of capital at the expense of working people and their families. The main obstacle to the success of the government's strategy is the trade union movement. The government's central purpose is therefore to overcome trade union opposition. Three methods have been chosen for this purpose:

First, by legislation: the Employment Act is drafted to weaken trade union power by imposing a host of legal restraints.[5]

Second, by deliberately raising unemployment. The fear of unemployment and the oft-repeated threat of redundancy, closure and dismissal is already having its effect on whole groups of workers, as in British Leyland and British Steel, and damaging the national interest.

Third, by using the resources of the state to persuade the public that the unions are to blame for the nation's economic problems.

Even supposedly non-political civil servants are being pressed into service to make highly political speeches on the same theme. A very senior British diplomat recently issued a press release which contained these passages: 'The sad fact is that there are people who regard trade unions as instruments to be manipulated in the service of Marxist policies . . . ' and later, he spoke of many people 'who are wondering whether the old British concept of trade unionism has not outlived its usefulness, and believe the British worker would be better off, in real terms, without the unions'.[6]

There are today, in Britain, many good people who have been persuaded that inflation caused by high wage settlements is the source of all our problems, who do not yet appreciate the real political motivation of those who are now attacking the trade unions. In parallel with these policies there has been a sustained media campaign against the trade union movement, its members, its industrial role, and its political aspirations. This campaign centres on the thesis that the trade unions, and the working people whom they represent, are mainly responsible for virtually all our economic difficulties. The methods used by the BBC and ITN newscasters to achieve this are, at last, being monitored and studied scientifically and the results of some of these studies have been published, for instance in two Glasgow University Media Group studies, *Bad News* and *More Bad News*.[7]

The class assumptions of the broadcasters are shown in their most basic and ordinary practices. In an industrial conflict the union side will be said to 'claim', 'demand' or 'reject' while management are more likely to be presented as making a 'plea', 'offer' or 'proposal'. Policies on wage restraint are justified by constant references to the alleged 'excessive' demands of the past. In the period of four months analysed by the Glasgow Group, there were only 17 occasions when someone appeared on the TV news and argued that wage restraint and lower wages were *not* the way to resolve the economic crisis. In the same period there were 287 occasions when someone argued that this was exactly what was needed.[8]

The language of industrial disputes often carries over to coverage of political issues, with the right wing of the Labour Party being cast in the role of management. The expression 'left-wing dominated' is often used to describe situations where the right do not have a majority. For example, an item on the BBC-1 Television News on 29th October 1980 included the following sentence: 'The left-wing dominated National Executive rejected pleas by Mr Healey and Mr Foot . . . ' The same language is not applied to situations where the right are in control. When did we last hear of 'the right-wing dominated' Shadow Cabinet or parliamentary Labour Party?

The unions are also attacked because some of their leaders are Marxists. But the plain truth is that some of the very finest and most dedicated men and women who serve the British trade union movement have been lifelong Marxists. It is one thing to disagree with Marxism. But it is quite another to try to discredit trade unionism because some of its leaders accept the Marxist analysis.

In short, it is hard to escape the conclusion that the policies now being implemented involve far more than having a Chancellor of the Exchequer who watches the movement of money supply very carefully; or having spending ministers anxious to cut down on wasteful items that may have crept into public expenditure. We are at the receiving end of a comprehensive strategy designed to end full employment, dismantle the welfare state, widen social inequalities and reduce working people to a state of greater subservience to their employers. To achieve all that, trade unionism as it has grown in Britain has got to be driven back and neutralised as a serious force in industry and politics.

The trade unions on the defensive

The inevitable response of the trade union movement to these developments will be – and is – to seek to defend the gains already made by campaigning publicly against unemployment and cuts in public expenditure, and for policies which would lead to economic expansion, a return to full employment and an extension of public provision. This campaign is already in full swing. The trade union movement is learning the lessons of its own history and preparing to refight battles that, a generation ago, were thought to be settled for ever. What then are those lessons?

First, that the right to organise free trade unions is a keystone of a free society; and that any attempt to reduce or remove it must be resisted vigorously. The dissenting belief that places conscience before the law is also a part of that tradition; and it would be unwise to assume that laws which purported to remove that right would be accepted without defiance. In this connection it is necessary to distinguish between revolutionary action to replace Parliament and law-breaking in pursuit of conscientious objection. Since the trade union movement believes itself, correctly, to have been a major founding force in parliamentary democracy through its support for the Chartists and others, it is not likely to reject its own history by seeking the overthrow of a government freely elected. But there will always be some individuals who would rather face jail than accept unjust laws which they believe would take away basic rights. The arrest of the five dockers in 1972, and their release after the TUC had decided upon national strike action, offers a recent example of what could easily happen again.[9]

One other lesson now being relearned is that the power of capital used the consensus period to strengthen its relative position at a time when the mass media were busy telling everyone that the unions were running the country. The consolidation of capital into fewer and fewer hands, and the development of multinational corporations, allowed the restraints imposed on capital by Parliaments, even with a Labour majority, to be sidestepped completely. The international bankers could move their money freely across frontiers and impose policies upon nation states by creating crises of confidence that were miraculously ended when capital had its way.

It is true that the trade unions had real power when they chose to use it, and had influence at the highest ministerial level, but with the passage of time it became clear that the loyalty of trade union leaders to consensus policies could make them unwittingly a vehicle for winning the consent of their members for policies which were not in those members' interest, as happened with successive pay policies introduced by Labour governments.[10] Seen from one point of view, trade union involvement in government decisions was a necessary condition for the maintenance of an economic system that is inherently unfair and chronically unsuccessful.

In the long sweep of history, the fact that capitalism now acknowledges that it requires the cooperation of labour if it is to retain its public acceptability, may be counted as an advance of a kind. But it has not escaped the attention of the Labour movement that such a sterile partnership was not what it set out to achieve, and that trade union involvement has not secured any lasting gains. Such an analysis has been reinforced by the knowledge that British capitalism, caught in a cycle of decline, de-industrialisation and slump, can no longer afford to be as generous in distributing its benefits as it was in the artificial boom years of Macmillan. There is now a growing realisation, within the unions, that no government, however well-intentioned, would be able to achieve full employment and maintain the welfare state within the limits set by market forces and this realisation has led to a renewal of interest in socialism.

But trade union anxiety goes deeper still. It is being seriously argued that the high level of inequality required to restart the old capitalist motivation to invest would be so unacceptable that it could not be carried through with electoral consent, and that parliamentary democracy itself – as well as trade union rights – may be threatened in the process. In one sense the threat has already materialised with the subordination of all parliamentary law-making to the Common Market under the Treaty of Rome. It is for these reasons that the election of May 1979 marked a real watershed for the Labour movement as well as for the nation. To put it in plain language, forty years of trying to pretend that welfare capitalism was possible, successful and permanent and could melt away the conflict of interest between labour and capital have proved that it cannot be done. If capital is to consolidate its electoral victory it must now go on to pulverise labour's power base in industry and neutralise its political voice and parliamentary prospects.

If labour is to recover its position it must withdraw from past involvement, rethink, regroup, and then advance again with a much more comprehensive strategy to secure its interests. For what we are witnessing is the reopening by monetarists of the class struggle. If the spokesmen for capital are now going back to Edmund Burke and Adam Smith to see what those famous Conservative philosophers have to offer them in planning their campaign, the spokesmen of labour are also rereading their socialist philosophers including Robert Owen, Keir Hardie and the latter-day Old Testament prophet, Karl Marx, to glean what they can from the collected wisdom of the socialist pioneers.

Now that the consensus of earlier years, which obscured these issues from our eyes, has broken down, we can see that the class system is still there with most of its privileges unchanged – and in some senses reinforced. This is why present policies can, by definition, never win general consent and it is to the reforms that will be necessary to secure consent that we now turn.

A wider perspective for the trade unions

It is widely accepted that unemployment will reach the three million mark early in 1982 and thereafter will continue to rise as a result of further de-industrialisation, cuts in public expenditure, an increase in the number of school leavers and the impact of the new technology. Forecasts of unemployment that rise as high as four million on the basis of the continuation of existing policies have also been published.

The social effect of such a situation cannot easily be grasped by those under fifty whose adult lives have been lived in the post-war period. When the monetarists have completed their task and have lost the public support which gave them their initial parliamentary majority, a new government will be elected to reconstruct the economy on a new basis. The task will be a massive one, comparable to the post-war task undertaken by the Attlee administration. The trade union movement will be looking to the new government to restore full employment by a massive programme of re-equipment and factory building, harnessing the oil revenues and public and private investment funds for the purpose within a pattern of planned trade.

If public support for this reconstruction is to be won, the trade union movement, in particular, has to rethink its own vision of its role in much bolder terms, if it is to widen its appeal to those beyond its ranks. Basic trade union rights must be re-established and entrenched in law; and these must include the right to organise, to be recognised, to negotiate pay and conditions, to withdraw labour as an ultimate sanction and to picket effectively. Without these rights those at work are deprived of their strength and their human rights within a free society. We know this from our own history, and from the experience of other countries which do not allow trade unionism to operate freely.

Wage negotiation by collective bargaining must necessarily remain a central feature of trade union activity because it is about the distribution of the surplus earned in the course of production of goods and services and it directly affects the living standards of those employed. Moreover, the arguments that surround wage negotiations also reveal the true power relations in industry and educate workers in the nature of that power structure and in the problems of the business. The fatal flaw in all permanent statutory incomes policies which seek to impose pay settlements from above is that they remove the authority of management as well as unions and frustrate the negotiations upon which all good industrial relations depend. However, it should now be clear that wage claims alone – however successful – do not necessarily alter the balance of power in industry. High wage settlements can be neutralised by inflation, offset by redundancies or clawed back in taxation, while industrial and political power remain in the same hands. Trade unionism confined narrowly to wage claims can become something of a dead-end. Moreover, because industrial disputes about wages involving the withdrawal of labour are essentially negative in character, they may not always command wholehearted support amongst the workforce and may alienate public opinion, without getting to the root of the problem, which is the uneven distribution of power between capital and labour.

For this reason the trade union movement has been pressing for many years for an extension of the role of collective bargaining to encompass the whole range of company decisions. Pressure for the joint control of pension funds – which are deferred wages – has so far not met with success. Next on the agenda for trade union negotiation must be an agreement for the joint planning of the whole range of company policy including decisions about research, development, marketing, investment, mergers, manpower planning and the distribution of profits, with a requirement to agree on all these matters before company policy is decided. This is not co-partnership which seeks consensus in the interests of the shareholders. Quite the reverse: it is to encourage the development of workers' initiatives, as at Lucas Aerospace, to promote industrial expansion.[11] Such decentralised decisions at the place of work will also inhibit the re-emergence of corporatism. For all these purposes planning agreements and full disclosure of information will be necessary and this will require legislation.[12]

To be effective in securing a share of power, the development of joint trade union or shop stewards' committees will have to go a great deal further, working closely with regional and national officers. Joint shop stewards' committees and combines offer the best hope for securing the degree of power and responsibility that must together comprise the basis of a new settlement.[13] Branch meetings at the place of work would also help to increase the involvement of all the membership.

All large organisations will, as they grow, come up against the problem of bureaucracy and be required to look at their power structures so as to be sure that they do not become top-heavy, undemocratic and corporatist. Trade unions are no exception to this rule and it is no accident that the issue of democracy within the Labour movement has been so keenly discussed in recent years. Democracy cannot be imposed from the top and from the outside by the use of law. It must be secured by devising institutions which guarantee the accountability of the top echelons to those they serve and not the disciplining of the rank and file by their leaders. Many unions, such as the National Union of Mineworkers, have provisions for ballots in their own constitutions, but these are the result of their own democratic decision and they work because they are accepted. They would not work if they were imposed from the outside.

Given the power which the unions have, and the degree of authority which they choose for practical reasons to vest in their national and regional officers, it would be quite natural if, within the unions, there was growing pressure to follow the experience of parliamentary democracy and increasingly provide for regular elections, for re-selection, for a full disclosure of information and for the strengthening of accountability and the democratic disciplines that that involves. All these issues will no doubt be hotly debated in the future. Democracy always arouses controversy because it is about real power.

It follows from all this that a massive expansion of trade union education will be required. Such an educational programme must be conceived on the broadest possible basis. The training of trade union officers and representatives is already conducted on a wide scale by many unions. But to be fully effective, sights must be set much higher. Children at school should be able to learn about the history, principles, organisations and work of the trade union movement to prepare them for their lives' work – in classes at which active trade unionists could speak. The public should have at least equal access through the media to the views and opinions of the trade union movement as they now have to the opinions of capital, management and the establishment.

This would require more programmes which allow the trade unions to speak directly to the people about their problems, aspirations and work, free from the present distortion and imbalance. In industrial disputes this is especially important, and some unions may find it advisable to seek professional help, to get their case across. The right to picket is basically a right to inform those who seek to enter the workplace about the nature of the dispute in order to solicit their support. The more picketing can be seen in its educational context and the less it can be presented as a mere show of force the better. The provision of printed material and the use of radio and TV in disputes would greatly help to get across the reasons why the dispute has occurred and why it is relevant to all concerned that it should be resolved satisfactorily. In this connection the decision by some trade unions to assume responsibility for maintaining essential services during the winter of 1978/9 was a significant advance on the alternative pattern of blank confrontation circumvented by the use of troops.

Above all, internal trade union education should be extended far beyond the immediate industrial issues into a study of the whole national and international background against which their industrial work is undertaken. Without a wide understanding of the political, social and economic situation the trade union response may appear to be narrow and ineffective.

One of the charges made against the trade union movement is that it tends to be too limited in its own perception of its task. This charge is in part based on ignorance of the real work that is carried out. The trade unions were, for example, the pioneers in calling for a proper concern with the environment at work including health and safety for employees and protection against industrial disease. The early campaigns which led to the

Factories Acts and the establishment of the Factories Inspectorate, and against pollution came from the unions. As technology intensifies, environmental problems have become of major importance for the whole community, as the issue of nuclear safety proves, and the unions could and should do even more to champion the public interest against the irresponsible use of commercial or industrial power. It is here that their cooperation with community groups should be developed. The unions are also deeply involved in regional policy and in pressing for job opportunities to be maintained and extended by the evolution of sensible strategies of development upon which communities depend for their lives and amenities. Another area of expansion lies in defending the interests of women workers, both at work and in the provision of nursery schools, crèches and the growth of flexi-time arrangements that allow mothers to take part-time jobs. Ethnic communities, as the Grunwick, Garner and Chix disputes revealed, also need to have their interests safeguarded by the use of trade union influence where it counts.[14]

A developed strategy along this broad front, and a public campaign to make people aware of what is being done, would go a long way to correct the thoroughly biased image of trade unionism that is now projected. One notable example of the success of such a policy can be found in the vigorous defence of pensioners mounted by the TUC which secured for that growing group of retired workers a regular increase in their real incomes even during the difficult years of 1975–9.

Towards a new constitutional settlement with labour

It follows from all this that a comprehensive strategy for modern trade unionism immediately takes it into the arena of Parliament and local government, and calls for reforms that together amount to a new constitutional settlement. The trade union movement is learning again that it needs a political party to represent working people in Parliament. Non-political trade unionism, on the American model, would fail here, as it has done there. For those without personal wealth or political authority a trade union card and a ballot paper are the only two routes to political power.

The whole history, tradition and ethos of the British trade union movement has been, and is, essentially democratic, seeing Parliament as its main hope for reform, and rejecting completely the authoritarianism which has characterised the regimes of Eastern Europe. That is why it is in the interest of labour to strengthen Parliament and the ministers answerable to it, as a countervailing force against those whose interests are incompatible with their own, including the Common Market authorities whose law-making and tax-gathering powers must be returned to Parliament. This is a very different view from the one widely publicised which always presents the state as the enemy.

If authoritarian, centralised, bureaucratic and remote, the state machine can threaten liberty and, when linked to the interest of capital, it often has done so, especially if the army, the police and the press are all harnessed together to repress the interests of working people. The Labour movement has always perceived the possibility of parliamentary power as a liberating force, driving back the unaccountable power of capital and permitting the advance of wider interests. It was in 1918 that the Labour Party, established by the trade unions, formally adopted a socialist constitution. But long before that the Labour movement had been influenced by socialist ideas. British socialism owes its inspiration to many sources, religious, cooperative, Chartist, Marxist and Fabian. Robert Owen, the first man to be called a socialist, based many of his ideas on a pamphlet published by a Quaker in 1696.[15] Socialism in practice has meant limiting, controlling, or replacing market forces as the main determinant of human activity. The health service offering treatment according to need and not wealth may be seen as pure socialism. So is comprehensive education which allows each child to have access to the main stream of learning. So are state pensions or other benefits which protect those who might otherwise go to the wall.

The same principle applies to industrial and economic policy, in the development of which the trade unions have a legitimate and continuing interest. If it is true – as the monetarists argue – that the pressure upon profits from union wage bargaining and public expenditure is destroying the motivation of capitalism, then the unions will press for direct ways of securing the necessary investment, by public enterprise. Indeed, the failure of past policies suggests that there is no other way. For if market forces are to be accepted as the ultimate determinant of economic development, capital can dictate the terms and insist upon compliance by Parliament and people. Public investment in industry, in the regions, in education, health and housing offers the only real alternative to a world run by bankers, multinationals, and the vast administrative apparatus and huge network of influence at their command.

One word of qualification is, however, necessary here about nationalisation. The Labour Constitution calls for common ownership – not nationalisation – and for the achievement of the 'best obtainable system of popular administration and control of each industry or service'.[16] In that sense the nationalised industries established after the war have been a great disappointment. It is true that they have proved that investment can be channelled in to equip basic industries such as railways, coal, electricity and gas. But the huge state corporations, run on the very same economic criteria as private corporations under authoritarian management, have altogether failed to realise the hopes of those who campaigned for public ownership – as workers in the steel industry are now learning to their cost.

But if the working people have been excluded from strategic decisions, so has Parliament which has quite wrongly accepted its own exclusion even from a supervisory role. That is no longer acceptable, and democratic control must be established at every level in the public sector in order to create a wholly new vision of what society could be like if we lifted the stranglehold of market forces. It is not state socialism run from the top with a centralised bureaucracy as its instrument. If common ownership is to replace capitalism, at least in the commanding heights of the economy – as will be necessary to secure the reconstruction of our economy – then it is to self-management that we must turn to provide the mechanisms of control.

The corporatist solutions used abroad have relied mainly on the disciplines of the law. The monetarist solutions which are now being applied in Britain rely upon the discipline of market forces. All societies, and all systems, require discipline if they are to work and the most effective of all disciplines is the self-discipline of real democracy. In this concept all power is held in trust and those who exercise it must be held to account for their stewardship by those over whom their authority is exercised. The basis of any new constitutional settlement must be the extension of democracy into the rest of our society, in industry, the public authorities and the public services, organised wherever possible close to the people and away from the dictates of the centre. This is also the best way to break the log-jam which has held back our industrial performance.

If the trade union movement is seeking to offer an alternative industrial, social and political perspective for the future of Britain, it will be called upon to provide a far more positive and constructive leadership than its critics believe is possible and there is no reason to think that it will not respond to that challenge. If the sights of the trade unions are lifted above the defensive battle on the industrial front to a bolder perspective, the alliance with the Labour Party will need to be strengthened at every level. But if the lessons of the past are learned, democratic socialism will be seen to be quite different from the consensus corporatism that marked the evolution of labour power in the post-war years.

What is at issue here is the whole future of Britain, its industry, its society and its quality of life. For if the people of this country are to realise their potential, and to be able to work constructively on the world scene, labour must come into its inheritance. There is no other route to the constitutional settlement we must seek, and there is no other policy that can meet our needs, or lay the foundations of a new democratic consensus more durable and more satisfactory than the old corporate consensus which has so clearly outlived its purpose.

10

The Need for Labour Party Democracy

The argument in outline

The debate going on now in the Labour Party is as important as any we have ever had. On the one hand it is about policy and on the other hand about party democracy, but above all it is about the inter-relationship between the two. Nobody should be in any doubt that we are discussing not only the future of the Labour Party, but the future of Britain – because the unity of the Labour Party depends upon greater democracy, and so do our prospects for replacing Mrs Thatcher's Government by a Labour government.

The Labour Party exists to protect working people, and we must never forget our prime responsibilities. With the unemployment figures higher than at any other time since the war; with the welfare state now being dismantled; with the trade unions under attack; with the risk of war increased by an accelerated rearmament programme, we must never forget that our job is to get the Tory Government out, to get a Labour government in and to get our policies carried through. This is the background against which all other issues must be seen.

The ballot box and free trade unionism are the twin instruments by which working people came into their own inheritance. The Labour movement and the Labour Party is the only route to power for people without wealth or influence. What we are discussing, therefore, is not just a dry, academic study for those who are doing an 'A' level in British Government. It is about how the Party can fulfil its historic task.

Those who argue that constitutional questions such as party

democracy are irrelevant to the political struggle against Mrs Thatcher's Government are misreading the whole history of our movement. If constitutional issues are irrelevant, why did the Chartists have to fight so hard in the nineteenth century? Were the twentieth-century suffragettes engaged in irrelevant activity when they were fighting for the vote? Constitutional questions are the key to power in a parliamentary democracy and have played a crucial role in the development of our party.

The Labour Party always argues but it will never split

The Labour Party always has argued and always will argue but it will never split. Our history proves that. Here is an extract from a resolution passed at the Trades Union Congress in Dundee in 1888:

> No progress can be made with dissension in the camp, and those who create discord are not worthy to associate with earnest men.

And who was the figure accused of creating this discord? Keir Hardie, who had argued that there should be a Labour Party to represent working people, whereas Henry Broadhurst, the Secretary of the TUC, favoured affiliation with the Liberals.

The *Book of the Labour Party* published in the 1920s shows how strong was the opposition to a centre party or to links with other parties.

> The Labour Representation Committee . . . quite early made it a constitutional offence for any of its Parliamentary members to identify themselves with or to promote the interests of any section of the Liberal or Conservative Parties.[1]

These quotes show how determined the Labour Party was to separate itself from the other political parties so that it could be free to undertake its own historic role.

We lost a few people even then. There was Mr Bell, who was the General Secretary of the Amalgamated Society of Railway Servants, now the NUR. The ASRS had moved the resolution which brought the Labour Representation Committee into being – but Bell, the Committee's first Treasurer and Chairman, left the Labour Party and joined the Liberals, we are told, because of a telegram of congratulations sent to him by the successful Liberal who had fought a Committee candidate in a by-election in Norwich.

The great Liberal establishment did all it could to check the growth of the Labour Party. On 6th March 1906 Mr Banks, the Liberal agent for Westminster, sent a letter to every Labour MP.

> Dear Sir,
> The opinion has been clearly expressed to me by Liberal leaders, who have promised considerable financial support, that a separate organisation should be formed to represent the views of the Liberal Labour Members in Parliament and to secure a substantial increase in their numbers in the next election. It is thought that the Labour Party, within the Liberal Party, will be a great source of strength to both and I am requested to ask your views thereon as a Labour MP.
>
> Would you please be good enough to send me a reply with suggestions during the week so steps may be taken to call an early meeting.[2]

Today we hear a lot about a break *out* from the Labour Party and the financial support there is for it. It often seems to be an echo of these early attempts to push the Labour Party *into* the Liberal Party.

We may lose a few people, as we have done in the past, but we will never split. The House of Commons Library prepared a list of all those who, having been elected as Labour members between 1914 and 1979, have defected from the party (for full details see Appendix B). It is a formidable list – 64 MPs, including 24 ministers. We have lost a prime minister, a Chancellor of the Exchequer and a Chancellor of the Duchy of Lancaster. We have lost Secretaries of State for Air, the Dominions and Education; we have lost a Foreign Secretary; we have lost seven departmental ministers, including ministers of Labour, Power, Transport and a Postmaster General; we have lost three law officers: a Lord Chancellor, an Attorney General and a Lord Advocate, and at least half a dozen junior ministers. But we have never split. And the defection in 1981 of the so-called Social Democrats has not created a split. They have not carried a single affiliated trade union or constituency Labour Party with them.

It may be a comfort to know that nothing we are engaged in doing now is any different from what happened in the earliest days of our movement. Against this background Labour people can relax a little when we come to discuss difficult questions that are now confronting the party.

How the Labour movement fought for parliamentary democracy

We should also see what is happening against the history of Parliament in our society. To hear some of the speeches made, or to read some of the leading articles in the newspapers, you would think Britain had enjoyed parliamentary democracy since 1066. But of course this is not so.

From 1066 to 1295 when the 'model Parliament' was summoned, Britain was run according to the system established by a king who had conquered the country. Anyone who wants to study William the Conqueror's view of how the government should be run, should read his Coronation Oath delivered on Christmas Day 1066 in Westminster Abbey. He was a dictator. We did not have parliamentary democracy under the Normans. Britain was ruled by the king alone until he lost absolute power at Runnymede.

For about another four hundred years after Magna Carta, the landowners ran the country from the House of Lords. These were the feudal barons and even the king had to be careful of them. All this culminated in the execution of Charles I in 1649, when Britain had the first of the bourgeois revolutions. People forget that 130 years before the American and French Revolutions all the ideas which inspired them had been fully formulated within the English Revolution led by Cromwell.

Our ideas are still much influenced today by what was written at that time by the Levellers and the Diggers in their famous pamphlets.[3] They too are part of our tradition. But at no stage in the seventeenth or eighteenth centuries was Parliament in any sense democratic.

Britain had a constitutional monarchy from 1688 to 1832, during which time the gentry, the merchants and others ran the country, increasingly using the Commons. The Lords became rather less important and the king had to accept the right of the House of Commons to have some say. But what we now call parliamentary democracy only began to be *considered* in 1832 with the first Reform Act, and then only in the most partial way. Neither women nor working men had the vote and MPs only represented a tiny minority of the total population.

Today we are sometimes pressed to accept Edmund Burke's argument that MPs are only accountable to themselves, as if anyone who takes a different view is challenging parliamentary democracy. Edmund Burke was my predecessor as an MP for Bristol two hundred years ago. He was the member for six years, visited Bristol three times and his electorate consisted of 2 per cent of the total population of the city, all men. His ideas have nothing whatever to do with parliamentary democracy. He was one of the great Conservative philosophers of the old order which ended with the Reform Act.

It was not until the mid-nineteenth century that the Labour movement began to try to establish a system of democratic government designed to meet the needs of working people. Power was not to reside with the king, nor the landowners, nor the entrepreneurs, nor the capitalists who had come to power under Adam Smith's liberal ideas; instead all the people were to be represented equally. How was it done? Let us examine our past strategy to understand what we have to do next.

The democratic strategy of the Labour movement

The Labour movement always has been and is a democratic one, and its strategy goes back far beyond the birth of the trade union movement to the idea that politics was about social justice and not about hierarchy or honours or titles, or even profit and loss. Social justice lies at the root of every Labour campaign. The campaign for the right to organise labour came later. People who had no wealth or power or influence in the land were forced to organise, and therefore the campaigns against the Combination Acts, to secure the right to organise labour, were also an inevitable part of our democratic development. The campaigns for the vote, by the Chartists and later the suffragettes, were parallel movements to establish the right for people to find a way of expressing their interests through the ballot box as well as through their unions. Then came the campaign for labour representation in the Commons, and the foundation of the Labour Representation Committee, launched with these words: 'It is the workers' reply to the aggressive action of Federated Masters and Trusts.'

The Labour Party itself was founded in 1906. Labour became a party in Parliament in its own right. The next step was to commit itself to socialism, which involved more than mere representation. The campaign for democratic socialism within the Labour Party did not begin in 1918 when it adopted socialist aims. It went back to the early days of the Independent Labour Party and the Social Democratic Federation and to all the original socialist thinkers. Robert Owen was the first man ever to be described as a socialist. Democratic socialism was embodied in the constitution of 1918 which committed the party 'to secure for the workers by hand or by brain the full fruits of their industry'. After 1918 came the campaign to get a Labour government elected. We have the ten-month 1924 Labour Government, the minority government of 1929–31, and finally the massive majority of 1945 which gave us the opportunity to put our policies into practice.

It is against the background of those long campaigns by the Labour movement, to achieve political democracy in Britain in order to pursue social justice, that we have to consider the campaigns now coming to the forefront of our debates within the party. We need to recognise them as a part of a continuing process: to re-establish democracy within the party so that we can develop policies strong enough to win social justice; to be sure of the commitment of the parliamentary leadership to those policies; and to be involved directly in the implementation of those policies when Labour has a parliamentary majority.

The reason why the Labour movement has never espoused a revolutionary alternative in Britain, as some socialists have done abroad, is because we ourselves fashioned the democracy which should express itself through a fully functioning democratic Parliament. Therefore to ask the British Labour movement to abandon democracy and go for the short-cut to socialism by some coup d'état is to ask us to repudiate our history. We will never do it, so long as the route to peaceful change through Parliament remains open to us.

What are the obstacles to democratic advance?

What then are the present obstacles to that steady movement which allows those who work by hand and by brain, and their families, to enter into their inheritance to replace the minority who own capital? Certainly the Conservative Party which has always represented wealth and power, first in land and now in capital, stands in our way, expressing its opposition, for example, in consistent attacks on the unions, from the Combination Acts to the 1980 Employment Act.[4] Today the Labour movement also recognises that much real power in a democracy lies with those who command the means of mass communication. Hence the media are now a major force working for the whole range of the political right against Labour.

But what about the obstacles to democracy that exist within the Labour Party. What about the blockage in our own system of party democracy that sometimes prevents the democratic decisions of our membership from being advocated by the Labour front bench or ending up in the statute book? How does this happen when the Labour movement has so many remarkable advantages? There are 13 million members of trade unions in Britain, six million of them affiliated to the Labour Party. We have one single trade union movement and we are not split into Catholic unions and communist unions, as they are on the continent. We have only one political party representing Labour in Parliament, and we do not have, as in other countries, two socialist parties and a communist party. The Labour Party also has clear aims, to which we are all committed as set out in our Constitution. Why, then, seventy or eighty years after the Labour Party came into existence are we witnessing the return of poverty, the return of mass unemployment, the destruction of welfare, and the risk of war?

First, we need to face the fact that what Labour inherits when it has a big parliamentary majority falls far short of real power. In democratic Britain the people are only allowed to elect half a Parliament. The other half is the House of Lords which all Labour governments know would try to bring them down if they ever tried to implement real socialist policies. Keir Hardie campaigned for the abolition of the House of Lords in the 1890s, but ninety years later we apparently still accept an electoral process which chooses only half the Parliament while the other half can frustrate a Labour majority at will. The power of the House of Lords should never be underestimated. It is enormous. When the Lords throw out a Bill, the Cabinet has the power to take the Bill through the Commons again. But what Labour government, involved in all the stress and strain of getting a great volume of legislation through the Commons, wants to take a Bill through a second session with three-line whips and late night sittings? The mere threat of Lords obstruction is therefore also very effective, especially near the end of a Parliament when the Lords' delaying power becomes a total veto. The House of Lords commands the parliamentary timetable when Labour is in power, but not when the Conservatives are in power, because then the Tories enjoy a majority in both Houses and have nothing to fear from the Lords.[5] Thus the Labour movement, after all its effort and all its commitment to democracy, has ended up with the electors controlling only half the Parliament. Britain is the only country in the world where democratic legislation can still be obstructed by those who have inherited seats in Parliament or sit there by the patronage of successive prime ministers.

The second major obstacle in the way of real democracy in Britain is the Common Market. British entry into the EEC in 1973 stripped the House of Commons of the power to legislate where that legislation runs counter to Common Market legislation. That is very important because when Labour next wins a majority in the House of Commons, we will be able to repeal every piece of domestic legislation that the Tories have enacted.

But we cannot repeal one single piece of Community legislation which the present Tory Government has assented to in Europe, for there is no provision for repeal, save by unanimity within the EEC Council of Ministers. Even if a Labour government supported by a huge majority in the House of Commons secures the passage of legislation that runs counter to Common Market laws, anyone, including the Commission or any citizen, who is aggrieved and favours the *Community* law, can take that Labour government to the *British* courts, and British judges will be obliged to find in favour of Community law rather than the laws passed by the elected House of Commons. That represents a major erosion of our democratic liberties.

A third threat for our democracy comes from international capital, the multinationals and the International Monetary Fund which dictated cuts in public expenditure to the Labour Government in 1976. The power of international capital is far greater than the power of domestic capital, from which the Labour movement sought to liberate the British people from the moment it was founded.

Finally, the British people have now lost the authority they once had through Parliament to decide the question of peace and war. This power has now been transferred to our American allies, who maintain on British airfields nuclear weapons which they can use without the explicit consent of an elected British government. They also exercise great influence behind the scenes.[6]

The House of Lords, the EEC, the IMF and American-controlled nuclear bases in Britain represent four major obstacles to democracy and deny our people the power to decide our own future, or shape our own destiny. The Labour Party's first four objectives must be to abolish the House of Lords, to change Section 2 of the European Communities Act in order to return the ultimate legislative power to the House of Commons, to adopt an alternative economic strategy to free us from the IMF, and to control our own defence policy so that we can determine our own response to the international situation. We cannot control world events, but we must be able to determine the foreign policy we wish to pursue: an internationalist policy. These four objectives, all necessary to secure Labour's aim of social justice, were all set out in detail in Labour's programme *Peace, Jobs and Freedom* which went to the Wembley conference and was carried by 6 million votes to 6,000 on 31st May 1980.

But how do we do it? That is the key question.

How Labour's manifesto is drawn up – and why the party should decide the policy

The first problem is how can the Labour Party be sure that its clear policies, agreed at conference, will ever get into the election manifesto, or be carried out if we win? Labour's ability to answer those two questions will determine the credibility of our party and our capacity to win electoral support. Let us analyse the relationship between the powerful Labour movement with its democratic traditions and its conference polices, and what actually happens when those policies come to be carried out by a Labour government.

How do we develop party policies in the first place? The National Executive Committee prepares policy statements that go to the annual conference, on the basis of its own working parties and sub-committees. The manifesto is the link which connects the policy motivation and democratic instinct of the Labour Party with the real power of government, by allowing the party to present its policy to the public, and seek support for it. But recent experience has taught us that the drawing up of the manifesto is not as democratic as we have a right to expect.

What happens when NEC policy proposals go to conference and get a two-thirds majority, as occurred when the party decided on the abolition of the House of Lords? How does the democratic Labour Party, having got its policies through conference, get them into the manifesto?

Clause V of the Party Constitution provides for the manifesto to be written by the NEC and the elected Parliamentary Committee (Cabinet or Shadow Cabinet). Let us turn to the historical evidence about how Labour manifestos are actually drawn up. Richard Crossman's diary for 6th February 1966 describes joint meetings before the general election of that year:

> After lunch in the somnolence of the afternoon with the weather growing more and more beautiful outside, all we had was a series of set declarations by ministers punctuated by a few mild comments. The net effect of all this was a vote of confidence in the Government and this will enable Harold Wilson and George Brown, as Chairmen of the Home Affairs Committee, to say to the Executive 'you've had it chums, we've given you your chance to complain – a whole day –you did nothing at all about it!' When the meeting was over, it was clear that writing the election Manifesto this time would be child's play. We would describe how we took the job on after 13 years of Tory rule and how we now want a mandate to finish the job. And we would insert a number of commitments to go a bit further than individual ministers intend. That is the job we have to do.[7]

Thus the NEC – and even Labour ministers – were reduced by the parliamentary leadership to a minimal role in the drafting of the manifesto. It was just the same before the 1979 election. For two years before the election sub-committees of the NEC and the Cabinet had been meeting to decide the policies that would go into the manifesto. When the government was defeated in a vote of confidence on 28th March 1979 it was clear there would have to be an election and that the final manifesto would have to be quickly agreed. The drafts already worked out by the NEC/Cabinet sub-committees should have formed the basis for the manifesto.

However, the day after the government defeat, No. 10 Downing Street revealed to the General Secretary of the Labour Party that the prime minister's office had already prepared a draft manifesto based 'to some extent' on the drafts already agreed. When the head of the Labour Party research department saw the draft he was horrified. Not only did it ignore entire chapters of party policy, it overturned and ignored many of the agreements laboriously hammered out at the NEC/Cabinet sub-committees. By the time the Cabinet met the NEC to draw up the manifesto in the way provided for under the terms of Clause V of the Party Constitution, the No. 10 draft had become the basis for discussion. If NEC members wanted to include items, they had to move additions. In the end commitments on such diverse issues as targets for unemployment, abolition of the House of Lords, the National Enterprise Board and freedom of information either had to be abandoned altogether or were included in a meaningless form.[8]

The commitment to abolish the House of Lords – overwhelmingly agreed by the 1977 Labour Party conference – was simply vetoed by the prime minister.[9]

There is no provision in Labour's Constitution for a veto. But the veto was exercised by the party leader. How did the idea of a leader's veto emerge? Let me quote Harold Wilson talking of 1973, when Labour's programme was being discussed prior to conference and the 1974 general election:

> At an all-day meeting of the National Executive Committee during the Whitsun recess of 1973, the opportunity was taken late in the evening when many Members had left, to force a snap vote on an outlandish proposal to commit the Party to nationalise 25 of the 100 biggest companies. It was carried by 7 votes to 6. *The following morning I issued a statement indicating the decision was inoperative. It would mean a veto.*[10] *[my italics]*

Anyone dissatisfied with any NEC vote should seek to have it reversed at the next meeting. This is the democratic way to act. Instead the leader invented a veto and asserted his right to use it whenever he disagreed with party policy. If the party leader claims control over the contents of the manifesto then its function as the expression of the policies of the party is frustrated.

That is why many people in the party are concerned with the way the manifesto is drawn up. Under the existing system the contents of the manifesto have to be agreed between Cabinet/Shadow Cabinet and the NEC. There is now strong pressure for the NEC alone to have the final say. We must decide whether we want the manifesto to come down from the leadership or to come up from the membership. That is the first crucial question.

The second is, how can we carry manifesto policies through when Labour is in power? For the policies put forward by the NEC can easily be undermined by the parliamentary leadership. Consider this passage from Harold Wilson's book *The Governance of Britain:*

> Under the Constitution of the Labour Party the Executive has a duty to work out policy for submission to the annual Conference. Inevitably, an Executive elected by Conference includes a substantial number, frequently amounting to a majority on particular issues in 1974–76, who were concerned to prepare policy statements on almost every subject under the sun at home and abroad inconsistent with, and sometimes sharply critical of, Government policies. This was liable to cause confusion in certain quarters, including national and international financial markets, where there are many who are singularly uninformed, not to say naive, about our political institutions and on where power really lies. Quite often, therefore, I had to make this point clear, by answers to questions in Parliament or published replies to anxious letters from City based financial institutions, such as the British Insurance Association or the merchant banking community, on more than one occasion, *drafting the letter to which I was at pains to reply myself.*[11]

Thus we are told quite clearly that a Labour leader, when he disagreed with the policy of the NEC, drafted letters addressed to himself for the City to send back to him to give him a chance to repudiate NEC policy. That is a very important illustration of one of the major blockages in our internal party democracy.

How Labour government policy is made

There is another issue – that of the prime minister who can exclude the party from any real power in policy-making, by appointing non-parliamentarians to advise him not about the carrying out of party policy, which is a legitimate and necessary use of advisers, but to determine policy itself. Here are four passages from what Bernard Donoughue, the chief adviser brought in to No. 10 by Harold Wilson, said on BBC TV's 'Platform One' on 1st April 1980:

> Then Mr Wilson asked me to come to Number 10 on the evening of March 4th. We went along to the Palace: he went inside and the team, we, stayed outside in the car, and then we went in to Number 10 on March 5th 1974. He formed the Government and I had very rapidly, under great pressure, to construct a policy in it.

The party is supposed to formulate the policy for a Labour government. Yet Mr Donoughue was told on his appointment that it was to be his duty as a political adviser to make the policy. He went on to spell it out: 'I brought in young outsiders with considerable expertise and they were able to feed into the Prime Minister an alternative policy view.'

This system was used not only to exclude the Labour Party and Labour MPs, but also against Labour Cabinet ministers:

> The power of the Prime Minister has increased relative to his colleagues and I think the media focusing on him tends to do that. He does have powers at his finger tips. For instance, he can load a Cabinet Committee by putting some people on it favourable towards a decision, or he might choose to leave someone off a particularly important Committee in order not to have problems.

Thus even Labour Cabinet ministers were isolated from real decision-making. Donoughue then went on to say something that was even more startling about what really happens when Labour is in office:

> The main areas of economic policy, monetary and fiscal, *were conducted without the ministers involved.*

Such a situation is simply no longer acceptable.

The danger of patronage in Labour government

Let me turn next to another unacceptable feature of government, which is an obstacle too. The Labour government in office is not a democratic organisation. It is entirely appointed by patronage, by the party leader. This issue is discussed fully in Chapter 2 but we must touch on it again here.

At every other stage in the Labour government, whether it be in trade unions, constituency parties, at branch parties or in Labour groups, there is an elected leadership. But when there was a Labour government in power, the prime minister, himself elected Labour leader by the parliamentary party, then dispensed his patronage over the parliamentary party and chose who is to form the Cabinet and all other ministers. Such a patronage system is inherently corrupting to donor and donee alike. If a prime minister has such power over the making and breaking of ministers and if Labour MPs are so dependent on the leader for ministerial office or for the peerages that they imagine make retirement agreeable, the balance of power between the rank and file in the parliamentary party and the leader gives that leader undue and unacceptable authority. That personal power represents another serious blockage in our democratic system.

But the situation is worse than that. Ministers who are appointed become subject to what is called 'collective Cabinet responsibility'. Collective Cabinet responsibility to implement the policy upon which the Labour Party was *elected*, would be understandable. But that is not the way collective Cabinet responsibility is interpreted. The Cabinet is held to be bound by all decisions including those which go against Labour policy as put to the electorate, and upon which Cabinet members were elected. What actually happens when a Labour government is elected is that the manifesto of the party is put into a pigeonhole and is only drawn out as and when the Cabinet determines that they will implement it. Therefore, any minister who publicly advocates the manifesto once Labour is in power runs the risk of breaking collective Cabinet responsibility if that part of the manifesto which he or she advocates has not yet been endorsed by the hand-picked Cabinet appointed by the prime minister. Moreover, collective Cabinet responsibility can be added to, or subtracted from, by the prime minister of the day according to his or her own inclination. It is, in fact, entirely within the prime minister's discretion and is used to reinforce his or her control over ministers.

The Official Secrets Act keeps the party in ignorance

The next blockage to party democracy is the Official Secrets Act. When a Labour MP becomes a minister and leaves the back benches he or she crosses the barrier of official secrecy. Everything he or she learns as a minister must be withheld from colleagues in the parliamentary Labour Party. The Official Secrets Act, which applies over a whole range of information, most of which should never be subject to it, is one of the major obstacles to the work of Labour in power. When there is a Labour government in power you will find two classes of Labour MPs: ministers who know and back-bench MPs who are not allowed to know. That is one reason why civil servants and Labour ministers, both of whom are protected by the Official Secrets Act, are sometimes said to have more in common than Labour ministers and Labour MPs who are divided by the Act. No wonder the party feels it is left out in the cold as soon as Labour governments are elected.

The Cabinet minutes dealing with the last eight days of the Ramsay MacDonald Government reveal that this secrecy was carried even into the Cabinet itself, as the minutes for 19th August 1931 record:

> At the outset of the proceedings special emphasis was laid on the vital importance in the national interest of safeguarding the secrecy of the facts and figures disclosed in the Cabinet, and it was agreed, that the copies of the most secret memorandum mentioned above should be returned to the deputy secretary after the conclusion of the meeting.[12]

But having sworn his Labour colleagues to secrecy, MacDonald discussed the situation in detail with the Tories; with the Liberals; with the American bankers, and French bankers. But the Cabinet was not allowed to warn colleagues in the Labour movement about what was really going on.

Thus, at the critical moment when, if the Labour movement had been alerted to what was happening, it might have responded in such a way as to influence events, it was silenced by official secrecy. This secrecy is a major obstacle to the development of parliamentary democracy. That is why we must have a Freedom of Information Act.

Labour MPs should have more power – and be more accountable for the use they make of it

Why do Labour MPs accept a position of so little influence or control over Labour front benchers in government?

The answer is simple. Labour prime ministers expect them to be loyal whatever the government or leadership does. If there is any criticism of the Labour government by Labour MPs they may receive a warning. I quote Harold Wilson speaking to Labour back benchers who had supported conference policy against a government decision:

> Every dog is allowed one bite, but a different view is taken of a dog who goes on biting all the time. *He may not get his licence returned when it falls due.*[13]

Thus, imperceptibly, perhaps without our appreciating it, we find that instead of Labour MPs electing a leader accountable to them, the leader decides the policy with the help of advisers and then threatens to remove the licence of the 'dogs' who are the elected members of Parliament. Nor is this an isolated or accidental reference. In the *Financial World* of 30th May 1980, Harold Wilson again commented upon Labour back benchers, indicating how easy he found it to keep them under control:

> Compared with the Conservative Party's terminal efficiency, the legions of Labour, left wing or right, are as innocent and innocuous as Labrador puppies.

The personalities involved here are not important, but it is often argued that Labour MPs are threatened with domination by conference, or the NEC, or local parties. In fact the real problem is that Labour MPs have fallen under the control of the parliamentary leadership through patronage, official secrecy and demands for total loyalty to the leader personally.

This interpretation of the present debate within the party is important if we are to understand what we are discussing. The main criticism of the parliamentary Labour Party is that it has not chosen to be strong enough to control the parliamentary leadership, and to see that it speaks for the party. For example, in March 1975 the Cabinet decided to recommend a 'Yes' vote in the EEC referendum. There was no consultation with the parliamentary party which, when it met, after the Cabinet had made its recommendation, came out in favour of a 'No' vote. The Cabinet took no notice. The special Labour conference also opposed our membership of the Common Market, yet those in the Cabinet who upheld party policy were described as 'dissenting ministers'. The question of the cuts in public expenditure was never put to the parliamentary party when the 1974–9 Labour Government was in power. The question of the 5 per cent wage policy was never put to the parliamentary party. In fact back-bench Labour MPs were given very little to decide. They were expected to accept whatever was decided by the parliamentary leadership, and that is not a situation that we can allow to continue in a democratic party. The same appears to have been true with the decision to develop Britain's nuclear weapons, about which not even the Cabinet was fully informed.[14]

The media all tell us that what we are now debating is a widening gulf between the parliamentary party and the conference. But to argue along those lines is to misread history. The gulf that should concern us lies between the party as a whole, including the back-bench MPs, on the one hand and the parliamentary leadership on the other. No one wants to see a Labour government weakened in any way by a revolt of the parliamentary party. That is the dilemma facing Labour MPs. They are not consulted and yet they must remain a key element in socialist reform. That is why they must have a more positive role. It is not good enough that we should have worked for a hundred years to get Labour members into Parliament only to see that when they get there they have little real power. One sign of this lack of power is that the parliamentary party, at its weekly meetings, had no real agenda, few votes, no circulated minutes, no proper consultation, no power to elect the Cabinet and no access to the information necessary to implement the party manifesto. No wonder some complain when, after the party in the country has worked desperately hard to get a Labour government elected, the government actually seems to be protecting the establishment against the party, thus preventing the party from achieving its objectives of social justice.

When Labour is in opposition similar problems arise in that the same mechanism, under which the parliamentary leadership has full control, may prevent the opposition from presenting party policy as the alternative to the policy pursued by Tory governments. It is a mistake to look for scapegoats in this situation or to seek to blame individuals or particular wings of the party. What is wrong is that there is a fundamental structural weakness in the way the party is organised in Parliament and in its relationship with the party in the country.

What is the answer of members of Parliament to this problem? Some just accept it, others do not. Others express a point of view that runs like this: 'Once I have been elected to Parliament, I represent everybody – not just the Labour Party.' But in what sense does a Labour MP represent everybody in his or her constituency? Geographically, of course he or she does. Everyone in the MP's constituency will come to him or her for advice. Labour MPs must try to help all their constituents impartially. But we do not represent the *views* of people who did not vote for us. This is a very important distinction that must not be blurred.

In no sense can election to Parliament give any Labour MP the right to abandon his or her political commitment or the manifesto policy upon which he or she was elected. It is just because some Labour MPs have seemed to argue that they can do so that there has been a move to secure the accountability of a Labour MP to his or her constituency party by mandatory re-selection. The object of re-selection is not to get rid of members of Parliament. It is to introduce that same element of accountability of an MP to his local party that we want the Cabinet to have in respect of the parliamentary party. It is to secure greater power for the Labour MPs over the parliamentary leadership, and greater accountability for the constituency parties over the use MPs make of that power. Political power must come from the electorate, through the party, up to MPs,

Cabinets and the parliamentary leadership in a series of unbroken links. If one or more links are broken, democracy itself is at risk.

The need for the parliamentary party and the party nationally to work very closely together

We have suffered from three waves of revisionism. The first was the attempt in 1959 to persuade the party to abandon its formal commitment to socialism and Clause IV.[15] That attempt failed in that Clause IV was not amended, but we ceased to try to implement it. The second wave of revisionism was in 1968 when Harold Wilson's Government introduced *In Place of Strife*, setting out plans for legislating against the party's own base, the trade unions. It was then argued by the parliamentary leadership that the unions were an embarrassment to the party. That attempt failed because there was a revolt among Labour MPs, but the damage done cost us the 1970 election. The third wave of revisionism seems to involve an attempt by the parliamentary party to reduce the influence of the rank and file on the leadership and party policy.

The danger of division is not between a left-wing party and a right-wing party; or a trade union party and a Labour Party; but between the party in the country and the parliamentary leadership. If the leadership were to claim its own right to develop its own policy it would be a recipe for disaster. We are already paying the price for twenty years during which socialism was muted in Parliament. All this helped to bring about our defeat in the 1970 and 1979 general elections and prevented us from offering coherent opposition to the Conservatives. We must reinstate the explicit socialist commitment and resist the pressure for revisionism.

The division between the parliamentary party and the party nationally has been growing for more than twenty years and we must look for a way of bringing them together.

Labour must be a broad-based and tolerant party

We must go back to our tested and tried strategy of strong trade unions, closely linked to the party, and a commitment to a socialist analysis, and the accountability of power through greater democracy. We need a broader party, not a narrower party. We must work with the trade union movement; establish workplace branches; strengthen the party itself; and attract community groups, many of which were formed because they did not see in Labour the instrument for realising their hopes. They must find that hope in Labour now. Labour must co-operate with and speak for the women's movements; the environmental groups; the ethnic communities; the peace movement. We must reawaken rural radicalism which is still reflected in the battles against the squirearchy. In many parts of England we have not made the political impact that we should have done. We need religious and moral inspiration. All who call themselves socialists and are truly committed to democracy should abandon their sectarian isolation and become loyal individual members of the Labour Party.

There are many different tendencies within the Labour Party. We are warned about infiltrators or 'entryists'. But there are also 'exitists', on the right – those who have gone. There are 'departurists' – those who are packing up to go. There are 'ultimatumists' – those who say they will go if certain things happen. There are those who are staying – to argue it out. There is the legitimate right, and the centre. Then there is the left: the Tribune Group, the Labour Co-ordinating Committee, Militant, the Institute for Workers' Control, the Campaign for Labour Party Democracy, Independent Labour Publications, the Socialist Campaign for a Labour Victory, Clause Four and the Women's Fightback. And outside the party, on the left, there are a myriad of socialist groups who do not want to work with the party.

The Labour Party must be a tolerant party. This is what the National Executive Committee had to say on the subject in a recent resolution:

> ... The Labour Party is and must remain a broad and tolerant party within which people of widely differing faiths and opinions can work together to secure the aims and objectives of the party as laid down in our constitution; and the policies agreed at our conference.

We believe in free and open debate, conducted in an atmosphere of goodwill, and in the right of all members of the party to speak and write freely and to seek to persuade others to adopt their views.

The constitution of the party lays down how decisions are to be taken in branches, constituencies, Labour groups, Parliament, at the NEC and at conferences. These are the democratic decisions of the party at the time they are made, but every member of the party must be free to change them by argument.

We also accept the rights of conscience when members are moved to follow it.

We appeal to the party at every level to respect this tradition of tolerance and not to resort to expulsion against those who differ from majority views, but those holding minority views should bear in mind the well-being of the party and the responsibility of the majority both at central and local level to carry out party policy.

The party has a duty to protect itself from those who put up candidates against the party, or make arrangements with opposition parties in defiance of party decisions, or stand as, or support, candidates for public election in opposition to duly endorsed candidates, who make the work of the party at any level absolutely impossible.

But we believe that in most cases of disagreement it is better for the majority to make their views clear, and where necessary to dissociate itself from the minority, and to seek to persuade the minority, than to expel those with whom they disagree. The NEC intends to exercise its constitutional role in examining all inquiries into all appeals against expulsion in the light of those principles. We appeal to party members to unite at this time of great danger for our people and to argue out their differences without resorting to expulsion.[16]

We do not wish to go back to the old days of intolerance. Stafford Cripps was expelled at the Labour conference in 1939. Aneurin Bevan had the Whip withdrawn, as did Michael Foot and Sydney Silverman. It was even argued that Bertrand Russell should lose his membership because he had not paid his sixpence contribution the previous month. We do not want to go through that again.[17]

Party democracy, party unity and Labour's electoral victory

We must rebuild our movement and organisation with strong unions and a strong party, with all power accountable, and democratic. We must be a campaigning party, winning by persuasion, and able to convince people that we will carry out our policy when we get there. We must reconnect with those people whom we were established to represent and who are represented by no other party. To do all that we need mandatory re-selection; the acceptance of an accountable parliamentary leadership of the party; and party control over the manifesto. Campaigning for democracy within the party will continue in the future because these reforms are indissolubly linked with Labour's integrity and credibility as a party trying to win popular support. We cannot convince others that we will establish social justice if we doubt our own capacity, as a party, to adopt an effective policy or to carry it out once we have adopted it.

The 1945 manifesto *Let Us Face the Future* said very clearly what Labour wanted to do, and the nation believed we meant it and they voted us in with a landslide victory.

> The nation wants food, work and houses. It wants more than that, it wants good food in plenty, useful work for all and comfortable labour saving houses that take full advantage of the resources of modern science and productive industry. It wants a high and rising standard of living, security for all against a rainy day, an educational system that will give every boy and girl a chance to develop the best that is in them. These are the aims. In themselves they are no more than words. All Parties may declare that in principle they agree with them. *But the test of a political programme is whether it is sufficiently in earnest about the objectives to adopt the means needed to realise them. It is very easy to set out a list of aims. What matters is whether it is backed up by a genuine workman-like plan conceived*

without regard to sectional vested interests and carried through in the spirit of resolute concentration.

If we are going to be called upon to rescue Britain again, we can only do it through a manifesto approved by all sections of the movement and implemented in close cooperation with the party and the trade unions. If Labour is to remain united to take up its historic task again, and to continue to advance democracy, here and abroad, this 1945 spirit of commitment will be required, not only to convince the electorate that we mean to do it but, more important, to promise ourselves that we will.

11

Europe: A New Perspective

The present division of Europe is symbolised by the Berlin Wall: on the one side the communist countries under the influence of Moscow; on the other the West under the umbrella of America. The two alliances, NATO and the Warsaw Pact, are both heavily armed with nuclear weapons, strategic, theatre and tactical. In all, there are between 10,000 and 15,000 missiles in position. Massive ground, air and naval forces are also deployed on both sides. Arms limitation talks are deadlocked and arms expenditure is now planned to rise still further.

The military establishments commanding these forces and this technology have access to huge industrial resources, and are getting more and more powerful inside each nation that sustains them and, as a result, are becoming harder and harder to control politically. Meanwhile, in the background the two superpowers have problems of their own which greatly influence their respective approaches to Europe. Mr Brezhnev is faced with a major revolt against Soviet domination in Poland, where working people are seeking greater democracy in their lives. The Soviet Union has also sent troops into Afghanistan in an attempt to secure the southern flank against what it perceives to be infiltration. Who knows what other revolts lie under the surface in and around the USSR?

President Reagan is faced with a major revolt against American dominance in El Salvador, and is demanding the use of Western European troops in a NATO Rapid Deployment Force, to safeguard Western interests world-wide. Who knows what other revolts against US power lie under the surface in and around the USA?

Both the superpowers have their own interests in Europe but the division of our continent is not quite as sharp and clear as might be supposed. Yugoslavia and Albania, each under a communist government, stand apart from their neighbours in the Soviet trading bloc, COMECON. The West is not monolithic either, for, even allowing for further enlargement to take in Spain and Portugal, the EEC does not include Sweden, Norway, Finland, Austria or Switzerland. The complex pattern of European systems is a product of the past: the First World War, the Russian Revolution, the growth of fascism, the Second World War, and the tension which has persisted since.

The 1914–18 conflict derived from a clash of imperial interests. It inflicted serious damage on all the participants, and laid the foundation for much of what has happened since. In 1920, the United States went into isolation, and the European economies, severely damaged by war, were thrown into slump and mass unemployment. First this brought Mussolini to power in Italy, then Hitler in Germany, Franco in Spain and Salazar in Portugal; and from 1940 to 1945 almost the whole of Europe came under the control of the Nazis. The Second World War drew the US back into Europe. It also encouraged great hopes for a new Europe amongst that generation – hopes which have never yet been realised.

The Russian Revolution has dominated the century as the French Revolution did its own era. It was a turning point in world history, and from then until now it has been the objective of various Western leaders to contain Soviet power or to overturn the regime itself. A British Expeditionary Force was sent to support the White Armies at Archangel in 1919. Twenty-two years later the German armies launched their blitzkrieg against the USSR, laying waste their territory and killing between 15 and 20 million Russians. As late as April 1948 the American Ambassador in London, in a despatch to the US Secretary of State, reported on his talks with Winston Churchill in these words: 'He believes that now is the time, promptly, to tell the Soviet that if they do not retire from Berlin and abandon Eastern Germany, withdrawing to the Polish frontier, we will raze their cities.'[1] It is necessary to remind ourselves of all these events in order to explain the developments of the last thirty years. After the Second World War the West built up its defences under the American umbrella, which gave rise to NATO, and built up its economies under the Marshall Plan, creating the EEC. In response the Russians looked to their defence system in terms of a *cordon sanitaire* of communist states on their western border and established the Warsaw Pact to protect themselves from another attack from the West.[2]

The fears of the superpowers

The dominant factor in European politics today remains fear of attack by both East and West from each other. In the West the Soviet control of East Germany, Czechoslovakia, Poland, Hungary, Bulgaria and Rumania is widely interpreted as clear evidence of Soviet intentions to expand its dominance over the whole of Europe, and the military arsenals of the Warsaw Pact, with their heavy preponderance of ground troops and tanks, add to these fears.

Viewed from Moscow the situation must look very different. Given Russia's past experience, the hostility of China, and the immense technical, industrial and economic superiority of the USA, the Kremlin calculates the balance of military forces on a different basis, which must appear a great deal less favourable to them.

The insecurity in America and Russia is not limited to their assessment of the external military threat as each sees it. For the Kremlin fears that the regimes in the Warsaw Pact countries would be unlikely to survive any genuine test of public opinion in a free election. And even at home, more than sixty years after the October Revolution, the repression of political opposition indicates that their system is still too vulnerable to survive the rigours of too much free debate. State communism is still not willing to put itself to the proof of public support, in a way that we would accept as democratic.

Nor is America without its own anxieties. In the years since the Second World War, the Americans have felt the need to establish and maintain – in Asia, Latin America and parts of the Middle East – a network of the world's most venal dictatorships. The purpose has been to make the world safe for American capital which requires access to cheap raw materials, cheap labour and free markets; and to stave off what it sees as the threat posed by social revolution. In recent years this American policy has suffered a series of reverses, in Cuba, Vietnam, Nicaragua and now in El Salvador. The election of President Reagan suggests that millions of Americans resent the evident decline of American power in the world and again feel the need to assert themselves militarily to stop the rot. The US is also now in the grip of a massive economic recession which poses acute internal problems and is not the best possible advertisement for the virtues of capitalism. This slump is also affecting Western Europe.

Europe is therefore caught up in the middle of this impasse between the superpowers, both of which show signs of being paralysed by their own deep sense of insecurity. But unless Europeans are content to remain pawns in a superpower chess game, we must seek to make our own judgments of what is happening, and why. It is necessary for us first to consider whether we really believe the warnings that issue from Washington about Moscow's intentions; or from Moscow about Washington's plans.

My judgment is that both the Pentagon and the Kremlin are mistaken if they believe that the other is seriously planning for world domination. Both appear to be behaving exactly as Great Powers have always behaved – determined to safeguard their own homeland and vital interests; and seeking to extend their influence and interests and their ideology as far as they can. That certainly was Britain's posture during the heyday of the Victorian Empire, and it even led Britain into repeated invasions of Afghanistan.[3]

It is not possible to believe, in the age of nuclear weapons, that either superpower is preparing for expansion in Europe by war. If either were to attempt it, by non-nuclear means, their plans would encounter such violent hostility world-wide and in the countries they occupied that they could not hope to succeed. Some judgment of the intentions of the superpowers has to be made if Europe is to look to its own future in its own right. As soon as we have cleared our own minds we can plan accordingly.

For those who believe that it is only a matter of time before the Red Army marches on the West, preceded by a bombardment from SS.20 missiles, mass mobilisation and a crash programme of nuclear rearmament and civil defence measures are the proper course. And if Russia really expects a direct attack on her security system she will activate her troops in Poland, establish military regimes in every Warsaw Pact country, and expand her nuclear weapons programme.

The links between East and West

The reality is, of course, very different. Despite the renewal of the cold war and the escalation of the arms race, the real Europe does not behave as if it believed in the inevitability of war. Nor does the pattern of life in Europe, as it is, correspond at all with the rigid division between East and West which the superpower strategists seek to impose upon it in their speeches and writings. This becomes clear as soon as any of the simple litmus paper tests are applied to the real world.

First, is it true that the conflict can be clarified in terms of ideology? Are we facing a holy war between Christian capitalism and atheistic communism? Those who argue that case would have a difficult task to sustain it. There is too much evidence which points the other way. Yugoslavia is a Marxist state receiving political support from the West. In Poland the church and the Communist Party have avoided confrontation, by accepting co-existence. Similarly, Marx has always been accepted as a towering socialist intellectual by most democratic socialist parties in the West. Many dissidents in Eastern Europe have denounced Stalinism on the grounds that it is a vicious distortion of the teachings of Marx. In Western Europe, the communist parties are no longer the monolithic blocs they were once thought to be. In Italy and Spain great changes have been made in organisational terms to allow more broad-based discussion, accepting political pluralism, and rejecting the doctrine of the dictatorship of the proletariat. This is similar to the demands made in Gdansk in 1980, in the Prague Spring of

1968, and in Budapest in 1956. No black and white division based on ideology stands up to examination. It would be truer to say that there is a growing demand for democracy in the communist states, and for socialism in the states which accept parliamentary democracy.

The second untruth is that the Iron Curtain is impenetrable. Look at the Ostpolitik, the policy initiated by the West German Chancellor, Willy Brandt, which led to closer relations with East Germany. Look at the special relationship between Austria and Hungary that benefits both countries. These contacts are also developing in the Balkans. Consider the pattern of trade between East and West. In 1978 Western Europe as a whole exported US$ 18 billion-worth of goods to Eastern Europe and imported US$ 20 billion-worth in return.[4] In 1980, in spite of the increase in international tension, intra-German trade remained high and profitable.

Even in energy which is of vital importance to the world economy, Soviet gas exports and Polish coal exports to the West, though temporarily reduced, are a part of the economy of the real Europe and play an important role in its mutual prosperity. Europe needs an energy plan worked out, in detail, between East and West. Following the Helsinki Accord, there is growing contact in cultural matters and exchanges of visits and delegations, although they could be increased still further. The BBC World Service plays an important part in the process. Many Western countries have technological agreements with the USSR and Eastern Europe. France pioneered them, then Germany, and I signed many of them myself as the British Minister of Technology in the 1960s. Later, my own direct experience as Secretary of State with responsibility for nuclear matters taught me that there is even a close accord on the issue of the proliferation of nuclear weapons, to which the Soviet Union is as strongly opposed as is the USA. The denial of human rights is by no means confined to the communist countries but was practised in Franco's Spain and Salazar's Portugal, and is still tolerated in today's Third World dictatorships backed by the West. Europe is living together, and working together, and changing its prospects by doing so. The restoration of democracy in Portugal and Spain is very significant in this context. This is the reality to which we must turn our eyes.

Europe is a huge continent: excluding the USSR, the traditional Europe consists of twenty-nine countries; ten in the EEC; eleven in the West but not in the EEC; and eight in the Soviet trading bloc COMECON. Its total area is nearly 6 million square kilometres and its total population is over 500 million. Together its national income added up in 1978 to US$ 27,700 billion.[5]

The present institutional framework within which today's Europe works is complex. In the West there is the Council of Europe, the Common Market and the European Free Trade Association; the North Atlantic Treaty Alliance; the Organisation for European Cooperation and Development; and the Nordic Council. In the East there is COMECON and the Warsaw Pact. But that is not all. The UN has its own regional commission, set up after the last war. The United Nations Economic Commission for Europe is, however, concerned with both East and West. Like the UN itself, its role has been ignored or down-graded in the West.[6]

To speak of the continent as a whole will be so strange to the ears of many people that to consider plans for its future, in cooperation, may seem visionary at this moment. But despite all that has happened, there is a strong common interest on which to build. The surest starting point must be the demonstrable desire of all the people of Europe for the achievement of certain minimum necessities of life itself. The people of Poland – like the people of Portugal, or the inhabitants of the two Germanies, or of Britain and Czechoslovakia – must necessarily hope and pray for peace for themselves and their families. Everyone wants work and good housing, health care and adequate schooling, opportunities for the young, dignity in retirement, and a fair distribution of wealth. And the majority would like to enjoy full human rights and political and trade union freedom so that they can organise and express themselves openly and without fear of victimisation. Women want equality and ethnic and cultural minorities want safeguards. Everybody would prefer to live in circumstances which allow them a real say over those who govern them. And the demand for regional self-determination is to be found in many countries. Unfortunately nowhere in Europe today are *all* these rights achieved or aspirations met. But for anyone who seeks to uphold these rights it is clear that there is a stronger common interest amongst common people in detente and disarmament than in tension and the arms race.

Dialogue instead of deterrence

If that is all true, and it is so obvious as to be beyond argument, we have to turn our minds to those policies which might move us towards their realisation. Any serious attempt to identify such policies must begin with the problems of security. Every government, of whatever political complexion, always makes security its first priority. That was the foundation upon which both the League of Nations and the United Nations based their charters. We must then ask ourselves how that security is to be achieved, and whether the balance of nuclear terror satisfies that requirement. I cite only one witness on this issue: Lord Mountbatten, a Supreme Commander of the Second World War, who, just before his death, delivered a remarkable lecture on this very subject.

> As a military man who has given half a century of military service, I say in all sincerity that the nuclear arms race has no military purpose. Wars cannot be fought with nuclear weapons. Their existence only adds to our perils because of the illusions which they have generated.
>
> There are powerful voices around the world who still give credence to the old Roman precept – If you desire peace prepare for war. This is absolute nuclear nonsense, and I repeat – it is a disastrous misconception to believe that by increasing the total uncertainty one increases one's own certainty.[7]

A growing number of Europe's half-billion population would share that judgment.

How can we reverse the drift to nuclear war? The most hopeful initiative that has emerged in Europe has been the growing demand for European nuclear disarmament to make our whole continent a nuclear-free zone. It has been canvassed by ministers over the years in both East and West, in speeches, by Poles, Czechs, and East Germans. The Irish Government touched on it in 1959 and the Swedes and Finns have also promoted it.[8]

In 1980 the European Nuclear Disarmament movement began to gather momentum in Western Europe, including Britain, and an appeal for support was launched in several capitals, where it has met with an encouraging response. This groundswell of opinion is growing as the arms race threatens to grow. It would be a mistake to present this argument in terms of pacifism. Many who are not pacifists now see nuclear weapons as a recipe for mass destruction and not as a defence policy at all. Others – like the British Labour Party – have decided to oppose all military strategies based upon the threat or use of nuclear weapons, and favour a non-nuclear defence policy, rejecting Trident, and cruise missiles, and the deployment of the neutron bomb. We want a defence policy that would safeguard our homeland and its people, not one which threatens to obliterate it. Here is a campaign which really does offer a future with some hope instead of the acceptance of fear as the main driving force for security. Moreover, experience since 1945 strongly suggests – as Vietnam and Algeria established, and Afghanistan and Poland may prove yet again – that a determined people is the best guarantee against permanent domination from outside. Decisions about peace and war cannot be sub-contracted to a man in a bomb-proof shelter with control over a nuclear button.

The Swedes and the Swiss have founded their defence strategy upon 'dissuasion' rather than 'deterrence' and it makes sense to examine that option carefully. Both countries have a large citizen army that can be mobilised very quickly and would inflict casualties on any invader, without nuclear weapons or creating a military elite that could organise a domestic coup.[9]

Security is not entirely an external problem. Internal security must necessarily rest in the end upon a foundation of popular consent. Karl Marx understood this when he wrote in *The*

Communist Manifesto in 1848 that, 'The free development of each is the condition for the free development of all.'[10]

And 140 years later we find Pope John Paul II making the same point in El Salvador: 'Any society which does not wish to be destroyed from within must establish a just social order.'[11] These beliefs, and the commitment to achieve them, inspired the British trade unions, when they demanded the vote for the working class in Britain more than a hundred years ago, just as the Polish trade unions have raised the same cry today. And it is the same voices from the Third World which are now demanding social justice and a new world economic order through the UN. The achievement of domestic justice and domestic security is a great deal easier when no external threat can be used as an excuse for internal repression. That too points to the desirability of detente, rather than a nuclear arms race. It also points to the importance of stimulating trade and commerce between East and West, and seeking to interlock the economies of the two blocs so tightly that interdependence makes conflict increasingly difficult and ultimately impossible. In this context we have to decide whether it is in our interests in the West for the economy of Eastern Europe to fail or to succeed. In the world we live in we have now a powerful interest in our mutual economic success, even if only to reduce the likelihood that any government, of the East or of the West, may be tempted to divert domestic discontent towards some foreign enemy in the hope of retaining public support.

If cooperation *is* to be achieved, how and where could we begin to discuss it? There is one body which we could revive. The United Nations Economic Commission for Europe is an agency with precisely the mandate we need. Delegations to its conferences could, and should, be raised to ministerial level, and made into a major forum for developing Pan-European cooperation.

Within that framework the proposals made by Mr Brezhnev for high-level East–West conferences on transport, energy, and the environment, could be made real. At least it would be a start, and could consolidate the many bilateral agreements which exist.

To be effective, contact must also be strengthened at all

non-governmental levels. Western businessmen have never allowed ideological differences to inhibit their search for markets as the East–West trade figures show, and Western multinational corporations have signed many agreements with state trading corporations from the East. But the formal division of the trade union movement world-wide remains much as it was when the World Federation of Trades Unions broke up at the height of the cold war. There are in fact 4,500 separate trade unions in the whole of Europe – 3,000 of them in one country, Greece.[12]

Allowing for the quite different trade union role in communist and non-communist countries, there are, in total, 105 million members of the trade unions in Europe as a whole.[13] Trade union delegations travel regularly between East and West, but there is no Pan-European trade union organisational forum at which the role of trade unions can be discussed.

Yet the concern of the unions in the West at the re-emergence of mass unemployment, and the possibility that Solidarity in Poland may trigger off parallel demands for free trade unionism in other COMECON countries, suggests that it would be in the interests of trade unions in the East and West to institute more regular and structural discussions.

Finally – and most important of all – we must supplement the present East–West cultural exchanges by encouraging a real political dialogue. The blanket acceptance that no dialogue on politics, ideology or religion could be meaningful is a by-product of cold war thinking. Yet the issues which concern us all must necessarily lead us in this direction. Politics is not *just* about personalities, parties or policies. It is about institutions and, above all, about values. In Latin America the liberation theology has brought priests, trade unionists and socialists into a close alliance of thought and action against poverty and repression. Europeans, East and West, should now have enough courage and faith to attempt to sort out some of Europe's problems by engaging in a similar dialogue in a forum created for that purpose.

An agenda for a united Europe

If such a future is to be sought, how do we get from here to there? What will happen to the European Community, to EFTA and to COMECON? Prophecy is a risky occupation, especially for those who are active in politics. Moreover, the existing institutional framework is well established and cannot be easily dismantled or quickly transformed. Yet there are already signs of pressure for change from within both East and West.

The peoples of Eastern Europe will not for ever accept their present role under the tutelage of Moscow, with internal bureaucracies claiming the right to govern. Rising living standards, better education and the emergence of a generation born after 1945, which does not remember the past, must necessarily lead to growing demands for liberalisation and democratic rights. Though the remnants of Stalinism hold few attractions for them, there is no reason to suppose that this new generation wants to reinstate capitalism, let alone the right-wing military governments which existed in some Eastern European states in pre-war days. The pressure for change is welcome so long as it is a natural growth from within the countries concerned. But if attempts are made from the outside to exploit these developments explicitly to destabilise Eastern Europe or to weaken Soviet security – in the sense that John Foster Dulles, the American Secretary of State in the 1950s, once threatened to 'liberate' Eastern Europe – the attempt to introduce democracy and self-government could end in tragedy for them, and for us. State communism and its international system must be transformed from the inside and it is in our interests to allow that to happen. These internal reforms are much more likely to succeed if they can take place within a framework of growing European cooperation and detente and without raising the spectre of a security threat for the Russians which their military leaders might then use as an excuse for intervention.

But pressure for internal reform is not confined to Eastern Europe. The Western economies are stagnating with high and chronic unemployment and cut-backs in essential services.

There are today 8.3 million unemployed in the EEC. Allowing for dependants, this could mean that 20 million people in the Common Market are now living in homes where the bread-winner is out of work and the family income is dependent upon social benefits.[14]

In the 1930s it was unemployment which paved the way for fascism and it was public expenditure in the form of rearmament that ended the slump and brought back full employment. It is against this background that the philosophy of the Treaty of Rome, which entrenches and sanctifies market forces, will now be judged. The most telling critique of that treaty is based not upon national interests but upon its inherent defects and the undemocratic nature of the Common Market Commission which operates against the true interests of the peoples in all member states.[15] As the Common Market changes by enlargement – or withdrawal – the pressure for a much looser and wider association of fully self-governing states in Europe is likely to be canvassed and could transform the nature of European cooperation in the West. Moreover, as the EEC needs to import a great deal of its energy, the necessity for oil and coal supplies from Norway, the USSR, Poland and OPEC, all outside the EEC, suggests a less self-sufficient posture than has been attempted in, say, agriculture.

While the people in the COMECON countries move to greater democracy, people in the EEC will be moving by democracy towards greater social planning combined with greater decentralisation and social accountability. These concurrent political movements will necessitate greater flexibility in both parts of Europe, and with a common interest between East and West developing simultaneously, new institutions for Europe as a whole could possibly be constructed to accommodate and assist the convergence of systems towards democracy and socialism. It may be too soon to think of the summoning of a Pan-European Peoples' Congress to allow this work to begin. But at some stage a real 'Council of Continental Europe' will need to be brought together to provide a true forum in which the future of Europe can be discussed. When that is achieved it must be seen as part of a United Nations strategy, because it is upon the UN that our hopes for world peace must ultimately depend. A whole generation of young people put their faith in the United Nations at the end of the Second World War and the revival of the United Nations role is of critical importance at this period in our history. Nothing less will be able to cement the sort of world-wide understanding reached through dialogue, upon which a secure and peaceful Europe will rebuild its confidence.

We are a continent with an ancient civilisation and history, rich with resources, human, material and mineral, including coal, oil and gas. We have a highly skilled people with well-established agriculture and strong industries. We have many religions, Catholic and Protestant, Jews and Muslims, and a rich tradition of political thought, including humanists, socialists, liberals, conservatives and Marxists. We have suffered grievously in war, and we are having to learn once more that we must live together, or die together.

This, then, is a draft agenda for discussing a new Europe that would be really worth working to build. We need talks about security and European nuclear disarmament, and more co-operation in trade, technology and energy under UN auspices – all supplemented by a real political dialogue that brings working people together. It is not too soon to begin thinking about Europe in the twenty-first century.

Our vision must be of peace, jobs and freedom, achieved between fully self-governing states within a security system ultimately replacing both the Warsaw Pact and NATO. We must envisage a multi-polar world well disposed to America and Russia, but under the control of neither. Europe must play a full part in the UN to realise the aims of its charter, and respect the demands for self-determination and independence in Third World countries with whom we must establish a constructive dialogue.

It is a vision for our children and our children's children, and in that spirit I commend it for your consideration.

Here is a text for tomorrow's Europe. It comes from Mahatma Gandhi, whose advocacy of non-violence makes him a fitting prophet for today:

I do not want my house to be walled in on all sides nor my windows to be shut.

I want the culture of all lands to blow about my house, as freely as possible, but I refuse to be blown off my feet by any of them.[16]

12

The Transition to Democratic Socialism

To prepare for the next stages of Labour's campaign, we must analyse some of the reasons for the failure of past Labour governments and reaffirm the need for a conscious policy of transformation towards democratic socialism.

Labour campaigns

The campaigns against unemployment and the cuts in public expenditure which have been so successfully organised will need to be extended and redoubled as the number of jobless rises and the foundations of the welfare state are still further undermined. Campaigns such as the People's March for Jobs give hope to those who would otherwise find themselves isolated as their factory closes, their services run down and their communities are progressively destroyed. They raise morale there, because trade unionists, Labour Party members and others come from all over the country in a gesture of solidarity. They are of major educational importance for those who attend them, watch them go by or hear about them, however inadequately they are reported by the mass media. This educational work focuses on the issues – peace, jobs, health and education – and helps to break the stranglehold of personalities which has characterised the coverage of political debates since the war. Through this work the Labour Party is being transformed into a campaigning movement, and is no longer the narrow electoralist machine which it had become over the years of revisionism. Party members no longer regard themselves simply as election workers shepherding the electorate in support of

Labour candidates who then govern the nation on their behalf, requiring nothing of the people in return but their loyalty. Election campaigns have become platforms from which democratic socialism can once again be preached, reinjecting into the consciousness of the people some of the values upon which any society claiming to be socialist must depend; and thus helping to destroy the rotten and shallow values upon which our present system rests.

All the work now being devoted to these campaigns is therefore well worth while. But it is not enough. If we are to win the support we need to dislodge Mrs Thatcher's Government, reverse its policies and defeat its philosophy, the Labour movement must offer an alternative that is credible, practical and capable of harnessing the people that our campaigns are beginning to awaken. This constructive task is much harder and all attempts to advance it may meet with opposition from within our own ranks.

Some will argue that it is unnecessary to work out future plans in detail, because we cannot know now what the situation will be when we come to power. Others will say that discussions about future policy will divide us and weaken the party. It will also be claimed that the most important job now is to get the Conservative Government out, and then we can decide what needs to be done. We will be told that policies revealed now may become hostages to fortune, exposing our flank to a Tory counter-attack, and could lose us the election. And, of course, we shall also have to listen again to those who believe that policy-making is the preserve of a leadership which 'understands the realities of power', and that the demands of the rank and file can be no more than aspirations to which all subscribe in the long term but which cannot be achieved within the lifetime of one Parliament.

The causes and significance of Labour's defeat in 1979

Before we accept that only leaders can make policy we should recall that this was the very argument which helped to get us into the situation which now confronts us. The crushing defeat which Labour suffered in the general election of May 1979 followed thirty years of anti-socialist revisionism preached from the top of the Labour Party, for over eleven of which Labour governments were in power. Throughout that period the membership of the party, and even our supporters in the country, were repeatedly given the same arguments. Then, when the final battle came, so many of them had deserted us that we could not carry the day.

But our defeat in May 1979 involved much more than a change of government. During the years when Labour ministers had actually been in power, the bastions of our political strength had been quietly surrendered, one by one, to the forces of our political enemies, without a shot being fired, and sometimes their Trojan horses had actually been welcomed in by the ministerial incumbent.

The erosion of Labour government support for trade unionism

First of all we should consider trade unionism, the existence of which is fundamental to the defence of the living standards of working people and their families. It was the trade union movement which secured the first major advances in the nineteenth century and which then broadened itself out to embrace the wider political aspirations of the working class, leading to the foundation of the Labour Party. Yet successive Labour governments, always elected with active trade union support, invariably ended up in direct conflict with the unions, as with *In Place of Strife* in 1969 or during the 1978/9 'winter of discontent', both of which disheartened our workers and disillusioned our supporters. Indeed, it went deeper than that, since trade union practices became the scapegoat used by some Labour ministers for all our economic ills, such as alleged low productivity and lack of competitiveness – the very arguments which the British establishment had long perfected as the explanation for Britain's decline.

The erosion of Labour government support for public expenditure

Public expenditure is another example. The Labour movement has always believed in the role of public expenditure as central to its economic and social purposes. Public housing, the health service, education, social benefits and local authority services have been seen as vital for the public welfare. Public services also narrow the inequalities which a market economy tends to widen, and do so by creating a social wage. Public expenditure also acts as an engine of economic development and helps to maintain employment, because public services are, in general, labour-intensive, and because much of the money finds its way into orders for the manufacturing and construction industries. It thus performs the same role as rearmament did in the 1930s when the world pulled itself out of slump by its massive purchase of military equipment.

Yet successive Labour governments found themselves increasingly under pressure to cut back on public expenditure plans and, in order to justify these decisions, Labour ministers began to adopt the arguments of our political opponents. The climax came in November 1976 when the IMF, with the active support of Treasury officials, actually persuaded a majority in a Labour Cabinet that severe cuts were necessary to save the pound. This decision led directly to the 'siege economy' of the so-called 'winter of discontent', and indirectly to the strengthening of the pound which is now responsible for so much unemployment.

In order to justify their policy, Labour ministers had to adopt some of the arguments against public expenditure which had been the stock-in-trade of the Tory Party for years. These included the official campaigns against 'scroungers'; the launching of a 'great debate' on education, which became a thin cover for an attack upon comprehensive education; a warning that 'the party is over' in respect of local government expenditure; and even a much-publicised claim made by the then Home Secretary, that public expenditure beyond a certain percentage of the national income could undermine personal liberty.

The erosion of Labour government support for democracy itself

From time immemorial, through the Chartist campaigns and up to the present day, the Labour movement at grass roots level has always fought to extend democratic control, first over political decisions, and then over industrial, economic and social decisions. Yet it is unfortunately the case that under successive Labour governments, democracy was gravely eroded by surrenders to the right.

The most serious of all was the majority decision of the Cabinet in March 1975 to recommend Britain's continued membership of the Common Market on the basis of an acceptance of the Treaty of Rome, the only written constitution in world history that entrenches the principles of capitalism and bureaucracy in the very centre of its provisions.[1] From the moment that the British people accepted that treaty, on the advice of a Labour prime minister, this nation ceased to be fully self-governing.

An erosion of democracy of similar proportions had occurred more slowly over the years with the acceptance of American nuclear bases in Britain, from which US atomic weapons could be launched without the explicit consent of the British Cabinet, thus stripping our own Parliament of the right to determine whether or not the nation wished to go to war. And more insidiously, the democratic control of our destiny was chipped away by the maintenance of strict secrecy over a whole range of key policy issues, from the secret modernisation of our Polaris weapons to the secret proposals to postpone the child benefit scheme. In terms of administration many of the policies that reflected our socialist objectives, in the extension of public ownership and the provision of public services, were so bureaucratically run and so tightly tied to capitalist criteria as to alienate the people they were established to serve. Thus the very freedom which true democracy is intended to advance actually seemed to some to be threatened by our public initiatives. As a result the monetarists were allowed to pose as the champions of personal freedom against the state, while in reality planning to subordinate true individual liberty to the jungle values of a market economy.

Assessing Labour's record in office

It was because Labour in office seemed to have given up some of its advocacy of trade unionism, public expenditure and democracy, that our election defeat in 1979 was of such massive significance. We had in effect surrendered many of the fundamental principles upon which the party was founded long before the election began, and the defeat involved a moral and philosophical reverse that will be far harder to recoup than we may yet realise. Seen in that light, the real failures of Labour governments since 1964 lay not so much in our apparent incapacity to achieve socialism in practice, for in the latter years we had no parliamentary majority for our measures, but in our apparent unwillingness to defend the interests of the people we were elected to defend, and our reluctance to espouse and advocate the principles upon which our long term success depended. Instead Labour came to present itself as a more competent and humane management team for an economic system which, of its very nature, cannot serve the interests which we came into being to advance.

It is necessary to remind ourselves of these deep-seated deficiencies in the record of recent Labour governments in order to identify what has to be done now. The purpose of describing them is not to denigrate the achievements of those governments, which compare favourably with the grim record of the Conservative governments of 1970–4 and the catastrophic policy pursued since 1979. Many Labour ministers did their best, sometimes in the most difficult circumstances, to protect the British people from the worst effects of the crisis in world and British capitalism. Any criticism there is must be accepted by all those who served, as I did, in the Labour Cabinets of the period; and there is no political purpose to be gained by seeking to place the blame upon individuals within them. That task can be left to future historians.

The incompatibility of a strong political democracy with a market economy

What went wrong? What must we do now to see that we get it right next time?

It is by no means easy to find the answer. Many factors were involved but at the root of our difficulties lies one key issue, which needs to be brought out and examined. It is that democratic power, acquired by working people in Britain through our long campaigns for independent trade unions and the right to vote, is now so great as to be capable of dislocating, or paralysing, the market economy upon which British capitalism still relies for its motive force. All Labour governments elected to advance that power very soon came to realise that fact through their practical experience of office. Labour governments, then, have to make one of two choices. They can either implement their manifesto objectives, paralyse the system still more effectively, and run the risk of being defeated as a result of the paralysis; or they can abandon their reforms and accept the dictates of the system they were elected to change, falling back upon their claim to be more humane and competent in administration. Most Labour governments have started their term of office pledged to implement the manifesto and have ended up ditching it and running the system at the expense of those who elected them. Neither choice is acceptable.

The impasse and how to get out

If that brief analysis stands up to examination – as I believe it does – then there is no prospect whatever for further advance in the interests of working people either by strengthening the trade unions, expanding democracy or extending the public services within the present economic system. While that system remains in crisis, its survival depends upon weakening the trade unions, restricting democracy and reducing the public services still further.

The Labour movement in Britain has therefore come to the crossroads. It must now decide whether the aspirations of British socialism are to be narrowly redefined as the desire to hold those gains we can expect as a by-product of a successful capitalism that can afford them in the rare boom years. The alternative is to set our sights higher, to decide to transform capitalism by democracy into socialism, and to set about the task of strengthening ourselves for that purpose.

The choice of transformation

Posed in that way, the choice of conscious transformation is the only practical course to adopt. This is partly because the likelihood of British capitalism recovering its dynamism again to the extent that it can once more afford socialist measures is now very remote; partly because if it did recover in such a miraculous way the case for a socialist transformation would be impossible to mount convincingly; and partly because if socialist policies could be mounted piggy-back on the shoulders of a revived capitalism, they would soon overburden it. There is, therefore, no alternative for us but to attempt a conscious policy of transformation, to work out how to achieve it and to win support for it. Then, having won that support, we have to carry it through with the active cooperation of those, at every level, who share the desire to see it happen.

It is one thing to decide to adopt a policy of transformation, and quite another to make it work. That will require the creation of a will which does not yet exist, and it will require public support that has not yet been sought, let alone won. It will require the creation of new institutions operating on different criteria, new machinery of government, and legislative authority from a Commons majority to bring them into being.

The need for institutional reforms

The institutions – international, national, regional, industrial and local – which govern our society were largely set up by the established authorities to uphold *their* interests. These institutions are by their very nature expressions of that mix of values and principles upon which the establishment depends for its power and its moral authority. Any strategy for transforming our society from a feudo-capitalist one into a democratic socialist one must therefore include an examination of those institutions and the theories which guide their role to see whether they can themselves be changed to serve different objectives or whether they need to be discarded and replaced. If they cannot be adapted, what alternative institutions operating under what alternative principles should be set up?

Institutional change has always featured prominently on any agenda for reform. Those who argue for it again must not be confused with those revolutionists who see no prospect of using any of the existing state apparatus for new and different purposes and wish to see it all swept away and replaced by a completely fresh set of structures, some of which could only be introduced at the expense of democracy. It is, however, indisputable that Labour governments which accept uncritically the institutions of a capitalist society completely programmed to serve one purpose, and then try to make them serve different ends, will find that ministers become the servants rather than the masters of the machinery which the electoral process has entrusted to them to control.

It is helpful in this context to consider the role of individual ministries.

The Foreign Office

The Foreign Office regards British foreign policy as being above party politics, evolving naturally out of the slowly changing interests of the establishment which in the nineteenth century was best served by the maintenance of Britain as the centre of a world-wide empire. In the twentieth, the interests of the establishment are best served by keeping Britain as a colony of a developing Western European federation.[2]

The Treasury

Similarly, the Treasury has its own view of the economic and fiscal policies necessary to maintain a market economy on an even keel, sometimes mildly Keynesian, and now mildly Friedmanite. This sets the framework within which marginally different policy options are prepared, from amongst which ministers of differing political parties may choose.

The industrial ministries

The industrial ministries in Whitehall have also created a mixed economy policy. Public ownership is considered acceptable if it upholds the prerogative of management vis-à-vis labour, and ties that management to the same criteria as are applied to capitalist enterprises. In this way, common ownership has been confined to one form of bureaucratic nationalisation, which has destroyed many of the purposes for which it was developed and alienated the whole system in the public mind.

The Ministry of Defence

The Ministry of Defence too has its own policy, designed to meet the twin dangers to the British establishment, posed by the existence of a powerful group of communist powers and the ever-present threat that domestic discontent triggered off by unemployment might call for military assistance to the civil power.

The BBC

The BBC has a similar perception of its own role, permitting the narrow range of official options to be discussed at length on radio and television but either censoring or denouncing any sustained discussion of the real choices that might be opened up by those who are seriously engaged in the promotion of democratic socialist reforms.

The House of Lords

The House of Lords welcomes with open arms those Labour politicians or trade union leaders who can be induced to accept peerages and then play out an active role in mildly regretting the Conservative policies of the majority there. Labour peers actually strengthen the Lords, for the true role of the upper house is to slow down or defeat any House of Commons majority which might attempt to use the Statute Book as an instrument of reform. Labour peers give legitimacy to the whole artifice.

The House of Commons

Even the ancient rituals and elaborate courtesies of the Commons have been known to dampen the reforming ardour of radical men and women who have been elected to work for real change. They find themselves buttered up by great parliamentarians or corrupted by prime ministerial patronage under which the Commons has surrendered far too much of its powers to the executive.

There are many other ways in which existing institutions can be and have been used to deflect political pressures and diffuse popular discontent until the energy they have generated has been dissipated into harmless channels, or diverted into minor measures of amelioration.

The issue of disengagement

These are not arguments in favour of revolution. They are arguments in favour of genuine reform, resolutely pressed, and against reformist rhetoric that is confined to the hustings and then immediately discarded when in office. They also raise the question as to whether or not a part of our strategy for transformation ought to begin with a conscious policy of disengagement by the Labour movement from those institutions which constitute a barrier to our policy.

Withdrawal from the EEC

One such example of disengagement can be found in the policy of outright British withdrawal from the Common Market when the next Labour government is elected.[3] This policy does not involve a withdrawal from close relationships with the countries which now make up the EEC or with those which are outside it. It requires instead a declaration that the Labour Party does not believe that those relationships can be developed, in a way that would meet the needs of the Labour movement here or on the continent, through the Treaty of Rome, but only on a completely different basis, through international institutions developed by international labour to meet its needs.

Abolition of the House of Lords

The decision to abolish the House of Lords and transfer all its revising functions to a reformed House of Commons is another important example of disengagement from feudo-capitalist institutions, and their replacement by extending the role of a democratically elected Chamber.[4] Meanwhile, no fresh Labour peers should be created, and it is arguable that those who are in the Lords should withdraw, thus stripping the Chamber in its remaining years of life of the legitimacy which it acquires from having a parliamentary Labour Party organised within it.

Removing the US missile bases

The decision of the 1980 Labour Party conference to require the removal of American nuclear missiles from the UK is a clear statement of intent to disengage from the role of aircraft carrier colony to the US, and to follow the Canadian example as a non-nuclear partner within the NATO alliance.[5]

Trade union disengagement from government bodies

We should ask ourselves if it makes sense any more for trade union leaders to continue to serve as lonely token figures on the boards of nationalised industries, charged under new statutes passed by the Conservative-dominated House of Commons with the task of selling off profitable public assets and closing down unprofitable parts of the business. We must question whether it is in the interests of the Labour movement that the TUC should continue to nominate six members of the National Economic Development Council, at which the Chancellor outlines his own monetarist strategy and seeks by the TUC presence there to acquire a legitimacy for policies that undermine the whole role of trade unionism.

The case for disengagement

A conscious decision by the Labour movement to disengage from institutions which consistently work against the interests of those we represent would have an electric effect upon the conduct of public affairs in Britain and abroad. Though our opponents would seek to present this strategy as an example of Labour sulking in its tent and refusing to come out and argue its case in Brussels, in NATO and in the House of Lords, it would in reality serve some very effective purposes of public education and political preparation. The institutions from which we disengage would be stripped of the artificial veneer of consensus legitimacy upon which they rely for their public support. Those who work within these institutions and know that they need a measure of real support if they are to survive could then become our allies, however reluctantly, in the process of bringing about the changes we want, by offering to reshape their policies in the hope of tempting us back into participation. But, more important still, the time and effort now devoted by the Labour movement to the largely fruitless work of cooperation with hostile institutions would be released to work on the evolution of alternative policies and alternative institutions to give effect to them. The choice we would offer the British people would be clearer and more credible than could possibly be the case if we were to ask them to believe that we could implement our programme through agencies now actively engaged in opposing us.

Conclusion

In this book I have tried to suggest practical ways in which many of our existing institutions can be adapted from their present role as props of the status quo. Instead they must become the agents of the profound changes necessary if we are to avert the serious economic and political problems which now confront us. I have set out ways in which the powers of the prime minister, the civil service and the security and scientific establishments can be made accountable. I have also looked at the role played by the media in perpetuating the values of the establishment at the expense of what is happening in the real world, and suggested ways in which we might move towards a free press in Britain. Finally, I have examined ways in which we can all play a part in the great tasks that lie ahead.

It will be noted that what is suggested in every instance

involves a diffusion of power through greater democracy and bears no resemblance to the structures of an East European state. On the contrary, the institutions at the disposal of the East European establishment have far more in common with the corporatism now consolidating itself in Britain and other capitalist countries than with any proposals made here.

There is no reason why the great institutions of the British state should remain at the disposal of any one social system, one class of people, or one set of values. In a democracy we need institutions that work for the benefit of all of us. The task of the Labour movement is to see that they do.

Appendix A

The Ownership of the British National Newspapers

The information below is taken mainly from Appendix A of the Royal Commission on the Press, 1977. See also Tables 1 and 4 in James Curran, 'Press freedom as a property right', *Media Culture and Society*, 1979, vol. I.

1 The *Daily Express*, *Sunday Express* and *Daily Star* are owned by Trafalgar House Investments, a public company in which Lord Matthews is a principal shareholder. Trafalgar House also owns the *New Standard*, London's only evening paper, and has interests in property, shipping and cement.

These papers were previously owned by Beaverbrook Newspapers Ltd. At the time of purchase by Trafalgar House, Beaverbrook Newspapers also owned 89 per cent of the voting shares in Associated Television Ltd and had much smaller holdings in Westward Television, Capital Radio and Radio Clyde.

2 The *Daily Mail* is owned by the Daily Mail and General Trust Ltd, about 56 per cent of the shares in which are owned or held in trust by Viscount Rothermere and the Hon. Vere Harmsworth. There are no other holdings of more than 10 per cent. The Harmsworths also own 48 provincial newspapers and other interests including Pizzaland Restaurants, self-drive hire cars, taxi cabs, North Sea oil, Australian Television and the docks at Purfleet. They also own National Opinion Polls Ltd.

3 The *Daily Telegraph* and *Sunday Telegraph* are the property of a private company in which 93 per cent of the voting shares are held jointly by Lord Hartwell and Viscount Camrose. They inherited the *Daily Telegraph* from the first Viscount Camrose.

4 The *Sun*, the *News of the World*, *The Times* and the *Sunday Times* are owned by a public company, News International Ltd, in which the dominant interest is held by Mr Rupert Murdoch. News International also controls 26 British provincial papers and three major Australian papers as well as the *New York Post*. The company also owns about 10 per cent of the voting and 40 per cent of non-voting shares in London Weekend Television. Until early 1981 *The Times* and the *Sunday Times* were the property of the Thomson Organisation – an empire which included 58 British provincial newspapers, over 60 magazines and 24 per cent of Scottish Television. Overseas assets include newspapers, television companies and radio stations in Canada and the United States, and about 30 magazines in South Africa. The Thomson empire also includes interests in North Sea oil, a chain of travel agencies and Britannia Airways.

5 The *Observer* was until November 1976 owned by the Astor family. For some twenty-five years its editor was the Hon. David Astor, son of the second Viscount Astor. The paper is now owned by an American oil company, Atlantic Richfield. In spring 1981 Atlantic Richfield proposed to sell the *Observer* to Lonrho, a multinational company with extensive interests in mining and finance. The deal was referred to the Monopolies Commission on the grounds that Lonrho already owned the *Glasgow Herald*, two Scottish evening papers and 25 weeklies. The Commission upheld the deal.

6 The *Financial Times* is owned by S. Pearson and Son Ltd. At the time of the Royal Commission Report 44·28 per cent of the voting shares were held by Broadminster Nominees Ltd which holds them for the descendants of the first Viscount Cowdray. The present chairman is Viscount Cowdray. S. Pearson also owns (through Westminster Press) 112 provincial newspapers, *The Economist*, *Investors Chronicle* and Penguin Books. It also has interests in oil, banking and pottery.

7 The *Daily Mirror*, *Sunday Mirror* and the *People* are owned by Mirror Group Newspapers Ltd, which in turn is owned by Reed International. Reed also owns 12 provincial newspapers and 174 weekly and monthly magazines; it had shares in Associated Television, Westward Television and Radio Clyde. Reed International's main interests are in the manufacture of newsprint. The *Daily Mirror* was originally the property of the Harmsworth family. At the height of their power the Harmsworths owned the *Daily Mail*, the *Daily Sketch*, *The Times* and the *Daily Mirror* simultaneously.

8 The *Guardian* is controlled by a trust established in 1930 by its founder, a former Liberal MP, C. P. Scott. Three of the ten trustees are members of the Scott family. Others include a former editor of the paper, a member of the editorial staff and the Liberal MP Jo Grimond. The Trust also owned the *Manchester Evening News* and four small provincial papers. Profits are either ploughed back or given to charity.

9 The *Morning Star* is owned by the People's Press Printing Society. The society, which has no other holdings, has a management committee with 15 members plus the secretary who is a member *ex officio*. Five members come up for re-election each year at meetings of the society's 29,000 shareholders. In 1981 these meetings took place in Glasgow, Sheffield, Birmingham, Manchester, Cardiff and London. A substantial percentage of the paper's sales are in Eastern Europe and the Soviet Union.

Appendix B

Labour MPs Who Changed Allegiance

The departure in March 1981 of 13 Labour MPs to set up a Social Democratic Party must be placed in historical perspective. There is nothing new about people elected as Labour MPs announcing after a period in Parliament that they no longer support the party in whose name they were elected. Some take the honourable course of resigning and fighting a by-election in the hope of achieving a new mandate; most linger on until a general election when they are usually defeated. Motives for departure vary. Some leave because of a genuine difference of principle with the party; some leave because, having used the Labour Party to achieve power and status, they wish to kick away the ladder up which they have climbed.

Whatever the reason, it is usual for departing MPs to claim that it is the Labour Party and not they which has changed. Before long many of them are writing articles on the leader page of the *Daily Express* advising readers to vote Conservative.

Where an MP leaves for reasons that place him to the right of the Labour Party, it is customary for him to be presented by the media as something of a hero engaging in an act of statesmanship or patriotism (see, for example, media treatment of Dick Taverne in the Lincoln by-election of 1973).

History records that although defectors from the Labour Party up to 1979 have included a long list of exalted people, they have, after enjoying a short outburst of media acclaim, sunk without trace. The Labour Party, on the other hand, has soldiered on. So it has been in the past, and no doubt history has a similar fate in store for the latest batch of Labour defectors.

Here is a record of those Labour MPs and Labour peers who left the party between 1914 and 1979:

Symbols and Abbreviations

*	elected as Liberal in earlier election(s)
Dem. Lab.	Democratic Labour
ENP	English National Party
exp.	expelled
ILP	Independent Labour Party
Ind.	Independent
Nat. Lab.	National Labour
NP	New Party
SLP	Scottish Labour Party

Name	*Constituency*	*First elected Labour MP*	*Changed allegiance*	*From*	*To*	*Next election*	*Ministerial offices under Lab. govts*
Johnson, William	Nuneaton	1906	Feb. 1914	Lab.	Lib.	—	
Kenyon, Barnet	Chesterfield	Aug. 1913	Feb. 1914	Lab.	Lib.	1918	
Hancock, John George	Mid-Derbyshire	1909	April 1915	Lab.	Lib.	1918	
Thomas, Sir Owen	Anglesey	1918	Oct. 1920	Lab.	Ind.	1918	
Saklavata, S.	Battersea N.	1922	1923	Lab.	Comm.	Comm. 1924–9	
Haden Guest, Leslie	Southwark N.	1923	Feb. 1927	Lab.	Ind.	Sought re-election March 27, lost	
Spencer, George A.	Broxtowe	1918	Feb. 1927	Lab.	Ind.	—	
Stephen, C.	Glasgow Camlachie	1922	1931	Lab.	ILP	ILP 1935–47 ret. Lab.	
Forgan, Robert	W. Renfrew	1929	Feb. 1931	Lab.	NP	—	
Mosley, Lady Cynthia	Stoke	1929	Feb. 1931	Lab.	NP	—	
Mosley, Sir Oswald	Smethwick	Dec. 1926 (1918–24, Unionist)	Feb. 1931	Lab.	NP	—	Chancellor, Duchy of Lancaster, June 1929–May 1930

Name	*Constituency*	*First elected Labour MP*	*Changed allegiance*	*From*	*To*	*Next election*	*Ministerial offices under Lab. govts*
Strachey, John	Aston	1929	Feb. 1931	Lab.	NP June 1931, Ind.; ret. Lab. 1945	—	Minister for Food 1946–50; Minister for War 1950–1
Baldwin, Oliver	Dudley	1929	Feb. 1931	Lab.	Ind.	—	
Brown, William J.	Wolverhampton W.	1929	Feb. 1931	Lab.	Ind.	—	
Aitchison, Craigie M.	Kilmarnock	Nov. 1929	1931	Lab.	Nat. Lab.	1931	Lord Advocate 1929–31
Amulree, Lord	—	—	1931	Lab.	Nat. Lab.	—	Sec. of State for Air 1930–1
Bennet,* Sir Ernest N.	Cardiff Central	1929	1931	Lab.	Nat. Lab.	1931	
Denman, Richard	Leeds Central	1910 Carlisle	1931	Lab.	Nat. Lab.	1931	
Gillett, Sir George	Finsbury	1923	1931	Lab.	Nat. Lab.	1931	Parly Sec., Board of Trade, July 1929–31
Hall-Caine, Derwent	Everton	1929	1931	Lab.	Nat. Lab.	1931 lost	
Jowitt,* Sir William	Preston	July 1929	1931	Lab.	Nat. Lab.	1931 lost	Attorney-General 1929–31
Knight, Holford	Nottingham S.	1929	1931	Lab.	Nat. Lab.	1931	

Name	*Constituency*	*First elected Labour MP*	*Changed allegiance*	*From*	*To*	*Next election*	*Ministerial offices under Lab. govts*
Lovat-Fraser, James A.	Lichfield	1929	1931	Lab.	Nat. Lab.	1931	
MacDonald, James Ramsay	Seaham	1906 Leicester	1931	Lab.	Nat. Lab.	1931	Prime Minister and Foreign Secretary 1924; Prime Minister 1929–31
MacDonald, Malcolm	Nottingham Bassetlaw	1929	1931	Lab.	Nat. Lab.	1931	
Markham, Sidney F.	Rochester, Chatham	1929	1931	Lab.	Nat. Lab.	—	
Sankey, Lord	—	—	1931	Lab.	Nat. Lab.	—	Lord Chancellor 1929–31
Snowden, Philip	Colne Valley	1906 Blackburn	1931	Lab.	Nat. Lab.	—	Chancellor of Exchequer 1924 and 1929–31
Thomas, James Henry	Derby	1910	1931	Lab.	Nat. Lab.	1931	Sec. of State for Colonies 1924; Lord Privy Seal 1929–30; Sec. of State for Dominions 1930–1
Buchanan, George	Gorbals	1922	Nov. 1931	Lab.	ILP	1935	Under Sec., Scottish Office, 1945–7; Minister of Pensions 1947–8

Name	*Constituency*	*First elected Labour MP*	*Changed allegiance*	*From*	*To*	*Next election*	*Ministerial offices under Lab. govts*
Kirkwood, David	Dunbarton	1922	Nov. 1931	Lab.	ILP ret. Lab. 1933	1935	
McGovern, J.	Shettleston	1930	Nov. 1931	Lab.	ILP ret. Lab.	1935	
Maxton, James	Bridgeton	1922	Nov. 1931	Lab.	ILP	—	
Wallhead, Richard C.	Merthyr	1922	Nov. 1931	Lab.	ILP ret. Lab. 1933	—	
Pritt, Denis	Hammersmith N.	1935	exp. 1940	Lab.	—	1945 Ind. Lab.	
Maclaren, Andrew	Burslem	1922	March 1945	Lab.	Ind.	—	
Walkden, Evelyn	Doncaster	Nov. 1941	Nov. 1947	Lab.	Ind.	—	
Platts-Mills, John	Finsbury	July 1945	exp. 1948	Lab.	Ind.	1950 lost	
Edwards, Alfred	Middlesbrough	1935	May 1948	Lab.	Took Con. Whip Aug. 1949	1950 lost	

Name	*Constituency*	*First elected Labour MP*	*Changed allegiance*	*From*	*To*	*Next election*	*Ministerial offices under Lab. govts*
Bulmer-Thomas, Ivor	Keighley	1942	Oct. 1948	Lab.	Ind., took Con. Whip Jan. 1949	1950 defeated at Newport	Parly Sec., Min. of Aviation, 1945; Parly Under Sec. of State 1946–7
Solley, Leslie	Thurrock	1945	exp. 1949	Lab.	Ind.	1950 lost	
Zilliacus, Konni	Gateshead	1945	exp. 1949	Lab.	Ind.	1950 lost	
Hutchinson, H. Lester	Rusholme	1945	July 1949	Lab.	—	—	
Blackburn, Albert Raymond	Northfield 1950	1945 King's Norton	Aug. 1950	Lab.	Ind.	—	
King, E.	Penryn and Falmouth	1945	1951	Lab.	Con.	Con. 1964–79	Parly Sec., Min. of Town and Country Planning, 1947–50
Acland, Sir Richard	Gravesend	Nov. 1947 (1935–45, Lib.)	March 1955	Lab.	Ind.	Sought re-election as Ind., 1955, lost	
Crawley, A.	Buckingham	1945	1957	Lab.	Con.	Con. 1962–7	Under Sec. for Air 1950–1
Robens, Alfred	Blyth	1945	—	Lab.	Ind.	—	Parly Sec., Min. of Fuel and Power, 1947–51; Minister of Labour and National Service 1951

Name	*Constituency*	*First elected Labour MP*	*Changed allegiance*	*From*	*To*	*Next election*	*Ministerial offices under Lab. govts*
Shawcross, Sir Hartley	St Helens	1945	—	Lab.	Ind.	—	Attorney General 1945–51; Pres. of Board of Trade 1951
Brown, A.	Tottenham	1959	March 1961	Lab.	Ind., took Con. Whip May 1962	1964 lost	
Donnelly, Desmond	Pembroke	1950	Jan. 1968	Lab.	Ind.	—	
Brown, George	Belper	1945	—	Lab.	Ind.		Joint Parly Sec., Min. of Agriculture and Fisheries, 1947–51; Joint Parly Sec., Min. of Works, 1951; Sec. of State for Economic Affairs 1964–6; Sec. of State for Foreign Affairs 1966–8
Ensor, David	Bury and Radcliffe	1964	—	Lab.	Lib.	—	
Marsh, Sir Richard	Greenwich	1959	—	Lab.	—	—	Parly Sec., Min. of Labour, 1964–5; Joint Parly Sec., Min. of Technology, 1965–6; Minister of Power 1966–8; Minister of Transport 1968–9

Name	*Constituency*	*First elected Labour MP*	*Changed allegiance*	*From*	*To*	*Next election*	*Ministerial offices under Lab. govts*
Wyatt, Woodrow	Bosworth	1945	—	Lab.	—	—	Parly Under Sec. of State and Financial Sec., War Office 1951
Davies, Stephen O.	Merthyr Tydfil	1934	1970	Lab.	Ind. Lab.	1970 died 1972	
Gunter, Ray	Southwark 1959	1945	Feb. 1972	Lab.	Ind.	—	Minister of Labour 1964–8; Minister of Power 1968
Taverne, Dick	Lincoln	1962	Oct. 1972	Lab.	Dem. Lab.	March 1973	Financial Sec. to Treasury 1969–70; Minister of State, Treasury, 1968–9; Parly Under Sec. of State 1966–8
Milne, Edward J.	Blyth	1960	Feb. 1974	Lab.	Ind. Lab.	Feb. 1974 lost in Oct. 1974	
Mayhew, Christopher	Woolwich E. 1951	1945	July 1974	Lab.	Lib.	—	Under Sec., Foreign Office, 1946–50; Minister of Defence (RN) 1964–6

Name	*Constituency*	*First elected Labour MP*	*Changed allegiance*	*From*	*To*	*Next election*	*Ministerial offices under Lab. govts*
Stonehouse, John	Walsall N. 1974	1957	April 1976	Lab.	ENP	—	Parly Sec., Min. of Aviation, 1964–6; Under Sec., Colonial Office, 1966–7; Minister of Aviation 1967; Minister of State, Min. of Technology, 1967–8; Postmaster-General (later Minister of Posts and Telecommunications) 1968–70
Robertson, John	Paisley	April 1961	July 1976	Lab.	SLP	1979	
Sillars, James	S. Ayrshire	1970	July 1976	Lab.	SLP	1979	
Prentice, Reg	Newham N.E. 1974	1957	Oct. 1977	Lab.	Con.	May 1979 for Daventry	Minister of State, DES, 1964–6; Minister of Public Building and Works 1966–7; Minister of Overseas Development 1967–9; Sec. of State, DES, 1974–5; Minister for Overseas Development 1975–6

Source: David Butler and Anne Sloman, *British Political Facts, 1900–79*, Macmillan, fifth edn 1980, pp. 215–20.

Sources

1. 'Britain as a Colony' – article in the first edition of the Labour Party journal, the *New Socialist*, Sept. 1981.
2. 'The Case for a Constitutional Premiership' – lecture due to have been delivered at Bristol University on 13 July 1979 but banned by the Vice-Chancellor and delivered instead at The Folk House, Bristol.
3. 'The Case for a Constitutional Civil Service' – lecture for the Royal Institute of Public Administration, Chatham House, 28 Jan. 1980; 'World in Action', Granada TV, 1980.
4. 'Civil Liberties and the Security Services' – introduction to the 1980 volume of the *Review of Security and the State*, published by Julian Friedman.
5. 'The Democratic Control of Science and Technology' – lecture delivered to the Danish Engineering Society, the Technical University, Copenhagen, 22 Jan. 1981.
6. 'The Need for a Free Press' – partly based on a talk given to the BBC Television Chapel of the National Union of Journalists at Lime Grove, 23 March 1981.
7. 'The Moral Basis for Democratic Socialism' – Sermon on revolutionary Christianity, Mansfield College Chapel, Oxford, Nov. 1979; lecture to senior church leaders at St George's House, Windsor Castle, 10 Feb. 1981.
8. 'The Way Ahead' – Newspaper Press Fund, City Chambers, Glasgow, 22 Jan. 1980.
9. 'The Trade Unions in the 1980s' – Granada Guildhall lecture, 15 May 1980.
10. 'The Case for Labour Party Democracy' – Herbert Morrison Memorial Lecture, House of Commons, 26 June 1980.
11. 'Europe: A New Perspective' – lecture delivered under the auspices of the Gulbenkian Foundation and the BBC World Service, Lisbon, March 1981.

Notes

1 *Britain as a Colony*

1 Interviewed by Desmond Wilcox, 'Profile', BBC TV, 14 Aug. 1979.

2 According to Harry Truman in his book *Year of Decisions 1945*, Doubleday, New York, 1955, p. 103, the State Department had prepared papers proposing the return of Hong Kong to China. Roosevelt also intended that French Indo-China should be decolonised; see George Rosie, *The British in Vietnam*, Panther 1970, pp. 31–2.

3 After the nationalisation of the Anglo Iranian Oil Company assets in Iran in 1951, American interests took advantage of Britain's weakness to establish a commanding position in Iran and reduce Anglo Iranian (now BP) to a 40 per cent share. See Ian Campbell, 'The Future of Oil', Union of Democratic Control 1957, p. 12; also Richard J. Barnet, *Intervention and Revolution*, Paladin 1972, pp. 230–3.

4 For details of the post-war loan negotiations between Britain and America and the terms sought by the Americans, see *Keesing's Contemporary Archives*, 15–22 Dec. 1945, pp. 7607–8. During the war Britain sold £1,118,000,000 of foreign investments (*Keesing's*, p. 7608).

5 For details of the collapse in August 1947, see *Keesing's*, p. 8779.

6 At a press conference on 14 Jan. 1963, General de Gaulle stated his opposition to British membership of the EEC and referred to the Bahamas Agreement between Britain and America under which Britain bought Polaris submarines from the Americans. He said: 'The English will have the preferential help of the Americans in building these [Polaris] submarines and these projectiles. I should mention in passing that this help was never offered to us and it should be known that, contrary to some accounts, we have never asked for it.' *Keesing's*, pp. 19197–9.

7 Following her visit to the United States in Feb. 1981 Mrs Thatcher told the House of Commons that she had discussed with President Reagan the possible creation of a Rapid Deployment Force for the Gulf and South-West Asia. She went on: 'I made it clear that if such a force were created, the United Kingdom would be ready to contribute to it, in the same way as, in conjunction with the USA and France, we have already stationed naval units in the Gulf in response to the situation arising from the Iran/Iraq war' (*Hansard*, 2 March 1981, col. 19).
8 See Ch. 12, n. 5.
9 On 28 Oct. 1971, the House of Commons decided by 356 to 244 votes in favour of British entry to the Common Market. The 356 votes for the government's motion included 69 Labour MPs. Another 20 Labour MPs abstained. The 244 votes against entry included 39 Conservatives. Had all Labour MPs voted in accordance with party policy, Britain would not have been taken into the Common Market.

2 *The Case for a Constitutional Premiership*

1 The 1832 Reform Act gave the vote to anyone owning property worth £10 a year or more and added 217,000 new voters to the electorate. In 1867 the franchise was extended to the better-paid urban male workers; in 1884 this was extended to the rural areas. Women received the vote on an equal basis with men in 1929.
2 The Labour Representation Committee was set up by the trade unions in 1900 and became the Labour Party in 1906.
3 During the meeting to draw up Labour's manifesto for the 1979 general election, the prime minister, James Callaghan, threatened to resign if a commitment to abolish the House of Lords was included in the manifesto. See also p. 183.
4 These figures and those which follow were supplied by the House of Commons Library.
5 Civil Service Department Record, 1978.
6 On 16 June 1977 Mr Callaghan was asked to say when collective Cabinet responsibility should apply. He replied, '. . . I certainly think the doctrine should apply, except in cases where I announce it does not' (*Hansard*, col. 552).
7 The Bill repealed Section 2 of the European Communities Act 1972 which gives the Council of Ministers the power to enforce European Community legislation in Britain, if necessary overriding the will of the British Parliament.
8 Figures prepared by the House of Commons Library in Feb. 1978.

Sources: C. H. Feinstein, *National Income, Expenditure and Output 1855–1965*, Cambridge University Press 1972, tables 12, 13, 34, 36 and 61; *National Income and Expenditure*, HMSO 1960 edn, tables 36–40; *National Income and Expenditure 1965–75*, HMSO 1976, tables 1.1 and 2.1; *National Income and Expenditure 1966–76*, HMSO 1976, tables 7.1, 7.2, 8.1, 8.2.

9 Civil Service Statistics 1971, table I, and Civil Service Statistics 1975, tables J and K.

3 *The Case for a Constitutional Civil Service*

1 For some suggestions as to how the power of the prime minister should be curbed, see Ch. 2.
2 See, for example, profile by Brian Connell, *The Times*, 15 Nov. 1976.
3 *The Economist*, 2 June 1979.
4 *The Times*, 15 Nov. 1976.
5 14 Jan. 1980.
6 Geoffrey Moorhouse, *The Diplomats*, Cape 1977, p. 385.
7 *Hansard*, 4 July 1972, cols 345–6.
8 Peter Jenkins reported in the *Guardian* on 28 Oct. 1976 that Treasury civil servants had been in touch with their opposite numbers in another European finance ministry saying, 'Don't bale the bastards out.' The Labour Government was at the time negotiating for an IMF loan.
9 *The Times*, 14 Jan. 1980.
10 Moorhouse, *The Diplomats*, p. 383.
11 Ibid., p. 384.
12 Ibid., p. 386.
13 *The Times*, 15 Nov. 1976.

4 *Civil Liberties and the Security Services*

1 See for example the front page headline in the *Daily Mail* of 1 Sept. 1980, 'Strike ends in triumph', over a story celebrating the success of industrial action by Polish workers.
2 According to Mr Chapman Pincher in his book *Inside Story*, Sidgwick and Jackson 1978, MI5 have files on more than two million people (p. 26) and our security services apparently believe that 59 Labour MPs in the 1974–9 Parliament had 'current or recent connections with Communist, Trotskyist and other Marxist organisations' (p. 28). The Special Branch also appear to take a close interest in politics and trade union affairs. For

example, during an occupation to prevent closure of a British Steel subsidiary in Greenwich, workers came across Special Branch reports on two of their colleagues. For details of this and other cases see Crispin Aubrey, *Who's Watching You*, Pelican 1981, pp. 36–7.

3 *Tapping the Telephone*, published in July 1980 by the Post Office Engineering Union.

4 Among those with reason to believe their phones were tapped during industrial disputes were eight members of the executive of the train drivers' union, ASLEF (Tony Bunyon, *The Political Police in Britain*, Friedman 1976, p. 182); and Jack Dromey, a leading member of the Grunwick Strike Committee (*Sunday Times*, 3 Feb. 1980). Papers now removed from the Public Records Office show that during the 1926 General Strike, Ernest Bevin, then leader of the Transport and General Workers' Union, had his phones tapped (*Sunday Times*, 3 Feb. 1980).

5 See Ch. 3, n. 8. No attempt was ever made to discover the accuracy or otherwise of this extremely serious allegation.

6 For a detailed account of links between British and American intelligence see Duncan Campbell, 'America's Big Ear in Europe', *New Statesman*, 25 July 1980.

7 The German government ban on employment as public officials of those whom they declare to be hostile to the German constitution.

8 See for example the Swiss defence system based upon civilian militia. The Swiss claim to be able to mobilise 625,000 troops or just under 10 per cent of their total population within 48 hours. This is double the total British armed forces and Britain has nearly ten times the Swiss population. Switzerland spends around 2 per cent of GNP on defence compared with Britain's expenditure of around 6 per cent. See Irvine Cohen, *Swiss Defence Profile*, available from Diplomatist Publications, Shooter's Lodge, Windsor Forest, Berks.

9 See Margaret Gowing, *Independence and Deterrence*, Macmillan 1974, p. 20. Ms Gowing writes, 'The Cabinet as a body was completely excluded from all the major decisions on atomic policy . . .'

10 See 'Mr Callaghan's secret bequest to Mrs Thatcher', *The Times*, 4 Dec. 1979.

11 For details of the US Freedom of Information Act (1974), see *Disclosure of Official Information: A Report on Overseas Practices*, HMSO 1979, and for an account of how the Act is working, see *The Economist*, 23 May 1981. The Act gives anyone the right to

request information from federal US government agencies, subject to certain exceptions which include national defence secrets, trade secrets and invasion of privacy.

5 *The Democratic Control of Science and Technology*

1 In his final report to Congress, see *Guardian*, 21 Jan. 1981, p. 7. As regards nuclear casualties in Britain, a British minister, Lord Belstead, said on 16 March 1980: '. . . if we had the sort of attack we think we can expect, about 15 million people would survive. We believe that if people took the measures in *Protect and Survive* that figure would be doubled . . .' The population of Great Britain is 56 million.
2 George Allen and Unwin, p. 367.
3 Tony Benn was Minister of Technology from 1966 to 1970.
4 As Secretary of State for Energy (1975–9) Tony Benn was responsible for the British nuclear industry.
5 In March 1979, at Three Mile Island, Harrisburg, Pennsylvania, an overheated uranium core in a nuclear reactor led to the release of radioactivity and evacuation of a large number of people from homes in the area.
6 In April 1979 the United States suspended development aid following reports that Pakistan was building a nuclear bomb using ingredients acquired by devious means.
7 See pp. 55–6.

6 *The Case for a Free Press*

1 See the Glasgow University Media Group, *Bad News* and *More Bad News*, Routledge & Kegan Paul 1976 and 1980. See also *New Statesman*, 26 Jan. 1979, for an analysis of media coverage of the lorry drivers' strike in January 1979.
2 For examples, see page 160.
3 In 1979 total advertising expenditure in national and local newspapers and periodicals was £1,496 million; a further £471 million was spent on television advertising. See *Advertising* magazine, No. 64, Table 4.
4 See pp. 136–7; for a more detailed analysis, see Tony Benn, *Arguments for Socialism*, Cape 1979 and Penguin 1980, Ch. 6.
5 See the Glasgow University Media Group, *Really Bad News*, Ch. 4, to be published in autumn 1981.
6 The Five Mile Act was a piece of seventeenth-century legislation which barred dissenters from preaching within five miles of city centres.

7 26 Feb. 1981.
8 For example, J. P. W. Mallalieu, a member of the Bevanite group of MPs who also acted as a sports commentator, had his contract curtailed.
9 For an analysis of the way the Rhodesian war was reported in the British press, see articles by Chris Mullin in the *New Statesman*, 25 Feb. 1977 and 19 Jan. 1979.
10 In April 1981 a letter signed by 74 Labour MPs, 23 trade union general secretaries and 20 academics, requesting that allegations of distortion and bias against trade unions be debated on the air, was sent to the BBC and the IBA. They both rejected this request.
11 *1949 Royal Commission on the Press*, p. 25.
12 The exception is the *Morning Star*, which has a circulation of 25,000 and cannot be said to be a mass circulation paper for the purposes of this argument.
13 James Curran and Jean Seaton, *Power Without Responsibility*, Fontana 1981, p. 48.
14 Ibid., pp. 118–19.
15 *Sunday Times* Business News, 3 May 1981.
16 Curran and Seaton, *op cit.*, p. 77.
17 Paul Addison, *The Road to 1945*, Quartet 1977, pp. 265–6.
18 For an analysis of media coverage of the 1979 general election, see articles by Paul Foot in the *New Statesman*, 13 April, 20 April and 4 May 1979.
19 Curran and Seaton, *op. cit.*, pp. 343–4.
20 For an account of the British distribution system, see *The News Trade and the Radical Press*, published 1980 by the Minority Press Group, 9 Poland Street, London W1; for an account of the French system, see *Press Distributors and Press Censorship*, also published in 1980 by the Minority Press Group.
21 *The Right of Reply*, available from the Campaign for Press Freedom, 272–288 London Road, Hadleigh, Essex, price 40p.

7 *The Moral Basis for Democratic Socialism*

1 Chapter 12, verses 29–31.
2 Wycliffe and the Lollards were persecuted for encouraging people to read the Bible, undermining the authority of the bishops and the priesthood, the King and the landlords.
3 The Levellers were one of several groups of radical pamphleteers who, in the wake of the English Civil War (1647–50), tried to promote far-reaching social revolution. They drew up a political

programme which anticipated by two centuries most other demands for radical change in Britain. They even made some headway in influencing Cromwell's army. This led to a mutiny in May 1649 which was quickly suppressed and a number of leading Levellers were executed.

4 Gerard Winstanley, *The Levellers' Standard Advanced*, 1649.
5 See p. 135.
6 *Encyclopaedia Britannica*, 1970 edn, vol. 7, p. 84.
7 SCM Press 1965, p. 46.
8 Delivered on 3 May 1968.
9 Darton, Longman and Todd 1975.
10 For the details of who owns the British press, see Appendix A.
11 Government Expenditure White Paper, 1981–2, Cmnd 8175.
12 Smith's best-known work, setting out the basis of capitalist philosophy, is *The Wealth of Nations*, first published in 1776 and available in Pelican.
13 Edmund Burke, *Thoughts on Detail and Scarcity*, a pamphlet published in 1795.
14 *The English Constitution*, introduction to second edn, p. xxiii.
15 H. G. Wells, *History of the World*, Pelican 1960, p. 157.
16 Winstanley, *op. cit.*
17 Robert Owen (1771–1858), *Report to the County of Lanark.*
18 Quoted in William Stewart, *J. Keir Hardie – A Biography*, ILP 1921, pp. 138–9.

8 *The Way Ahead*

1 A former Tory Colonial Secretary, Chamberlain made his call for tariff reform in a speech in Glasgow on 6 Oct. 1903.
2 Assistance to the private sector totalled about £5,000 million between 1 April 1974 and 1 April 1979. *Hansard*, oral answers, 2 Feb. 1979.
3 According to the Bank of England Information Office a gold sovereign was worth £7.35 in June 1973 and £77 in June 1980.
4 For a detailed account of Labour's economic programme, see *The Alternative Economic Strategy*, published in 1980 by CSE Books, 55 Mount Pleasant, London WC1.
5 A very rough estimate based upon 10 per cent unemployment which is assumed to be 8 per cent above the 'natural' level; every extra 1 per cent unemployment is assumed to result in a loss of 2 per cent of output; an extra 8 per cent unemployment, therefore, results in a 16 per cent loss of output; Gross Domestic Product is about £250 billion, therefore a 16 per cent reduction in GDP is

about £40 billion; government revenue in terms of income tax, VAT, excise duties, Corporation Tax, etc., is reckoned at about one-third of GDP; one-third of £40 billion is £14 billion. (Calculated with the help of Francis Cripps of the Cambridge Economic Group.)

6 This is made up of £1.238 billion unemployment benefit and £2.463 billion in supplementary benefit of which about £2 billion goes to the unemployed. Government Expenditure White Paper, 1981–2, Cmnd 8175.

7 *National Income and Expenditure*, HMSO 1980 edn, table 13.3.

8 *Sense About Defence*, Quartet 1977, pp. 28–9.

9 *Sunday Times* Business News, 15 March 1981.

9 *The Trade Unions in the 1980s*

1 Macmillan 1938; reprinted by EP Publishing (Wakefield) 1978.

2 John Maynard Keynes's *The General Theory of Employment, Interest and Money*, Macmillan 1936, sets out what became known as Keynesian economics, upon which all post-war governments before 1976 based their economic policy. William Henry Beveridge was the author of 'Social Insurance and Allied Services', 1942 (Cmd 6404), which laid the basis of the modern welfare state.

3 The National Economic Development Council, established 1962, meets monthly and brings together representatives of government, the employers and the unions.

4 On 17 Jan. 1969, the Labour Government published *In Place of Strife* (Cmnd 3888), a paper containing proposals for discouraging strikes. Among the measures proposed were strike ballots and a conciliation pause; breaches of the proposed legislation would be dealt with by the courts. *In Place of Strife* was abandoned following protest from the trade unions and Labour MPs.

5 The 1980 Employment Act, among other things, restricts the powers of trade unions in respect of picketing and payment of benefits to strikers.

6 Sir John Ford, British High Commissioner in Canada, speaking in Winnipeg, 25 Feb. 1980.

7 Routledge & Kegan Paul, 1976 and 1980.

8 *More Bad News*, p. 57. For details of 'plea', 'offer', etc., see Ch. 4 of *Really Bad News*, to be published in autumn 1981.

9 The dockers were imprisoned in July 1972 following their picketing of the Stratford cold storage depot in defiance of the 1971 Industrial Relations Act introduced by the Conservative Government.

10 The 1975, 1976 and 1977 Trades Union Congresses endorsed the economic policy of the then Labour Government, in which wage restraint was a major factor. In 1978 the TUC rejected wage restraint.
11 Workers at Lucas Aerospace have produced detailed plans for converting their factories away from the manufacture of military equipment to socially useful products such as kidney machines.
12 Planning agreements were an important (but unimplemented) part of Labour's 1974 election manifestos. Under such agreements, leading companies would be obliged to disclose both to their workers and to the government their investment, employment and other plans.
13 Joint shop stewards' committees or combines consist of workers' representatives from different unions working together on a company- or industry-wide basis in order to present a more effective negotiating team. The most successful and best known is probably the Lucas Aerospace combine. Combines are not always popular with full time trade union officials who see them as undermining their authority.
14 These disputes involved Asian workers employed at very low wages by employers who refused to recognise their right to belong to a union.
15 Robert Bellers, *Proposals for Raising a College of Industry*, first published 1696, reissued by the Institute for Worker's Control, pamphlet no. 68.
16 Clause IV(4).

10 *The Need for Labour Party Democracy*

1 Caxton 1924, Vol. I, p. 124.
2 Ibid., Vol. I, p. 128.
3 The Levellers and the Diggers were groups of radical pamphleteers; see Ch. 7, n. 3.
4 The Combination Acts were introduced in the early nineteenth century to prohibit workers from organising trade unions. The 1980 Employment Act restricts the power of the trade unions with respect to picketing and prevents the payment of benefit to strikers.
5 For example, the House of Lords was used by the Tories to block nationalisation of the steel industry in 1948 and the dock labour scheme in 1975. In 1948 the House of Commons voted on a free vote to abolish the death penalty for a trial period of five years; this

was thrown out by the Lords and the death penalty remained for nearly twenty years.

6 For an account of the terms under which US nuclear weapons are based in Britain, see Professor Robert Neild, 'Why Britain must say "Non" to being America's Aircraft Carrier', *Guardian*, 11 May 1981. See also Professor Neild's *Making Up Your Mind About the Bomb*, Deutsch 1981.

7 *The Crossman Diaries*, edited by Anthony Howard, Magnum 1979, p. 178.

8 For a detailed account of the way the 1979 Labour manifesto was compiled, see a chapter by the head of the Labour Party research department, Geoff Bish, in *What Went Wrong?*, Spokesman Books 1979, pp. 187–206.

9 Bish, *op. cit.*

10 Harold Wilson, Final Term, Weidenfeld & Nicolson and Michael Joseph 1979, p. 30.

11 Michael Joseph 1976, p. 75.

12 Reproduced in the Institute of Workers' Control Bulletin no. 34, Nov. 1976.

13 At a meeting of the parliamentary Labour Party, 2 March 1967.

14 For an account of how Mr Callaghan kept the decision on the third generation secret from most members of his own Cabinet, see Peter Hennessy, 'Mr Callaghan's secret bequest to Mrs Thatcher', *The Times*, 4 Dec. 1979.

15 Clause IV (4) of the Labour Party Constitution commits the party 'to secure for the workers by hand or by brain the full fruits of their industry and the most equitable distribution thereof that may be possible upon the basis of the common ownership of the means of production, distribution, and exchange . . . ' It is printed on every Labour Party membership card.

16 This resolution was passed at the July 1980 meeting of the National Executive Committee.

17 When the right wing were in control of the party, dissenting MPs regularly had the Whip withdrawn. In 1939 Sir Stafford Cripps and five other MPs were disciplined in this way for advocating a united front with the Communist Party; on 16 March 1955 Nye Bevan had the Whip withdrawn because, in the words of Hugh Gaitskell, his attitude fell below 'the standards of loyalty to be expected from ourselves – Labour MPs – to party decisions, to the party leader and to one another'; on 16 March 1961 five MPs, including Michael Foot, had the Whip withdrawn for voting against the Air Force estimates.

11 *Europe: A New Perspective*

1 *Foreign Relations*, 1948, Vol. II, p. 895, despatch dated 17 April.
2 NATO was set up in 1949; the Russians waited until 1955 before setting up the Warsaw Pact.
3 Britain has invaded Afghanistan three times in the last 150 years. Ironically, the reason in each case was to counter Russian influence. The invasions and occupations occurred in 1838–2, 1878–81 and 1919–21. For details, see *Encyclopaedia Britannica*, 1970 edn, pp. 243–4.
4 *UN Monthly Bulletin of Statistics*, July 1980, tables 2 and 18.
5 *World Bank Atlas* for figures of national income (based on average prices and exchange rates for a three-year period).
6 The UN Economic Commission for Europe was set up in 1947 to study economic and technical problems in Europe and to recommend action.
7 Stockholm International Peace Research Institute, 11 May 1979.
8 For details see Ken Coates (ed.), *Eleventh Hour for Europe*, Spokesman Books 1980, pp. 17–20.
9 For details of the Swiss defence system, see Irvine Cohen, *Swiss Defence Profile*, 1977. Available from Diplomatist Publications, Shooter's Lodge, Windsor Forest, Berks.
10 Penguin 1967, p. 105.
11 *The Times*, 7 July 1980.
12 *Europe Yearbook*, 1980, Vol. I; *ILO Yearbook of Labour Statistics*, 1979, table 3.
13 Ibid.
14 Figures for May 1981, EEC Press Office, London.
15 For a more detailed summary of the case against the Common Market, see Tony Benn, *Arguments for Socialism*, Cape 1979 and Penguin 1980, Ch. 4.
16 As copied from a plaque in Mahatma Gandhi House, London.

12 *The Transition to Democratic Socialism*

1 Articles 30–4 of the Treaty of Rome outlaw all restrictions on free trade; Article 67 provides for the abolition of all restrictions on the free movement of capital; Article 92 declares that any measure which 'threatens to distort competition' is 'incompatible with the Common Market'.
2 See Geoffrey Moorhouse, *The Diplomats*, Cape 1977, pp. 383–4, cited in Ch. 3, pp. 62–3.
3 The 1980 Labour Party conference passed by 5,042,000 votes to

2,097,000 a resolution urging the Party 'to include the withdrawal of the United Kingdom from the European Economic Community as a priority in the next general election manifesto; to disengage Britain from the European Economic Community institutions and in place of our European Economic Community membership to work for peaceful and equitable relations between Britain and all nations in Europe and the rest of the world'. *Report of the 1980 Labour Party Conference*, p. 297.

4 The 1977 Labour Party conference passed by 6,248,000 to 91,000 votes a resolution calling for the abolition of the House of Lords. See *Report of the 1977 Labour Party Conference*, p. 362.

5 For details of Labour Party policy on nuclear disarmament, see composite resolutions 44 and 45, *Report of the 1980 Labour Party Conference*, p. 299. For details of Canada's renunciation of nuclear weapons, see Christopher Hitchens, 'Canada's Nuclear Departure', *New Statesman*, 13 June 1980.

Index

More About Penguins and Pelicans